THE INSPIRED TEACHER

ASCD cares about Planet Earth.

This book has been printed on environmentally friendly paper.

THE INSPIRED TEACHER

How to Know One, Grow One, or Be One

CAROL FREDERICK STEELE

**Association for Supervision and
Curriculum Development**
Alexandria, Virginia USA

Association for Supervision and Curriculum Development
1703 N. Beauregard St. • Alexandria, VA 22311-1714 USA
Phone: 800-933-2723 or 703-578-9600 • Fax: 703-575-5400
Web site: www.ascd.org • E-mail: member@ascd.org
Author guidelines: www.ascd.org/write

Gene R. Carter, *Executive Director;* Nancy Modrak, *Publisher;* Julie Houtz, *Director of Book Editing & Production;* Sara Felice, *Assistant Editor;* Reece Quiñones, *Senior Graphic Designer;* Mike Kalyan, *Production Manager;* Valerie Younkin, *Desktop Publishing Specialist;* Kyle Steichen, *Production Specialist*

All Web links in this book are correct as of the publication date below but may have become inactive or otherwise modified since that time. If you notice a deactivated or changed link, please e-mail books@ascd.org with the words "Link Update" in the subject line. In your message, please specify the Web link, the book title, and the page number on which the link appears.

PAPERBACK ISBN: 978-1-4166-0742-7   ASCD product #108051   n3/09

Also available as an e-book through ebrary, netLibrary, and many online booksellers (see Books in Print for the ISBNs).

Quantity discounts for the paperback edition only: 10–49 copies, 10%; 50+ copies, 15%; for 1,000 or more copies, call 800-933-2723, ext. 5634, or 703-575-5634. For desk copies: member@ascd.org.

Library of Congress Cataloging-in-Publication Data
Steele, Carol Frederick, 1946–
    The inspired teacher : how to know one, grow one, or be one / Carol Frederick Steele.
        p. cm.
    Includes bibliographical references and index.
    ISBN 978-1-4166-0742-7 (pbk. : alk. paper)   1. Teaching.   2. Teachers.
3. Motivation in education. I. Title.

    LB1025.3.S7342 2009
    371.1—dc22

                                                    2008048899

20 19 18 17 16 15 14 13 12 11 10 09   1 2 3 4 5 6 7 8 9 10 11 12

To my grandmother

Clara B. Inscho Frederick

and all the other people who helped me grow

THE INSPIRED TEACHER

How to Know One, Grow One, or Be One

Preface

I try to continue learning at each step of my teaching journey. Although inspired teaching is always my goal, I can manage it only part of the time. I have inspired moments, and sometimes, I have inspired days. In between are extended periods of competence, times of struggle and, I suppose, evidence of blindness. I am delighted and relieved that I have progressed from my original state of ignorance. I am capable of teaching adequately most of the time and fabulously upon occasion. Because I still try to improve, I may be even better tomorrow. The journey from ignorance—mine and others'—to inspiration is the subject of this book.

I am not a researcher, though I read widely and pan for gold in everything I encounter. I see myself as my best research subject. At various stages of my teaching career I can recall how I felt and can identify input that changed me, helping me to think like a teacher. I remember both successes and fiascos. I celebrate hard-earned successes because great moments in teaching are a gift and a source of joy. I try to let go of shame or guilt about the worst moments, knowing I had limited knowledge at the time.

Several great teachers inspired me. Looking back their skills fit the definition of inspired teaching, though the term didn't occur to me at the time. But when I set out to emulate them, I hadn't a clue how to do it. This is the book I wish someone had given to me when I started teaching.

I prepared as all teachers-to-be do; I took the required education courses and earned a teaching certificate. With little classroom experience, I couldn't apply what I was learning.

In terms of Bloom's taxonomy, I gained knowledge and some comprehension, but most higher-order thinking was missing. Analyzing situations, applying information effectively, evaluating what I saw or did, synthesizing what I learned—these skills were beyond me when I was a student teacher. Even though some assignments in my education courses required these skills, I answered abstractly and didn't effectively transfer the learning to future situations.

I also felt frustrated in my teaching seminar. The professor assigned unit plans with goals and objectives. Trying to imagine where to begin, I peppered her with questions. How could I write lesson plans when I hadn't even met the students and didn't know what they needed? Looking back, the professor and I were both right. She was trying to impart knowledge about how to plan lessons (covered here in Chapter 2), how to make the classroom productive (Chapter 5), and how to cover material in depth (Chapter 12). I felt I needed to know how to understand the students and the setting (Chapter 7), how to assess what students know (Chapter 8), and how to solve problems I observed (Chapter 3).

Could the professor and I have effectively discussed all six of these areas, and others, simultaneously? It's unlikely. My struggles are not an indictment of my college instructors or my courses. I am sympathetic to the challenge my professor faced as she tried to shape me into a teacher. Until I gained experience, nothing my professors could have said or done would have reached me at the level of deep understanding. I needed context and time to incorporate real-life experiences.

When I was first hired as a high school teacher, teaching four different courses was frustrating. I never had enough time to competently prepare for each of them; sometimes I hardly tried. At the end of the year I went home—fled, really—to start a family.

I thought I was done with teaching, but I maintained my teaching certificate. Later I worked in a community education program for homebound adults who wanted to earn a high school diploma. Despite feeling unsuccessful as a high school teacher, I reasoned that I could successfully teach one person at a time because I wouldn't have to manage group behavior. While teaching in this program and later at a Job Corps center, I encountered a variety of students and life stories that shaped my idea of the typical student. These experiences were the first of many that deepened my understanding of what teaching really means and stimulated me to look at all learners, ages 5 to 95, as more alike than different.

My next major opportunity to grow as a teacher came when I participated in a study team on teaching writing more effectively. A team of 24 teachers spent a week during the summer with facilitators who bombarded us with up-to-date research and best practices. For the next year, we met monthly for day-long workshops with experts on various aspects of teaching in general and teaching writing in particular. My notion of teaching writing became more complex and multifaceted, as I learned the reasons behind various methods and recommendations.

When the study team ended, I was still hungry for more, so I found another way to grow my teaching: a series of effective instruction courses offered by my district's staff development center. One particularly enlightening day I remember thinking that I had no business teaching without knowing this stuff! How had I functioned without it? Not well, but at least I could see myself improving. When a few of us finished the series of four courses and still wanted more, the district responded by offering an independent study for our small group to pursue further information.

Thereafter I worked in the staff development center leading workshops to help others improve their writing instruction. Later I worked in a large high school in our district. I had come back full circle to high school teaching, but now I experienced some success. Besides teaching, I became involved in school improvement efforts and mentored teachers-in-training. Young intern teachers taught me as much as I taught them; the experience constantly enriched my thoughts and actions in the classroom.

As a mentor to intern teachers, I found it hard to explain the reasons for the teaching actions I chose moment by moment. I made choices that were nearly intuitive as I scanned the room to check the attention level of students, paused to rephrase an explanation, glanced at the clock for pacing, or considered how to react to student questions and comments. No matter how many books I read or how many workshops I attended, however, my ability to explain my mental processes was frustratingly limited. Novices did not think about classroom events the way I did—they overlooked things I thought were significant. We also approached planning differently; most beginners thought of just one idea, not a range of possible ideas. Bridging the gap in our thinking processes was hard, and it made me think about how I had learned and changed as a teacher.

One thing that significantly changed my thinking about teaching was peer coaching and scripting. When my peers first scripted my lessons as part of a staff development series, I was amazed at the details they pointed out to me. Colleagues transcribed a whole lesson as I taught, and then we discussed it line by line. My peer coaches named what I was doing at various points and cited what the research suggested about such actions. Soon my teaching choices, previously motivated by "educated guesses" stemming from a shallow mix of education and experience, became known techniques I could use at will. Even better, I saw my specific strengths and weaknesses all folded into the same performance. At last I could begin to tease apart the various aspects of my own teaching performance to discern effective practices.

I began scripting the student teachers' lessons to point out the implications of their teaching choices and actions. To my surprise, scripting others accelerated my own understanding. The effects of different teaching decisions became clearer to me. I learned to pay more attention to student learning, not merely teacher presentations.

Later in my career I heard about the National Board Certification process. The idea of measuring myself against an objective standard to find out if I was really a good teacher appealed to me. I signed up for the certification process and worked harder than I could have imagined. Never had I been asked to look so carefully at every detail in my assignments or presentations, or to ponder and analyze the various results, or lack of results, that my teaching produced with learners. The certification process pushed me to a new level of consciousness. To perform well was not enough; I had to evaluate the effect each choice had on learners, not generally, but in specific gains that I could reasonably credit to my teaching. Once again I developed new awareness and was more capable of excellent teaching. My certification took two years to complete, but the effort was more than worth it. The experience increased my ability to reflect upon my own efforts to effectively instruct students.

A National Board for Professional Teaching Standards (NBPTS) validity study (Bond, Smith, Baker, & Hattie, 2000) provided me with a framework to understand excellent teaching. Based on the study's identification of 13 research-based criteria and related measures, I began focusing on separate teaching skills and how to identify growth—in other words, better performance—in each one. The more clearly I understood each skill, the better I assisted the developing teachers with whom I worked.

Looking back on my own growth, I agree that experts redefine problems and "reach ingenious and insightful solutions that somehow do not occur to others" (Sternberg & Horvath as cited in Bond et al., 2000, p. 41). I am aware of the pitiful lack of problem-solving skills I displayed as a first-year teacher. The data other writers and presenters shared, and more important, the thought-provoking and revealing questions they asked, triggered a rearrangement of the ways I thought about teaching. Over time, as my knowledge expanded, I witnessed myself using skills that would have been impossible when I was a beginner; the growth and its results felt terrific. Better, the fact that I could create assignments and settings where students learned more was delightful and deeply satisfying to me. I invite readers to join me in an ongoing journey toward teacher self-improvement.

For Information and Inspiration

National Board for Professional Teaching Standards, www.nbpts.org

---

Bond, L., Smith, T., Baker, W. K., & Hattie, J. A. (2000). *The certification system of the National Board for Professional Teaching Standards: A construct and consequential validity study.* Greensboro, NC: Center for Educational Research and Evaluation, University of North Carolina.

Sternberg, R. J., & Horvath J. A. (1995). A prototype of expert teaching. *Educational Researcher, 24*(6), 9–17.

Acknowledgments

To my editors, Genny Ostertag and Sara Felice, my deep gratitude for showing me how to eliminate the unnecessary and enhance the indispensable.

To Norma Oly, Ruth Nathan, Margaret Kroon, Betty Spahr, and Gary Rackliffe, thank you for believing in me while I was learning to believe in myself.

To John and Mary Harberts, Joyce Garcia, Teresa Arpin, Steve Barone, Dr. Patricia Newby, Sue Maturkanich, Ken Folkertsma, Marsha Potter, and the staff at Grand Rapids Opportunities for Women, thank you for helping me build skills I would never have had the chance to develop without encouragement from you.

To Heather Christian and Ellen Montle, thank you for years of useful feedback about my writing.

To the National Board for Professional Teaching Standards, thank you for a certification process that helped me grow, for excellent research that helped me know more about great teaching, and for permission to build on your work.

To all my students and interns, you are so beautiful.

To family, friends, and dearly connected individuals, thank you for being a heartwarming part of my life.

Introduction

I have seen dozens of checklists, evaluation grids, and scoring rubrics over the years. All were static rather than dynamic, often composed of categories such as Poor, Fair, Good, and Excellent. Each implied a once-and-for-all categorization, whereas real people move up and down the charts, constantly fluctuating.

I questioned how anyone could be effective in all areas at all times; I knew I wasn't. As teachers, we often see ourselves improving in some areas and not changing much in others. Inservice training and conferences provide practical ideas for many aspects of our teaching, though such information comes to us piecemeal and may be hard to sort into a meaningful, considered approach to better teaching.

I wondered what thoughts or behaviors could move me, or any teacher, from fair to good or from good to excellent. When I asked for suggestions, I often received platitudes: "You're doing fine." "I have no complaints." "Keep up the good work." Despite the reassurances, I sensed that changes in my teaching were needed. I didn't know what new approaches to use, however, and helpful mentoring was rarely available.

Because teaching is incredibly complex, it cannot be described by a simplistic checklist of discrete behaviors (Bond et al., 2000, p. 35). Every feature of the classroom context affects all others. This complexity is part of the reason why we often cannot imagine what to do differently in the classroom to improve instruction.

In working on this book and reviewing the four levels of teaching identified in the NBPTS validity study (Bond et al., 2000, Appendix F.1), I spent months thinking about how to name the different levels of teaching performance; I wanted to illustrate the gradual, developmental nature of self-improvement. In most rubrics the lowest level describes a deficiency in knowledge, yet the teacher, often a beginner, is not willfully poor at a task; rather, he is ignorant, blind to what experienced practitioners see. For this reason, I named the first level "unaware." This stage precedes everything found on Bloom's famous taxonomy (Bloom, 1984). Before we know or comprehend anything, we are unaware that the information exists.

Teachers leave their unaware state when they are introduced to new information and begin to comprehend it. The process is labored and awkward at first. Whether learning how to check for understanding or organize successful group activities, the first attempts are mere approximations of the desired behavior. This second level I call "aware."

After we become aware and have practiced for a while, performance can improve. Teachers learn to do a competent job if they thoroughly prepare and concentrate as they work. They remember to include key points and impart information clearly, if not always, at least often. This is the normal level of experienced practitioners, provided they continue to make a serious effort to perform well. I call this stage "capable."

Teachers can go further, though not all do. Some continue to seek new information and implement it throughout their careers. They learn to anticipate student reactions, and they fine-tune every lesson to ameliorate problems they expect will arise. They take inspiration from everything and, in turn, inspire their students and colleagues. Whether quiet or effusive, they have a profound effect on student learning. These teachers perform at a level that I call "inspired."

Being an inspired teacher is not "dancing solo on the ceiling," a phrase from Marge Piercy describing a flamboyant individuality without appropriate and necessary interaction with other individuals or a community. Inspired teachers notice and absorb what students, colleagues, or contexts offer and use the data as their raw material. They process the information and then act responsively—animating, influencing, or stimulating others to creative effort.

Inspired teaching has two important characteristics. First, inspired teachers have absorbed and developed a large body of knowledge about their subject and about teaching well. They have mastered this information and use it effectively with ease. Second, they take inspiration from their students; every student reaction is a subtle signal used to mold more effective instruction. Inspired teachers read students and environments so well that their teaching appears intuitive. If asked why they chose a particular instructional method, they will describe reasons based on pedagogical wisdom, not whim. Because so many decisions are instantaneous, however, they discover the reasons as they explain them. Only later, when time permits, do they unpack all their thinking.

Identifying highly effective teachers can be challenging, in part because they are often quite different from one another. Using credentials or years of experience to determine who might be placed in the top category is tempting. This shortcut is unsatisfactory, however, because teaching is a complex activity. Some teachers are excellent at one part of teaching, and others excel at a different aspect. Can a person be partly excellent? Does that qualify her for inclusion in the inspired category?

No teacher is likely to excel at every aspect of teaching. By using a model of excellent teaching—and identifying various aspects of it—we can create a clear picture of outstanding instruction and identify how various teachers approximate it (Sternberg & Horvath as cited in Bond et al., 2000, p. 36). Thus, one teacher may be highly proficient at planning lessons, managing the classroom, and monitoring learning, while another possesses an expert grasp of the subject matter and spontaneously uses helpful analogies to answer student questions. We can identify both teachers as excellent if their behaviors are a good match for our prototype of inspired teaching.

But how does one progress from unaware to aware to capable to inspired? Mostly, teachers learn to think differently. Experts recall pertinent information in chunks and disregard information that they judge is not relevant (Chase, 1983; Chase & Simon, 1973; Reitman, 1976). What experts attend to and ignore is markedly different from what beginners notice. The growth continuum ranges from initial ignorance (unaware) to comprehension (aware) to competent application (capable) to great expertise (inspired). The Appendix beginning on page 233, adapted from the NBPTS study rubrics (Bond et al., 2000, Appendix F.1), summarizes a growth path for each of the 13 skills.

Teachers' learning experiences parallel those of their students. Believing that teaching is simple and straightforward often leads to frustration, discouragement, and self-loathing. Practitioners may think the problem is personal, that they are unintelligent or inferior; the truth is that teaching is difficult and cannot be mastered quickly. Warning beginning teachers that they will only gradually achieve mastery can prepare them for the challenges they face.

We ask beginning teachers to master pedagogy; this is the traditional name for the teaching of the young. We are learners at all ages, however, and no learner is a blank slate; we bring experiences and personal goals that influence the experience of learning. Perhaps if we refer to the art and science of teaching as andragogy—the teaching of humankind, not merely the young (Knowles, 1980)—our minds will be open to essential similarities between ourselves and our students. I find the term a useful aid to my thinking, leading me to ask how each classroom event might have affected me had I been in the role of learner. The idea of andragogy also allowed me to cull information about adult learners for inspiration as I tried to reach students of all ages.

All learners begin by simply becoming aware of information, naming and describing things or ideas. Next they learn to use and dissect the information through application and analysis. The most complex thinking involves assessing and recombining the information through evaluation and synthesis. Underlying the whole of Bloom's taxonomy is one unstated assumption: learners start out unaware. Whether we are referring to students, future teachers, or veteran instructors, we all begin in relative ignorance—a simple not knowing.

The growth pattern for teachers parallels Bloom's taxonomy, as shown in Figure 1.1 on the following page. Lack of awareness occurs before Bloom's categories. The awareness stage is a fair match for Bloom's stage of knowledge and understanding. Teachers at the capable stage use application and analysis well. Educators who reach the inspired stage have become skilled at synthesis and evaluation in regard to their thinking about teaching and learning.

Bloom described the six progressively more sophisticated thought processes that learners can reach. Most educators assume that the majority of students will require some assistance from teachers to reach the higher levels. A question arises: Who helps educators develop?

In the past, teachers pulled themselves up by their own mental bootstraps. Some teachers succeed in self-development of their knowledge. When they do, their development becomes a spiraling improvement, similar to a helix, repeated over and over again (Shulman, 1987). This endless process of self-transformation creates the best teachers.

Figure 1.1	**Teacher as Learner**
Teacher Growth Pattern	**Bloom's Taxonomy**
Inspired	Evaluation Synthesis
↑	↑
Capable	Analysis Application
↑	↑
Aware	Understanding Knowledge
↑	↑
Unaware	[Unaware]

Many research projects have pointed out significant differences among novices, advanced beginners, and highly skilled teachers. Great teachers demonstrate differences in both thought and behavior. As I've come to understand, based on the NBPTS validity study (Bond et al., 2000), inspired teachers demonstrate a level of mastery over 13 different skill areas that is significantly more effective than that typically shown by beginners. Below is an overview of the 13 skills and the NBPTS study research, which I will discuss in detail in the chapters that follow using the measures identified in the NBPTS study (Bond et al., 2000, Appendix F.1). The 13 skills are distinct aspects of teaching behavior, yet they are often used simultaneously; we separate them here to make sense of the complex job of teaching. Although contemplating each skill individually can be helpful, the 13 skills are interdependent and interrelated and probably cannot be separately mastered. They surround us as we teach, yet we usually have only one or two at a time in our conscious awareness. For each skill, I will explore how individuals may gradually move from a lack of awareness to an impressive expertise that we can confidently label as inspired.

Knowing the Subject. We cannot teach what we do not know, so knowledge of subject matter is essential. In general, subject-matter knowledge increases with experience. Unlike their less skilled peers, inspired teachers have a rich understanding of the subject and are able to organize and reorganize their knowledge to be accessible to learners. Teachers think about what they know and then the idea must be "shaped or tailored until it can in turn be grasped by students" (Shulman, 1987, p. 13).

Using Knowledge of Teaching and Learning. This skill is more than simple awareness of pedagogy, or andragogy, and technique. The greatest teachers merge information about learning in general with teaching approaches and then adapt their plan to fit a specific class, as well as the groups and individuals within that class. Experts in this area are selective in their awareness, remembering information mostly related to planning and instruction rather than the random behaviors or physical characteristics of their pupils (Carter, Sabers, Cushing, Pinegar, & Berliner as cited in Bond et al., 2000, p. 19).

Solving Instructional Problems. Solutions to problems that relate to curriculum and instruction are a constant concern of expert teachers. Unlike novices or less expert colleagues, inspired teachers solve problems all the time—before teaching, while teaching, and after teaching. They are better able to imagine the learning task from the student perspective and to adapt lessons in advance because of their awareness of a larger number of instructional goals. These teachers notice student behavior during the lesson, which provides clues to the lesson's effectiveness, and they may adapt their plan based on these observations. After teaching, they reflect on whether they have achieved their goals and met students' needs and then make further modifications if necessary in future presentations (Westerman, 1991).

Improvising. Insufficient background in a subject or lack of thorough preparation may cause presenters to mask personal limitations using a "highly didactic, teacher-controlled, swiftly paced combination of lecture and tightly-controlled recitation" (Grossman as cited in Shulman, 1987, p. 18). In contrast, inspired teachers can comfortably use the Socratic method or other highly interactive approaches because they can draw from their broad and deep understanding of subjects. These experts are able to field wide-ranging questions and quickly develop effective explanations or metaphors for unexpected queries.

Managing a Classroom. Inspired teachers prevent problems by "using their voices and body language along with well-practiced management strategies to motivate students and control their attention" (Westerman, 1991, p. 297). They sense the reasons behind students' behaviors and adjust their teaching to increase the likelihood that learning will occur. Part of their management skill lies in developing routines that make aspects of the classroom automatic, comfortable, and reliable for teacher and students alike.

Interpreting Events in Progress. Experts use more elaborate schemas and greater metacognitive skills. These abilities allow them to notice more of what is occurring in the classroom and to consciously make choices that change the direction of interaction and instruction. These are teachers who seem to have eyes in the back of their heads and who remain constantly aware despite numerous distractions and interruptions (Westerman, 1991).

Being Sensitive to Context. Inspired teaching "involves complex judgments of balance between ideal and possible practices" to determine the best option in a given situation using practical wisdom (Shulman, 1987, p. 13). The wisest teachers understand themselves, and they understand the personal, social, and cultural characteristics of their students. They make continual adjustments to balance the complexities that connect these factors, aware that one size never fits all.

Monitoring Learning. Expert teachers are flexible in how they move toward instructional goals. They constantly sample students' understanding to determine their comprehension level and also observe whether students are attentive moment by moment and adjust accordingly. These teachers usually present lessons in a highly interactive manner. In the classroom they show a "superior ability to see meaningful patterns in the stream of ongoing events" (Sternberg & Horvath, 1995, p. 13). They also give students useful feedback and often teach students to monitor their own learning.

Testing Hypotheses. Experts concentrate on identifying a problem before they advance hypotheses or attempt solutions. They are far more likely to consider and evaluate a number of alternative hypotheses, rather than use the first one that comes to mind. Inspired teachers continually learn through experience and welcome challenges as opportunities to expand their knowledge and competence (Swanson, O'Connor, & Cooney, 1990).

Demonstrating Respect. Inspired teachers believe in and work at "growing persons, perceived as *persons*, not as 'typical high school classes,' or 'the shy,' or 'the boisterous,' or for that matter, 'the gifted,' 'the disruptive,' or the 'slow learner'" (Sockett, 1987, p. 217). Respect contains an element of caring. Those who practice respect have, and constantly demonstrate, a concern for the best interests of each individual with whom they have contact.

Showing Passion for Teaching and Learning. Inspired teachers are committed both to teaching and to encouraging student learning; to them teaching is more a mission than a mere job or career. They demonstrate responsibility, a strong code of ethics, and a deep love of the subjects they teach. In addition, they express more emotion than nonexperts when discussing successes and failures in the classroom (Berliner as cited in Bond et al., 2000, p. 58).

Helping Students Reach Higher Levels of Achievement. Inspired teachers do more than guide students to complete assignments just for the sake of finishing or earning a grade; they help students find intrinsic satisfaction in learning. Thanks to the efforts of outstanding teachers, students see that their own efforts affect outcomes. As a result, students develop more confidence in themselves as learners. Inspired teachers show students how to try harder in order to help students learn more (Locke & Latham, 1990).

Helping Students Understand Complexity. While inspired teachers help students learn and store more facts in long-term memory, they also help students find a "new way of seeing" (Marton, Dall'Alba, & Beaty, 1993). This new type of understanding cannot be retrieved from memory but must be created. Students build a dense mental matrix representing entire systems, rather than discrete, unrelated facts. Thus, the best teaching allows students to mull over facts, synthesize their meaning, and form their own interpretations based on those facts.

Adapted from an NBPTS validity study (Bond et al., 2000) with permission from the National Board for Professional Teaching Standards.

Inspired teachers develop an unmistakable inner strength. Even in a professional work environment considered inadequate by objective standards, expert teachers sustain outstanding performance. Keith Campbell (as cited in Bond et al., 2000, p. 23–25) describes eight qualities shared by expert teachers: a strong sense of mission, a desire to improve their teaching, a holistic sense of teaching to develop individuals as well as impart facts, a high degree of confidence in their own personal and professional views, a peer support system that reinforces their sense of mission, a form of support from significant others, a sense of professional autonomy, and a refusal to permit interference with their teaching mission.

Such personal success does not develop haphazardly. Teaching qualities grow over time, and building such competence can be a daunting task. The purpose of this book is to show that feeling lost or incompetent is not a permanent personal indictment. Discouragement is the disequilibrium that precedes growth; it can be a friend and motivator, however uncomfortable it feels. We can grow past unawareness to become aware and then capable. And finally, we can learn to be the inspired teachers we long to be.

For Information and Inspiration

Berliner, D. C. (1988, February). *The development of expertise in pedagogy.* Paper presented at the annual meeting of the American Association of Colleges for Teacher Education, New Orleans, LA.

Bloom, B. S. (1984). *Taxonomy of educational objectives.* Boston: Allyn and Bacon.

Bond, L., Smith, T., Baker, W. K., & Hattie, J. A. (2000). *The certification system of the National Board for Professional Teaching Standards: A construct and consequential validity study.* Greensboro, NC: Center for Educational Research and Evaluation, University of North Carolina.

Campbell, K. P. (1990–91, Winter). Personal norms of experienced expert suburban high school teachers: Implications for selecting and retaining outstanding individuals. *Action in Teacher Education, 12*(4), 35–40.

Carter, K., Sabers, D., Cushing, K., Pinegar, P., & Berliner, D. C. (1987). Processing and using information about students: A study of expert, novice, and postulant teachers. *Teaching and Teacher Education, 3*(2), 147–157.

Chase, W. G. (1983). Spatial representations in taxi drivers. In D. Rogers & J. H. Sloboda (Eds.), *Acquisition of visual skills* (pp. 391–405). New York: Plenum.

Chase, W. G., & Simon, H. A. (1973). The mind's eye in chess. In W. Chase (Ed.), *Visual information processing* (pp. 215–281). New York: Academic Press.

Danielson, C. (2007). *Enhancing professional practice: A framework for teaching* (2nd ed.). Alexandria, VA: ASCD.

Knowles, M. S. (1980). *The modern practice of adult education: From pedagogy to andragogy.* Wilton, CT: Association Press.

Locke, E. A., & Latham, G. P. (1990). *A theory of goal setting and task performance.* Englewood Cliffs, NJ: Prentice-Hall.

Marton, F., Dall'Alba, G., & Beaty, E. (1993). Conceptions of learning. *International Journal of Educational Research, 19*(3), 277–300.

Reitman, J. S. (1976). Skilled perception in go: Deducing memory structures from inter-response times. *Cognitive Psychology, 8*(3), 336–356.

Shulman, L. S. (1987). Knowledge and teaching: Foundations of the new reform. *Harvard Educational Review, 57*(1), 1–22.

Sockett, H. T. (1987). Has Shulman got the strategy right? *Harvard Educational Review, 57*(2), 208–217.

Sternberg, R. J., & Horvath J. A. (1995). A prototype of expert teaching. *Educational Researcher, 24*(6), 9–17.

Stronge, J. H. (2007). *Qualities of effective teachers* (2nd ed.). Alexandria, VA: ASCD.

Swanson, H. L., O'Connor, J. E., & Cooney, J. B. (1990). An information processing analysis of expert and novice teachers' problem solving. *American Educational Research Journal, 27*(3), 533–556.

Westerman, D. A. (1991). Expert and novice teacher decision making. *Journal of Teacher Education, 42*(4), 292–305.

1

Knowing the Subject

Let's start with a paradox: Teachers should know their subject matter thoroughly, but it is impossible for one person to know any subject completely. Teachers are always traveling toward complete knowledge but never arriving. Of course, every person follows the same road, whether he notices or not. It's a good road to travel though, always fresh and challenging. Every day we can stretch again to reach a noble goal.

We meet people with vast stores of knowledge: computer technicians, doctors, financial planners, mortgage bankers, housing inspectors, auto mechanics. Some speak in a jargon so dense we struggle to grasp a fraction of what they say.

Why don't they make their knowledge comprehensible and usable? Maybe they don't know how. If my accountant said, "Here are 11 things to know about quarterly tax returns," my stomach would knot. To do 11 things, I need a checklist and time to comprehend each item. However, if he told me to do two things so that he could do the rest, I could confidently take appropriate action.

Communicating with the uninformed requires sorting key facts from less important details. The accountant above knew that two factors were absolutely critical, so he asked me to take action on these two only. From experience he knows that other factors are of second-tier importance. Factors that are central to basic understanding are called critical attributes. Wise experts concentrate on those things first.

Some experts choose words and examples so memorable that we can recall their words and concepts later. When we meet these jewels, we rave about the experience because it's unusual. Its rarity hints at how difficult it is to know and impart complex knowledge well.

Many issues are complex. It is difficult, using linear speech, to capture the multifaceted relationships within any given subject. We need to simplify to build understanding, yet we must also "re-complexify" the same subjects as our knowledge grows, or we remain partially ignorant. Consider a toddler learning about the kitchen stove. Although his mother warns him away, he touches it anyway, learning that hot stoves are dangerous. He has a simplistic understanding: Stove-hot-danger-stay away. Later in life he needs to know more. As he matures, he will "re-complexify" the original knowledge: A stove may be hot and might burn me (bad), but the heat can be used to cook food (good), so follow safety procedures around stoves (balanced).

Knowing exists on many levels, and understanding deepens as people gather more information over a lifetime. Communication skills influence how well people convey what they know. Every subject-matter teacher needs excellent writing and speaking skills, but even teachers may have learning difficulties or communication barriers. A teacher with dyslexia, for instance, may teach well, yet spell poorly on the board. In such cases, he must find coping skills to compensate for his limitation. As a teacher deepens his knowledge and develops his communication skills, he will teach facts differently.

The Unaware Teacher

Everyone is unaware of something—cheesecake recipes, quantum physics, properties of tanzanite. When the photocopy process was first developed, businesses were unaware of its useful value; the inventor leased machines to offices to create awareness. With hindsight the value seems clear, yet we surely remain blind to certain things that will someday be obvious.

The unaware teacher knows the subject and organizational methods incompletely

Novices begin with much to learn. Although they have completed the education department's coursework (or earned the HVAC certificate, MD, or BA), they are still wet behind the ears because there are thousands of facts and nuances that can be mastered only through experience. Incomplete knowledge is the normal state of the beginner.

Beginning teachers must study and then attempt to effectively organize the material. Their first efforts are often clumsy.

They need to forgive themselves for not being perfectly pre-pared. We have learner's permits for young drivers, internships for doctors-in-training, and probationary periods for most new hires. No newcomer is as knowledgeable as a 20-year veteran in the same field. New doctors, consultants, and foremen all strug-gle to master details. With steady effort, teachers know more every year and present it better.

••• **TIP** •••

For a quick introduction to the main ideas of a subject—butterflies, nutrition, Mayan math—look at children's nonfiction. Authors distill and simplify information for young readers, offering a brief, accurate over-view we can appropriate.

Limited knowledge of the subject matter triggers anxiety. Beginners lament, "I never studied this in college." Neither the beginners nor the college failed. The body of knowledge in every subject is so deep and so wide that no matter what beginners have studied, it never matches what they need for all teaching assignments. Colleges offer a broad education, but in-depth mastery is a lifelong task.

Ms. Shinozaki, a preservice teacher who majored in history in college, offers an example. When she taught U.S. history for the first time, she read each section in the student textbook sev-eral times. She looked up additional information on the Inter-net and assembled lesson plans for hours, and she still made occasional factual errors. She couldn't predict what her students already knew or how to connect their knowledge to the new information; these skills develop through experience and exper-imentation. Provided she taught the course again and contin-ued her efforts to grow as a teacher, her expertise in those areas would develop over time.

We hope that novices find out what they don't know. Nor-mally, only students will hear a teacher's lectures, and only a few students will challenge the teacher's instruction. Either some-thing—a student, a colleague, the media—challenges a novice's assumptions and gaps in knowledge, or, through continual vol-untary study over time, a teacher reaches a broader and deeper understanding. Very knowledgeable teachers are usually those who feed their own curiosity, building knowledge year after year.

Beginners also lack skill in organizing information to increase the likelihood that students learn. Novices have a limited range of approaches. Because many have just experienced four years of college lectures, they gravitate toward lectures. Unfortunately, we recall only about 5 to 10 percent of what we hear; merely telling is a poor way to ensure student learning. Would a short video clip clarify the information? Is it best to go from a big idea to supporting details or start with details to lead to the big idea? Will a group discussion work? Should the teacher provide questions for students, create a diagram to be filled in, or invite personal experiences? Are kinesthetic materials needed?

Novices don't know how to organize their knowledge for learners because they are still sorting out their own understanding. Beginners have a hard time recognizing which facts are critical, which are fairly important, and which can be safely ignored. Although they may learn to prioritize facts for their lessons, dealing with the unexpected is still difficult. Preparing well to teach adjectives and adverbs, for instance, does not prepare them to explain gerunds to an inquisitive student.

The unaware teacher rarely makes connections

New teachers don't yet see clearly how knowledge fits into a bigger picture. College courses cover separate aspects of a major field. Integrating the information takes time and effort. Unaware teachers don't integrate various subject areas, and they rarely connect their own general knowledge to the subject matter or to other courses students are studying.

My second year as a high school teacher was my 14th year of teaching. In between I spent six years teaching adults seeking a high school diploma, six years teaching Job Corps students, and nearly two years leading workshops for teachers. I knew how to teach but was still a novice in teaching U.S. history to 10th graders. I had little idea of what students were learning about in other subjects from other teachers. Not until I had many teacher-to-teacher conversations did I understand what teachers of biology, math, art, and physical education were teaching in my high school and how these areas might connect to what I was teaching. As I learned, I connected history lessons to the other coursework students were taking. I teamed with the English teacher who taught the same students. Students read stories in English class about personal liberties while we studied the U.S. Constitution. They read the work of Native American writers or women writers or 18th century writers that dealt with issues covered in the history text. My partnering teachers and I gradually learned to use themes to improve our teaching.

The unaware teacher fails to link what students know to the subject

Beginners rarely check to see what students already know. Novice teachers often follow a plan developed by someone else—usually a textbook or a prescribed curriculum. Such outlines imply that the information must be covered in the order in which it's presented, so novices plunge forward. It may take months to notice that many students already know the material or that some lack the background information needed for full comprehension.

Novices avoid asking what students know because they want to avoid a very real problem: If everyone already knows this material, the teacher will have to teach another lesson entirely. This is an intimidating challenge for new teachers. Who could possibly prepare alternative lessons for every class? With experience, beginners become aware enough to assess student knowledge and brave enough to deal with the related difficulties.

Questions to grow by

☐ Do you read several sources to make sure you understand material thoroughly before planning lessons?

☐ Do you discuss with other teachers which issues seem most important in a given lesson or unit?

☐ Do you ask students to tell you what they already know about the subject under consideration?

☐ Have you tried asking students what they want to know or what they are curious or confused about?

☐ Do you help students connect what they are learning to ideas from other subjects or previous years?

☐ Do you write down what worked and what didn't so you'll teach the material more effectively next time?

The Aware Teacher

At the aware level, teachers are still spending a great deal of energy assembling facts and mastering intricacies of their subject matter because it is relatively new to them. They rarely think about the order that facts are presented in, how those facts relate to other matters, or their students' current understanding. Their knowledge of subject matter, while fairly broad, is still incompletely processed.

The aware teacher knows the subject adequately but organizes poorly for learning

When I took 10th grade biology, I was taught by Mr. Hammond, a recent college graduate. I remember the day he explained genes and chromosomes.

"Genes are located on the chromosomes," he said, "like beads on a string. During reproduction, they duplicate themselves before the cell divides. That way each of the new cells is just like the old cell."

My mind rebelled. *How could beads on a string reproduce themselves?* I memorized what he said without understanding how the process could possibly work. Perhaps he repeated to us the explanation he received in college. Still, I felt dissatisfied; his explanation didn't make sense to me. My knowledge of actual beads was a barrier.

The aware teacher sometimes checks prior knowledge

What the learner already knows is referred to as prior knowledge. Why would beginning teachers ignore prior knowledge? One reason is a human tendency to make assumptions: *If the curriculum expects me to teach this, then the students must not know it.* Another reason is that teachers fear coping with the results, such as inventing a whole new approach on the spot.

The knowledge of novice teachers is often tentative. Beginning teachers may be able to comprehend the material well enough to take a multiple-choice test or understand summaries and studies, yet they find explaining it to students much harder and they may stumble. At the aware level, teachers know more information and have some memorable ideas about organizing lessons, but they can do this only with focused effort. There is limited time for improving every lesson. Novices' lessons sometimes enhance learning; other times they don't.

We may be in a similar position after attending a seminar, a sales presentation, or a conference. An interested person asks what we learned and what seemed crystal clear as incoming data now sounds muddled and confusing as we hear ourselves trying to explain. Why is this true?

When we first hear or read new information, we have only a surface grasp of it, no matter how attentive we are. To have a deep understanding we must gradually construct a web of comprehension. On first hearing, we follow the line of thought as presented by the speaker or writer. This may be a good introduction, but it is a single strand of thought. We have not yet built a matrix of understanding.

Consider how memory works. If we hear "3rd grade" or "first job," a whole set of memories pops up. We remember things in sets and groups, with attached sensations and emotions. Sometimes a long-forgotten aroma will take us time traveling. We construct our own understanding by gradually making mental connections to the cognitive structures we have previously built.

Gary Rackliffe (1998) has used an activity with teachers-in-training to demonstrate how people construct knowledge.

"Form a group of four or five people," he says. "Then draw a poster to show the idea of a tree."

Each group creates a complex poster that includes many details: leaves, bark, branches, and seeds; green, brown, yellow, and red; birds, nests, squirrels, and nuts; swings, yards, and fences; sun, rain, clouds, and soil. All the posters are different, yet all do exactly the same thing. Each poster reveals dozens of facts that relate to trees, and each shows a complex understanding of what trees are, what they do, and where they come from. It is a re-creation of the sort of connections people have in their minds.

Rackliffe explains that we create mental filing systems for information. He compares the process to an old post office. The postmaster sorts all the incoming mail—into each box goes mail for one family. Similarly, in our minds we put new information into existing, related categories. When we first hear about birch bark canoes, the information may be filed with trees (because of bark), or with forms of transportation (because canoes are boats), or both, but every fact attaches to existing knowledge structures. Barring physical deterioration of the brain, people construct new knowledge for as long as they live.

What level of understanding can we expect for teachers who are still constructing knowledge in the subject area that they teach? Most states require incoming teachers to pass a test in their major and minor before receiving a teaching certificate. The tests may contain 200 multiple-choice questions on facts or issues that cover a whole field of study. To pass, candidates must answer three-fourths of the questions correctly. Some states also require essays or language proficiency tests. Future teachers must be familiar with a wide selection of details in order to pass, but how dense their matrix of understanding may be is not measured. We have to hope that they will continue to develop after they begin their jobs, in the same way that new drivers improve over time.

Beginning teachers are still in the process of constructing a complex matrix of understanding; they are often unaware of details regarding today's lesson and connections between those topics and other matters. Because they overlook interrelatedness, they are unable to guide students toward connections.

My daughter taught college courses as she worked on her PhD. She worked hard the first semester and received positive evaluations from her students. Nonetheless, when she started the second semester, she had a clearer idea of what students needed to know and how to present it. After the first week of the second semester she told me, "I feel like I should find all the students I had last semester and apologize to them!" This sentiment is familiar to many who have struggled through their first teaching experience and then seen growth in themselves. It can be embarrassing to look back at those first efforts.

Adequate knowledge means that presentations are free from major errors in fact and congruent with other information students are gleaning from text, handouts, authoritative Internet sites, and other reliable sources. If we state an error, we catch ourselves in the midst of it or have the guts to come back later and admit the error so it can be corrected in the students' notes and minds. Adequate knowledge means knowing basic grammar, dates, key definitions, correct procedures, and whatever else is central to the subject at hand. Although every teacher will occasionally make mistakes, adequate knowledge means that such errors are rare rather than pervasive. By this measure, my daughter's teaching displayed adequate knowledge, but for her, being merely adequate wasn't enough. She wanted to grow beyond that baseline.

The aware teacher may link the subject with other knowledge

Each time teachers or presenters point out how a subject connects to information we already understand, the new information is more firmly attached in memory. For most people, teaching this way is not automatic. Only through time and experience do we see these connections and learn to point them out. Teachers who are building this skill will gradually point out more and more of these links. They will also notice which links help learners most and which ones help very little. Naturally, over time teachers will reuse the effective examples and try to find good replacements for those that don't work well.

When I first heard about punctuating with colons in 7th grade English, I didn't understand their use. Mrs. MacFarland stood in front of us and explained, "A colon precedes something, like a list." We must have looked confused, so she tried a new approach. "Think of it as a warning light at a railroad crossing." She held one hand above the other, each index finger rhythmically poking the air as if in time with an imaginary flashing light at a crossing. "Something's coming. Something's coming. Something's coming," she chanted.

Instantly, the colon's job seemed perfectly clear. I never forgot her example and repeated it when I became a teacher. Mrs. MacFarland didn't teach the other punctuation marks in clever ways, but when it came to colons, she gave us exactly what we needed.

The absolute beginner rarely shows deep, broad knowledge or makes connections well; however, the person who has begun to improve does both at least part of the time. As teachers improve, the incidence of these two factors goes from somewhat rare to more common. When teachers connect new information to students' existing knowledge, the new information makes more sense to students and they remember it better. Connections contribute to congruence—the smooth fit between the old and the new. Information that doesn't overlap what is already known is harder to acquire. Information that conflicts with what is already believed to be true is integrated even more slowly or not at all. Therefore, if teachers point out overlaps with existing knowledge and also discuss perceived conflicts between new and old information, learners can better grasp and recall the lesson.

Events from the daily news may be used as a tie-in to a lesson. For instance, the actions of a well-known sports figure may illustrate a point in the lesson or appear as a character in a math problem. The teacher may refer to topics covered a week or a month ago and add new information from the current lesson to deepen understanding. Apparent contradictions are mentioned, clarified, and discussed so learners see a web of connections and build a place for these connections in their own minds. Teachers who take these steps are working to connect new knowledge to students' prior knowledge. Nonetheless, aware teachers still need extensive planning and comprehensive notes to make it happen. They deserve congratulations; they are working to develop greater skill.

Questions to grow by

☐ Do you subscribe to a magazine in your subject area?

☐ Are you reading books that broaden and deepen your subject-matter knowledge?

☐ Have you taken advantage of all the training opportunities your employer or school district offers?

☐ Do you seek out additional materials from the Internet, a regional resource network, or your library system?

☐ When your school district adopts new texts or materials, do you attend the introductory training sessions?

☐ Do you ask other teachers how they present various topics or issues?

☐ Is sharing lessons, materials, handouts, and ideas a part of the culture of your workplace? If not, what can you do to change this?

Self-Development

• Assume there are things you do not know. Keep assuming this for as long as you teach. If you hear a fact that is "wrong" from students, friends, or the media, look it up to verify your own interpretation. Sometimes you will be humbled, but improved.

• Make a plan for deepening your knowledge and follow your plan. Read or listen to books. Subscribe to useful sources of information. Take a course. Join a professional organization and attend conferences. This will take time you do not have. Do it anyway.

• When you make an error, admit it to students, so they can know the truth. They may already know you were incorrect. If they don't, their respect for you will grow, along with their factual knowledge. Remember, you are their role model for lifelong learning.

Collegial Support

• Share information and lesson plans with others. Build a culture of mutual assistance. There is so much knowledge in every field that no one has it all. Everybody benefits from sharing information.

• If mentoring an inexperienced person, you are likely to hear numerous errors in one session. Resist the urge to jump on every one. This will paralyze the person. Prioritize. Be sure to mention strengths. Then bring up only two or three significant errors. When a person comprehends significant concepts, smaller errors tend to disappear. If they don't, deal with errors during later sessions.

The Capable Teacher

A major difference between the aware level and the capable level has to do with ease and frequency. Aware teachers are like new drivers who recite the steps for shifting gears as they try to implement them. It takes a great deal of focused effort. At the capable level, drivers can rely on their hands and feet to shift fairly smoothly most of the time in normal driving situations. To carry the analogy further, not until they reach the inspired level will they instinctively downshift for control or master the shifting necessary to get out of a snowdrift.

The capable teacher knows the subject and organizes for learning

A teacher with extensive knowledge has probably studied several sources and holds a lot of information clearly in mind, more than will actually be used in a given lecture or explanation. She is aware of complexity and contradictions within the material, and she emphasizes important points to help students understand. She answers questions correctly and confidently. If the question is unexpected or slightly off track, she may promise to look up the answer and get back to the inquirer (and remember to do so). There is no hesitancy in the presentation because the information has become quite familiar. Notes are mostly unnecessary, used to help keep track of where she left off last time, not as a crutch. Teachers at this level may display a calm demeanor that springs from comfort with the topic. Nervousness abates because they no longer worry that they'll forget, become confused, or get lost.

The capable teacher connects information to prior knowledge

Think back to my story about being taught that genes and chromosomes resemble beads on a string. In college the topic came up again. My botany professor, Mr. Nebel, explained the process of cell division quite differently:

> "Genes are components of chromosomes, like building blocks. During reproduction the paired chromosomes sort of unzip down the center and each gene on the chromosome attracts a new partner from the nuclear soup inside the cell, almost like a magnet. Once the new partners are all attached to the existing genes, you have two zippers, or chromosomes, one for each new cell."

I thought, *Wow, that makes sense!* Building blocks, zippers, soup, magnets—these were things I was familiar with. I had also been familiar with beads, but the examples in this analogy helped me picture the actual process of replication much better than the beads had. Mr. Nebel's explanation worked for me because the comparison was not contradictory: The reproduction of beads is not an idea that makes sense. A zipper actually does open down the middle. From there, attracting a new partner from the nuclear soup Mr. Nebel described, while an odd idea, was not completely unimaginable.

Many science students are given a paper with shapes representing genetic building blocks like adenine and guanine. They color each type, cut them out, and paste them on a sheet to demonstrate the way the replication occurs. The first time I saw teenagers doing this I envied them, wishing I had been taught this way by Mr. Hammond.

Both Mr. Hammond and Mr. Nebel used a technique very helpful to learners—analogy. The best analogies present unfamiliar information by comparing it to familiar things and then pointing out similarities and, where appropriate, differences. Analogies use learners' prior knowledge. The beads-on-a-string analogy that Mr. Hammond provided gave a picture of the sequential nature of genes on a chromosome, but it didn't go very far to explain other characteristics of cell reproduction. Mr. Nebel combined the ideas of building blocks, zippers, and magnetism to describe a process. His comparisons stimulated in me a real understanding. He demonstrated higher skill in the use of subject-matter knowledge by organizing it in a way that greatly enhanced learning—definitely putting him at the capable level, or maybe even higher.

The capable teacher connects the subject with other knowledge

Capable teachers have a mental road map of today's lesson, the unit it belongs to, and the semester plan. This road map supports the making of connections. Teachers recall where they have been with this class and foresee where they will go next. They understand the relationship between the parts of the subject and the course. Such teachers often refer back to a previous lesson or experience to reinforce a point. They may promise to delve into a certain issue in the next unit, not to put students off but because these teachers know some matters will be better understood at that point. These teachers may answer the relevant part of a question, promising to cover more details at a future time. They actually do cover them later, because they teach their way along a mental road map and don't skip any important sites along the way.

Capable teachers have built a repertoire of examples and links that are held in memory. Tried and true ways of making information understandable enrich the lessons. A variety of links will be used to help students connect new knowledge to old, and to do so more often and more thoroughly.

Good teachers are open to unexpected connections that students make spontaneously. Thus, if May Belle blurts out that today's fraction lesson about eighths reminds her of Grandma, instead of squelching her, the teacher may ask why. May Belle can explain that Grandma always cuts pies into eight pieces so all the cousins can have a piece. This provides a chance for the teacher to discuss a complicated idea: the smaller the denominator, the larger the pieces. The larger the denominator, the smaller the pieces, but the more pieces there are. This concept is made more memorable when Grandma's pies and May Belle's clamoring cousins enliven it.

Questions to grow by

☐ Do you look for new ideas everywhere, even from presenters who repeat things you have already learned?

☐ Does your school or department make mutual assistance and learning a part of every meeting?

☐ Have you formed a support group with other teachers to brainstorm new approaches to each topic?

☐ Have you read research to ensure your understanding matches developments in the field?

☐ Do you design assessments before planning lessons in order to guide your explanations?

The Inspired Teacher

Inspired teachers' subject-matter knowledge is extensive, and they know from experience how to organize and present information to make it interesting and memorable to students. They integrate their subject-matter knowledge with other fields and help students to do the same. These teachers pay attention to students' prior knowledge and help students make connections to the topic under study, so that students' previous understandings are linked and integrated with new information.

The inspired teacher understands the subject and organizational methods deeply

If you have ever heard it said of someone that they "live and breathe" physics or Civil War history or psychology, that individual is likely to demonstrate an inspired command of a topic. When the individual is a teacher, this deep interest and curiosity can be sensed by students, and such interest is contagious. An impressive command of the subject underlies all planning, comments, and responses to questions. For the learner it feels like a guided tour through a complex maze—difficult but delightful.

Sometimes when experts try to answer questions or explain points, their eyes drift upward as they pause briefly to formulate their comments. I imagine that they are mentally poring over mounds of data to choose just those specific items that are needed by a specific listener with a specific question. When the answer is clear and responsive, I marvel at how much knowledge experts have brought to bear in that simple but effective answer. The inspired teacher has this kind of grasp of what makes lessons work and uses this knowledge constantly.

The inspired teacher integrates knowledge of the subject with other fields

Inspired teachers' deep, clear understanding includes thousands of facts, but facts alone are not enough. These teachers also see the relationships within a subject and across subject boundaries. They may point out similarities between parenting and the presidency, sociology and nuclear physics, economics and courtship rituals, or basketball and typing, not because these comments are required in the curriculum outline, but because such teachers perceive that pointing out the relationship will clarify some points for learners or help keep them interested and on track.

Questions from students are no longer interruptions but wonderful invitations to explore more deeply along some related trails of thought. The inspired teacher asks the student what he already knows or what he guesses the answer might be. Or the teacher answers by telling the class two or more theories or interpretations and asking students to evaluate each. This teacher is willing to explore complexity and is comfortable with the possibility that neither theory can be proven "right" or "wrong," yet both make interesting points. Such reactions are possible only if the teacher has command of a large body of knowledge.

Imagine a geography teacher with a deep understanding of cartography. Rather than merely presenting a list of the strengths and weaknesses of various map styles, she may present a series of situations to the class, asking how maps might be made to meet certain criteria. A map that attempts to show the relative size of nations looks very different from one that is designed to maintain the grid lines of latitude and longitude. A map designed to demonstrate the populations of nations rather than the land masses is distorted and odd-looking, yet still correct for its own purpose. Discussion based on a book like *How to Lie with Maps* (Monmonier, 1996) will give students a deeper understanding of the strengths and weaknesses of maps and the multiple purposes they might serve. This is a very different experience from memorizing one map and moving on.

> ### • • • TIP • • •
>
> Teachers often say they have no time to read. An average 5th grader reading at the 50th percentile for just 11 minutes a day would read, over the course of one year, about 465,000 words (Nathan, 1990). Maybe every teacher could find 11 minutes a day. That might be enough.

The inspired teacher guides students to link prior knowledge to the subject

It is important to work from what students already know, adding new information along the way. Repeating the known can lead to boredom and mischief; telling only the unknown soon overwhelms the listener. A technical writer once told me that he tried to structure his sentences so the new information was at the end of the sentences. He said that people seemed to follow his instructions best when he started sentences with something he'd already covered and added new details at the end.

Starting with the known and moving to the unknown sounds relatively simple—if everyone in the group has a similar level of existing knowledge. But everyone in a given audience or classroom brings a different set of experiences and thus a different body of existing knowledge. In some cases the difference is relatively small; in other cases it is immense.

Great teachers develop the ability to find the heart of the lesson, the few key factors that cause the subject to make sense. We already named these key factors as critical attributes. Key factors form the skeleton upon which all the rest of the details hang. For example, the moment a toddler can tell a dog from a cat, she has isolated the key attributes of "dogness" and "catness." People of all ages can identify attributes but may find it challenging when faced with a brand-new subject. A great teacher identifies critical attributes and points them out as soon as possible to help students comprehend. The teacher must sort through a mountain of details and isolate those few that are central to understanding.

It can be tempting to include too many details too soon or to dwell on exceptions. But teachers who can concentrate on the critical attributes make every topic accessible. Students who are studying under such instructors say that the topic is "easy" without realizing that it might seem impossible if presented by a less skilled teacher. Some say it is possible to teach very sophisticated ideas—philosophy, for instance—to very young children as long as ideas are presented at an age-appropriate level. To do this, finding and pointing out critical attributes is indispensable.

Mentioning critical attributes at the beginning of a presentation takes a fairly short time. This is not boring to the knowledgeable listener, who may just nod in agreement, while his completely uninformed neighbor may be able to absorb enough at the onset to make the rest of the discussion intelligible. If the presenter follows with diversified assignments, then all levels of understanding can be served. Admittedly, diversifying is quite difficult. One method is to provide work stations for student learning. The teacher must spend time preparing these learning experiments, but once class begins, students do all the work.

Inspired teachers also sense that sometimes it is best to begin with interesting facts that are peripheral to the core subject because they rivet the attention of the learner. Choosing an effective approach hints at how inspired their work is. A thorough grasp of best practices feeds an intuition about when to disregard the typical approach and when to use it.

It's easy to forget that how we teach is as important as what we teach. A teacher, speaking as a parent, related this experience: "When my son was in 11th grade," she said, "our high school hired a retired chemist to teach chemistry. We were all delighted because he really knew his stuff. But once he started teaching, the kids were lost. He was the worst teacher my son ever had. After that year the teacher quit. What a disappointment."

This chemistry teacher had a deep understanding of his subject without an accompanying ability to use and organize the information to effectively guide learners. Even the teacher-parent overlooked how important this skill is and that the skill must be developed over time. Effective teaching is not automatic, but rather a set of habits assembled through reflective practice. Reflective practice means thinking back on one's own work with questions: *What reaction did each of my actions get? What might I do differently to elicit different responses?* Inspired teachers know that when they change their own behaviors, they have the power to cause new responses and increase learning.

Donald Cronkite, a science professor at Hope College, consciously designs activities to increase learning. When studying the brain, his students wear shower caps bearing labeled diagrams of the brain. His students perform square dances based on cell division and create costumes to illustrate important features of various phyla (Reinstadler, 2005). No wonder Cronkite was named Michigan's College Teacher of the Year.

Tests given to potential teachers can show us whether they have a basic command of their subject; however, there is no written test to show us whether they can see connections or guide students to make them. These skills emerge over time in the context of the classroom. We learn whether teachers can demonstrate this skill by observing. Are connections made over hours, days, weeks, and months? Teachers develop these skills through daily consideration of whether their lessons and approaches achieved the desired results. If the answer is yes, the teachers will repeat or adapt the approach. If no, they will try something different.

Actions to grow by

☐ When you read, mark all terms or references that are unfamiliar. Look them up to increase your depth and breadth of knowledge.

☐ Compare several versions of the material about a subject—preferably unfamiliar versions—looking for differences and contradictions. Ponder what these variations tell you.

☐ To test your own knowledge, take the tests associated with your class's textbook before preparing any lessons.

☐ Be a mental adventurer. Expose yourself to fields you have never studied before.

☐ Ask listeners to share their knowledge of the subject before giving yours.

☐ Look for connections between the subject at hand and other courses, events, or memories listeners are familiar with. Mention connections as you teach.

☐ Think of three or more ways to present a concept and then select the one that seems most effective.

☐ Write notes to yourself about the experiences of your audience. For instance, people born after 1980 will understand comparisons to iPods and cell phones, but not record players or *Sputnik*.

For Information and Inspiration

The following professional organizations offer teachers a forum for improvement in various curriculum areas. Joining such organizations, reading their publications, and attending their conferences can inspire and inform teachers.

American Alliance for Health, Physical Education, Recreation, and Dance, www.aahperd.org

American Council on the Teaching of Foreign Languages, www.actfl.org

Association for Career and Technical Education, www.acteonline.org

International Reading Association, www.reading.org

National Art Education Association, www.naea-reston.org

National Council for the Social Studies, www.ncss.org

National Council of Teachers of English, www.ncte.org

National Council of Teachers of Mathematics, www.nctm.org

National Science Teachers Association, www.nsta.org

Brooks, J. G., & Brooks, M. (1999). *In search of understanding: The case for constructivist classrooms*. Alexandria, VA: ASCD.

Monmonier, M. S. (1996). *How to lie with maps* (2nd ed.). Chicago: University of Chicago Press.

Nathan, R. (1990, May). *Improving writing instruction*. Presentation for Grand Rapids English teachers, Grand Rapids, MI.

Rackliffe, G. (1998, October). Finding the heart of the lesson [Seminar]. At Fire Up Conference, Grand Rapids, MI.

Reinstadler, K. (2005, March 3). Hope science teacher, pupil win state honors. *The Grand Rapids Press*, p. B4.

2

Using Knowledge of Teaching and Learning

In addition to subject-matter knowledge, teachers use pedagogical knowledge—familiarity with effective teaching methods. Universities offer courses in educational psychology to explain how we learn and react. Methods courses describe techniques and approaches for teaching effectively. Other courses examine the beliefs or philosophies that underlie our assumptions about students and about effective instruction. The novice teacher must put learned theory into action and develop an approach that will match the students and their situation, and the teacher's own style and comfort zone. An introverted teacher will not become an extroverted one, but both sorts of teachers can find methods that make their teaching work well.

Teachers must also learn to observe response patterns of listeners and interpret those responses accurately. Teachers must see gaps and misunderstandings in students' comprehension, correct students and expand on their prior knowledge, relate existing knowledge to other pertinent ideas, and help learners integrate the new information.

The Unaware Teacher

Novice teachers are like salespersons who have memorized the selling points but never make a sale. Novices don't know how to make knowledge stick in a student's mind and aren't adept at reading students and reacting effectively.

The unaware teacher sees events in a disconnected way

At the unaware stage of teaching, the practitioner doesn't yet notice the relationship between teachers' actions and students' reactions. A novice teacher knows his job is to teach, but only in a general way. He misses the idea that every moment in the classroom can be structured for student learning.

Regardless of a written lesson plan, some teachers will talk about peripheral topics for most or all of the class, failing to teach their subject. Perhaps they think students will teach themselves, providing assignments are given.

"I didn't finish my algebra homework," mutters Emily.

"Don't worry," Jack responds. "Just ask Mr. Trenton about the Lions game last night. He'll get so worked up, he'll forget to ask for homework. You can turn it in tomorrow."

This teacher thinks being in the classroom is equal to teaching. Students can bring up any topic and relax while the teacher chatters on, subject matter forgotten. This teacher "wings it" and sees little connection between his actions and student learning.

Unaware teachers don't yet understand that lessons need to be interactive to work well. What the students grasp, or don't grasp, determines the direction for tomorrow's lesson. Unaware teachers just hope to be assigned bright students, not understanding that all students are bright to teachers who know how to teach well.

Teachers who stay on topic may still have problems. The first time I taught high school U.S. history, I studied every night so I could present the next day's lesson. I gave notes for each topic and wrote them on the overhead. Students copied my words and phrases, but many did not do well on the tests. I believed that the students who got low test scores must not have studied hard enough. I tried a variety of approaches—games, discussions, studying in pairs—hoping to help kids who were flunking my tests.

One day, Ian, a student leader and a hard worker, stopped by my desk. He had a *B* average in my class.

"I take notes every day and study them," he said, "but it doesn't help. The notes just don't seem to help me know the things you ask on tests." He wasn't whining, but he sounded discouraged.

Ian offered me important information. I realized that the notes I gave were neither clear nor a good match for the content

I tested. I had gone through the motions but had not taught effectively. I believed that poor test performance meant that students hadn't studied, not recognizing that I hadn't taught in a way that effectively prepared students for the test. When I felt frustrated, I just tried some other activity—any other activity. I was not analyzing the effect I got from each effort or predicting what any given presentation or activity would trigger in students. I certainly hadn't learned to analyze lesson results and make logical adjustments. It took some time for me to learn how to adjust my teaching methods in response to what was actually happening in the classroom.

Later, I learned to identify critical attributes before teaching a lesson. Once I began to identify what was truly essential, I emphasized that rather than a flood of less important details. The notes I gave and the tests I designed improved.

Changing our teaching takes great effort and considerable time. A well-meaning critic's advice to "Give better notes" or "Use meaningful activities" is only marginally useful. Beginning teachers do as well as someone with a basic level of training and experience is likely to do. The work still lies ahead. Teacher improvement has a lengthy and challenging learning curve.

The unaware teacher rarely makes sense of classroom events

The first weeks of teaching are like attending a carnival for the first time. Ferris wheels, bumper cars, and the calls of midway barkers overwhelm the senses. Time is needed to absorb what the carnival offers before deciding which part of the experience to engage in.

In a classroom filled with 20 or 30 learners, a teacher hardly knows where to begin. She may concentrate on the lesson and not the learners. Students' responses are regarded as interference. She may imagine that each child is a clean slate, devoid of knowledge, and simply start at the beginning and plow through. Children are never blank slates, however; they are already shaped by culture and personal experiences and bring information—or misinformation—on many topics. Furthermore, students never learn equally easily or equally thoroughly. Students always have individual differences.

Students also have reasons for what they do, no matter how hard it is for teachers to discern them. Some student motivations can be clearly stated; others are unconscious. Kids who misbehave, cry for no visible reason, or refuse to participate may be reacting to or protecting themselves from threats that the teacher can't yet identify.

Inexperienced teachers are frustrated by things that appear random and unreasonable from the front of the room. Ask unaware teachers to describe what happened in class today, and they will have difficulty making much sense of classroom events. They will respond with general comments: "The kids were awful today," or "After recess they were hyper," or "For once, they were angels." Such teachers do not see patterns in the classroom disorder. Maybe students paid attention during the explanation at the beginning of the math lesson, but started to talk and misbehave as soon as they were asked to do sample problems. Were they confused? Maybe the teacher hasn't taught them to work independently. Unaware teachers cannot recall exactly what happened when, nor can they consider what patterns of student behavior might reveal. Because such patterns are invisible to unaware teachers, they cannot respond to them.

The unaware teacher adjusts lessons randomly

The unaware teacher doesn't know which teaching approaches will work. Basic structures for effective lesson design exist, but it takes time to learn these protocols, and there are thousands of procedural options. Experience can teach us which ones are more useful, but only if we pay careful attention. Some protocols will yield good results and some will not. Some teachers with many years of experience still struggle to construct highly effective lessons or procedures. They use criteria with little payoff: "We haven't tried this in a while," "I'm in the mood for a change of pace," "I'm tired so I'm giving them a worksheet," "There's an assembly later and I don't like it when one class gets ahead of the others." Having an instructional reason for decisions is necessary for effective lessons.

Random teaching approaches may sometimes yield good results. Over a period of time, trying new things can lead to insights and increase a teacher's repertoire of methods. Whether the ideas work well or not, at least the teacher is gathering some new information. Still, most inexperienced teachers have to endure a period where they do the best they can but feel discouraged when they fall short of their goals. Good mentors can give helpful feedback and teach beginners to think more analytically. No teacher can skip the learning process, but having a mentor can accelerate progress.

Questions to grow by

☐ If your district offers a mentoring program, are you taking advantage of it?

☐ If your district has no mentoring program, have you tried e-mentoring or Internet discussion groups?

☐ Are you building a support group of teachers willing to brainstorm more effective approaches?

☐ Have you ever asked another person to observe your teaching and give suggestions?

☐ Do you ever observe other teachers' classrooms?

☐ Are you willing to videotape your teaching in order to observe yourself?

☐ Have you made an audio recording of your teaching voice to critique your volume, tone, and vocal mannerisms?

☐ Are you willing to ask students to evaluate your teaching of a lesson or unit, letting them tell you what would help them learn better?

The Aware Teacher

Aware teachers have begun to discern student learning. While their ability to observe is still limited and tentative, aware teachers can focus on significant matters one at a time, at a minimum recalling the surface details of student responses. These teachers make small changes in their teaching, at least occasionally, in response to student behaviors.

The aware teacher sees events and issues one at a time

Consider Ms. Milanowski, a middle school student teacher. To start students thinking about the day's topic, Ms. Milanowski writes a question on the board before class every day. Students are supposed to answer it in their notebooks as soon as they enter the classroom, but most students chatter or move around the room for several minutes after the bell rings. She reminds them to get started, reprimands horseplay, and loans pencils, while she tries to complete roll call. Several weeks into the semester students are still not settling down quickly, so she discusses the problem with her supervisor.

"They need to come in and get to work, but they don't," she says. "I don't know what to do."

"From the students' point of view, what happens if they just talk instead of getting started right away?" the supervisor asks.

Ms. Milanowski looks confused. "Well, they don't get the assignment done."

"And?"

"Well, they lose points."

"When?"

"I collect the notebooks every month."

"How many points do they lose?"

"One point for every question not answered."

"Wouldn't you rather talk to a friend now instead of earn one point next month?" asks the supervisor. "How can you change the dynamics here?"

"I'm not sure," says Ms. Milanowski. "Offer more points for each?"

"How else?" the supervisor asks.

Ms. Milanowski looks puzzled.

"There is no time pressure," her supervisor points out. "Questions stay there all hour unless you need to use the board. You could erase them after five minutes. Or use the overhead projector and turn it off after five minutes. Using a timer would also add urgency."

"I'm going to try that," says Ms. Milanowski.

"Think about your grading, too. Waiting a month to receive a grade is a long time for some kids. You could check the questions more often to see if that makes any difference," says the supervisor. "Maybe you can work up to a monthly interval as students learn the process."

"But they're in 8th grade," protests Ms. Milanowski. "Shouldn't they follow instructions by now?"

"Ideally, yes. But that's not what matters. For you, what they *should* do is less important than what they *actually* do. They are reacting to the circumstances right here, right now, in your classroom. Alter their circumstances and their behavior will follow."

Ms. Milanowski nods slowly.

"You have lots of options," says the supervisor. "For some kids, grades mean less than attention does. You'd be surprised how much harder they might work if you praised students when you caught them working, or noted improvement in their work. Everyone likes to be noticed."

When Ms. Milanowski tries these suggestions, each causes a slight improvement in student effort. Used together, they produce a big improvement. Ms. Milanowski is adding new understanding to her previous knowledge. Her opening questions are a good way to begin class promptly and to point students toward what is about to be covered, but even good ideas need fine-tuning for maximum effectiveness.

Sometimes a student acts out in reaction to a lesson—throwing a pencil, scowling, refusing to work. The student's actions need to be addressed immediately and perhaps continually. At the same time, such students may act as warning beacons, revealing important implications for planning. Was the material too advanced? Too simple? Does it appear irrelevant to the student? Does it contradict the student's current beliefs? Misbehaving students can help us become more effective. A room full of completely compliant students would lead us to believe all our teaching was perfect, when in fact, there is always room for improvement.

Ms. Milanowski is learning how to teach her subject effectively. Creating urgency and planning meaningful lessons are essential to effective teachers, who rarely waste instructional time. They usually start class with something that grabs attention and turns students' thoughts to the subject and then move through a series of helpful and engaging activities.

The aware teacher recalls surface details of events or timing

"I guess they hate maps. They never pay attention when I pull one down."

"Whenever I put them in groups, they act terribly."

"First I passed out the vocabulary lists, then I assigned the review and homework sheets. After that Connor and George got smart with me, so I gave them a time-out."

Teachers who make these remarks don't look beyond the details of presenting the material. If students are uninterested in maps, how is the teacher using them? Are students confused, frustrated, or bored? Does the teacher turn her back, talk softly, or block the students' view? Experimenting and observing student reactions can show the teacher how to use maps more effectively in lessons.

If students misbehave during group activities, did the teacher coach students in the roles they must play in group dynamics? Does every person have a task to complete? Are there clearly stated expectations? Does the teacher redirect or discipline offenders? If the answers are no, then the teacher's omissions are part of the problem.

Though teachers may be able to describe classroom events chronologically, interpretation of the teaching and learning relationship is often missing. What triggers Connor and George's misbehavior? Do they usually act up when faced with successive reading or writing assignments? Are these weak areas for them? What are their strengths? Such questions occur to teachers who look beyond the surface. To address only the surface misbehavior and not the cause encourages recurrence of the problem.

The aware teacher may see the need to make minor adjustments

Teachers often say, "They didn't get it." That is only partly correct. More accurately, students didn't learn what the teacher hoped they would or didn't give the desired answer on a test or evaluation. According to Rackliffe (1998), a more useful response from teachers would be to ask, "What *did* they get?"

Students with the lowest reading scores on standardized tests were the most likely to fail my history tests. Logically, either they weren't able to read the words in the assignments or they didn't understand and remember the words they had read. I began to provide a study guide for each chapter. I asked them to read the terms and questions before they started the chapter. This practice focused attention on important concepts that would be covered in class and on the test. Because some improvement occurred, I felt the study guides were worth continuing.

Aware teachers recognize when things go badly but can imagine few solutions. When I teach college classes to education majors, I ask my students to brainstorm a variety of ways they might present a given lesson. They can generally think of only two or three options, and one of the options usually requires students to look something up. Aware teachers imagine basic solutions because that is the only type they can foresee. That's why I push my future teachers to generate a wider variety of approaches.

For instance, how might one teach the Preamble to the U.S. Constitution? Many students are required to memorize it, but memorizing it is not the same as understanding it. We know from the previous chapter that teachers need to know the material they are teaching; in this chapter we are looking for ways to lead students to comprehension and application of the material.

Knowing the words of the Preamble does not guarantee the ability to interpret or apply its meaning. When I point this out to teachers-in-training, they seem to grasp the idea. However, if I invite them to brainstorm a list of ways to teach the Preamble, they are perplexed. Other than suggesting that students look the words up in the dictionary, they have few others ideas. Though the best solutions come from weighing numerous options, aware teachers rarely develop more than two alternatives. What are some ways we might teach the Preamble?

Translation. "Look it up" is the first suggestion we make when students don't understand, but the dictionary eats up learning time. Using a triple-spaced version of the Preamble on an overhead transparency, one teacher wrote synonyms above the difficult words. Then she assigned one phrase each to small groups and asked them to dream up a second synonym in "teen talk." Next, each group was told to write all three versions of their phrase on a poster and each version was read aloud: the original wording, the teacher translation, and the teen translation. The posters were hung in the classroom and referred to throughout the unit on the Constitution. Because each group worked on only one phrase, the work went quickly, yet the results built a much deeper understanding as each group absorbed the work of other groups.

Cartoons. For several decades, *Schoolhouse Rock!* has been circulating in schools, allowing teachers to convey important information through song. The Preamble has been set to a lively tune and illustrated with animated figures. Humming the song makes it easy to recall the wording. To make the historic phrases meaningful to students encountering them for the first time, one teacher asked students to note the pictures that animators used to represent the six main purposes of the Preamble and then create four-panel cartoons to illustrate each.

Drama. A government teacher wanted her students to analyze how the six purposes of the Preamble played out in daily life. Each student created a superhero from one of the purposes and wrote a story about the hero in action. The results were stirring tales about characters like Domestic Tranquility Man, Justice Boy, and General Good Woman. Laughter and enthusiasm suggested that the students would not forget the six purposes of government and how they unfolded in everyday life.

Poetry. An English teacher used the Preamble to illustrate the construction of powerful, persuasive writing. She asked students to rearrange the words into poems that revealed the relationships between phrases by their location on the page. Because each poem was different, interesting arguments developed about how well each arrangement revealed the meaning of the Preamble.

Which approach is best? Each is effective and meets the goals of a particular teacher's curriculum and contains organized steps that help learners succeed. Each respects learners' abilities, enlisting their participation and resulting in deeper learning. All the approaches demonstrate a teacher's knowledge of learning processes and teaching methods. Each teacher conveys information to students in understandable, memorable ways. There are dozens of other good approaches to this or any topic.

Questions to grow by

☐ Do you attend workshops on methods for presenting the material you teach?

☐ When a new method feels awkward the first time you use it, do you keep experimenting until you become comfortable with it?

☐ Have you studied concepts like lesson design, motivational techniques, communication, listening skills, assessment, developmental psychology, and other areas that will improve your teaching?

☐ Can you list areas in which you think you would benefit from more training?

☐ Can you name the components of effective lessons?

☐ Do you keep up on new research about how the brain works in order to apply it to your teaching?

Self-Development

• Perhaps you had methods classes in college and found them uninspiring, but revisiting methods with a new set of personal frustrations and questions can stimulate fresh insights.

• Learn about effective instructional techniques, as described by Madeline Hunter (1982). You will be able to use them at will when you deem them appropriate and helpful.

Collegial Support

• Scripting an entire lesson for other teachers can be helpful to them. Scripting requires that you jot down as many of the statements, questions, answers, and student comments as possible during a lesson, much like a transcription. Use the transcript to go back over the lesson and identify things that worked and things that didn't. Compliment successes. Discuss a few alternatives for less successful sections but don't overwhelm the listener with suggestions.

• Listening is another valuable skill you can use with other teachers. Because you know both the triumphs and the frustrations of teaching, your interest and feedback can help teachers achieve professional insights.

The Capable Teacher

Capable teachers have begun to recognize patterns in student learning, sensing which patterns are significant. They plan each new lesson based on students' reaction patterns in previous lessons. They have developed the ability to choose from a variety of methods and materials for teaching based on students' responses.

The capable teacher sees patterns in student understanding and events

Earlier Ms. Milanowski learned a basic lesson. Teachers can raise a student's level of concern by structuring assignments and feedback effectively. This is just one aspect of learning how to teach material. In time, we can see, interpret, and use the reactions of students to become more effective teachers.

A few years into my career I taught English courses at a Job Corps center. All the students in my classes had dropped out of high school. They were at Job Corps to learn job skills. They voluntarily signed up for high school completion classes in hopes of earning a diploma alongside vocational certification.

Whenever I started a grammar lesson, I noticed my students' body language and comments changed. Grammar made them apprehensive; they believed that they didn't get it and never would. One day I prefaced my lesson with an activity I thought would reassure them.

"Write your age down. Good. Now think about how old you were when you started speaking English. Were you two? Three? Whatever age it was, I want you to subtract that number from your current age."

Comments and jokes abounded.

"OK, what number did you get? That is the number of years you have been speaking English—and successfully! Your friends understand you, right? And your teachers, right? So you already know how to use English, don't you? What you don't know is the names we give some things. So, when we do today's lesson, remember that you are just learning to name the stuff you can already use."

I was troubled that English-speaking teenagers believed they couldn't understand grammar, so I tried a new approach. No miracles occurred, but students had a better attitude and we had more successful lessons.

A few months later in a professional development course, a presenter introduced the law of requisite variety. He explained that if things get too familiar and boring, humans seek novelty and variety, yet if we are surrounded by too much novelty, we get stressed and seek the familiar. By way of example, he pointed out that if a French person comes to town, we are intrigued, so we seek him out. But, if we are vacationing in France, surrounded by French speakers, we may feel overwhelmed. If we hear an English speaker in that setting, we seek familiarity and may introduce ourselves.

Reassuring my students that they could handle the unfamiliar terms in grammar transformed what seemed daunting to them into something more familiar, and thus, less stressful. My foggy awareness of class problems was transformed by the presenter's explanation into a tool I could use in many situations. I was able to analyze whether any given lesson was too familiar and needed variety, or so unfamiliar and threatening that it needed a bridge from the familiar to the new.

Students' Level of Concern

Great teachers think deeply about what is going on in a classroom. Awareness of students' level of concern is one way teachers can alter and improve their teaching. Too much concern in students is paralyzing; too little may lead to boredom. Because teachers want to increase students' sense of involvement, they may consider the following:

• Accountability. Will this assignment be graded, reported on, or presented in front of the class? Is participation monitored? Constant evaluation is impossible, but group activities that arouse enthusiasm tend to make students accountable to one another, especially if each has a separate responsibility. Spot checking is important, even for adult learners. However, if everything is rewarded extrinsically with grades or points, students lose the intrinsic pleasure of satisfying work.

• Time. A moderate time pressure is usually motivating, but too much can be debilitating. Many students give up if the time sounds impossibly short. Time limits usually increase productivity, yet caution is needed. Time pressures are quite difficult for students with certain processing problems or learning disabilities. Carefully experiment to find the optimal range for various students or classes.

• Visibility. Will work be displayed? Is a performance in front of the room required? Will grades be posted? Will completed assignments be graphed? Like time limits, visibility motivates some and frightens others. Giving students invisibility—at least temporarily—is sometimes necessary to keep anxiety under control.

• Predictability. If a teacher always calls on people in the same order, some students tune out until their turn. When a teacher calls on only disruptors or raised hands, well-behaved or shy students may become less involved. Calling on everyone randomly holds attention better; students wonder if they will be next.

• A caution. Beginning teachers might apply the idea of raising level of concern by making daily threats; however, skilled practitioners apply only as much pressure as needed, without overstressing kids. They seek optimum performance from individuals and the class by making controlled adjustments with logic and awareness.

The capable teacher uses student reaction patterns to plan lessons

Capable teachers use patterns of student understanding in order to plan better lessons. Experience taught Mrs. Mitchell that identifying verbs was difficult for many students, but she found a way to help students pick out verbs.

"Does this sentence take place in the past, the present, or the future?" Mrs. Mitchell asked. Students invariably gave the correct answer.

"Which words tell you that?" Again the students would choose the right answers.

"Those words are verbs. They are always verbs. No other words tell us whether things are happening in the past, the present, or the future. Remember this and you will always find the verbs."

When explanations from grammar books confused students, Mrs. Mitchell sought a more effective tool. She adapted her instruction by combining two patterns. She noticed what students didn't understand, and she pointed out a grammar pattern that would help them. While we often plan to present things sequentially, when today's lesson reveals something that tomorrow's lesson must address, changes are necessary. Capable teachers get better every year because they are always seeking and using new approaches based on their general and particular knowledge of students.

The capable teacher varies methods and materials based on student responses

Beginning teachers are sometimes told not to smile to let students know that the teacher means business. Better-informed teachers prefer to respond to the actual situation instead of using a rigid approach.

Fear and anxiety inhibit learning. For that reason, a capable teacher attempts to keep a positive tone. At the same time he knows that a negative tone is indispensable as a tool for teaching individuals or groups when they have made serious mistakes in judgment. If, after days of pleasant exchanges, the teacher expresses disappointment to the class for bullying on the playground, punishes them sternly for cheating, or scolds them for sneaking out of the assembly early, the contrast in tone magnifies the effect of the reprimand. Students understand they have violated his expectations.

Once the negative feeling has made a point—for minutes or maybe an hour, but not for too much longer—the teacher resumes a neutral attitude, no longer angry, but not yet transitioned to his normal cordiality. The class has time to shift gears. Then, punishment over, lesson learned and now forgiven, the regular positive feeling is again introduced to the classroom. A teacher's tone can be used to influence and motivate students.

Skilled teachers use a feedback loop to teach. Student responses help determine whether the material has been assimilated or needs to be clarified or taught again. Skilled teachers say, "After I read your papers I realized ..." Then they use a new method or approach to ensure a deficiency is addressed. Methods vary from day to day. Even though the teacher may be an auditory learner herself, she remembers to provide visual, tactile, and social components for students whose learning styles don't match her own. Over time varying experiences are provided: writing assignments, three-dimensional products, art, group presentations, individual speeches, music, computations or statistics, graphs or visuals, drama, simulations, speakers, hands-on activities, field trips. These are not frills; they are legitimate opportunities for students with different interests, abilities, and learning styles to participate fully.

There is an important reason for varying both methods and materials based on student responses: Teaching what students already know is unproductive, and talking above students' knowledge base is frustrating for them. Capable teachers know they need to present material in a way that is familiar enough to be manageable and unfamiliar enough to be interesting for the whole class. The chosen teaching strategy must also be suited to the focus of a given lesson. The authors of *The Strategic Teacher: Selecting the Right Research-Based Strategy for Every Lesson* (Silver, Strong, & Perini, 2007) offer useful strategies for building effective lessons for mastery, understanding, self-expression, or intrapersonal purposes. Capable teachers develop and use such approaches; this is why their teaching is more effective than that of aware teachers.

Questions to grow by

☐ Do you frequently check the design of your own lessons to see if any components are lacking that would make them more effective?

☐ Do you brainstorm multiple ways to approach a given lesson or unit?

☐ Do you discuss lessons with other teachers to exchange ideas?

The Inspired Teacher

The National Board for Professional Teaching Standards requires at least three years of experience before a teacher can attempt to pursue certification as an accomplished teacher. Most teachers I have talked to tell me it took them more than three years in the classroom before they began to feel highly skilled. During the first few years novice teachers must learn about and then learn to use a vast array of methods to effectively present material.

Truly inspired teachers must do something even more significant; they must learn to be inspired *by* students before they can be inspiring *to* students. Being inspired by students requires using individual and class responses as a unique source of information based on pupils' skills, talents, and history. Inspired teachers observe their students closely and make effective instructional decisions based on response patterns they see. Inspired teachers are continually enriching the learning experience for their students, moving beyond a simple curricular outline to a three-dimensional learning environment. They expand on the basics and help students make exciting connections.

The inspired teacher notices detailed responses to instruction

Inspired teachers notice nuanced responses in students. They observe, recall, and speculate on the meaning of students' reactions. Great teachers remember these responses and pick out patterns over time, whether in a single individual, a group, or a class. A teacher might notice, for instance, that William performs slowly when asked to handwrite an assignment but finishes before his peers when typing on the computer, using complex sentences and original examples not present in his handwritten essays. The teacher speculates that William may have anomalies in the area of the brain that coordinate handwriting. Whether or not this is verified by tests, his teacher knows that his responses range from poor to superior depending on which delivery system he is asked to use. Awareness of this pattern allows her to work with William more effectively, using his strengths and shoring up his weaknesses.

After noticing the responses of individuals, groups, or whole classes, teachers make assumptions and predictions that they use for the next lesson or lessons. Assessing exactly what patterns mean or what response they demand from teachers is a continual learning challenge. Inspired teachers reflect on the effectiveness of each part of the lesson in relation to classroom events. Teachers gather data, formally or informally, and use it; they maintain order while encouraging students and helping them to learn things they are not convinced they are capable of; they show high regard and high expectations while being sensitive to the nuances of the social setting and the culture of their students; and they spontaneously improvise responses and solutions to situations not outlined in manuals. The teacher's knowledge is a filter for what will and won't work pedagogically with a given group. Lesson planning, and the whole world of teaching, is rich with possibilities that novices never see.

The inspired teacher uses response patterns to predict what will help students learn

The inspired teacher has built a vast memory of possible lesson approaches available for ready access. Choosing well, in ways that meet the needs of *these* students in *this* setting, is the mark of an expert.

Great teachers stimulate learning in two ways. They build on students' strengths; knowing students' natural talents allows the pupils to shine. Most students are eager to work in their areas of strength. Great teachers also help students develop competence in areas that do not come naturally, areas that seem boring, frustrating, or agonizing. Including both types of experiences for students is a balancing act to keep them involved and learning.

Over time teachers learn to predict what response a lesson will get before it is presented. They also look for responses during instruction that allow them to determine whether to alter the lesson or some part of it. The alteration may take place in the middle of the lesson, or may simply be noted so the next day's lesson can be designed to make up deficiencies in student knowledge or teacher presentation.

The better the teacher is at planning and presenting strong lessons, the easier the results appear. A great teacher's presentation keeps students attentive and involved, yet the same students may dissolve into frustrated confusion if someone else takes over. Neither the students nor the material changed, but the method of delivery makes all the difference.

One year I noticed my history students making negative comments about English language learners from other countries in our high school. Whenever ELL students laughed and joked in their native languages, my students complained that ELL students were laughing at them. My students didn't consider that others might laugh and talk about interests of their own. Because they separated themselves from ELL students, they never had a chance to test their assumptions.

I decided to put some face-to-face experience into our unit on immigration during the 1800s by asking students to interview ELL students who had recently immigrated to the United States. I arranged for my students to visit a bilingual class, filled with recent arrivals studying basic English. When my 10th graders came to class I let them choose a partner and gave each pair an assignment sheet that contained three tasks: interview a student from another country using questions provided, learn two phrases in his or her native language, and create a simple map of the route the ELL student used to get here.

Even with a partner to help, they looked nervous. When we entered the classroom, I had to escort pairs of them over to their interviewees.

Things started slowly. There were language barriers and wide-eyed paralysis for the first several minutes. Three adults circulated to get things started. The classroom noise began to rise from near silence and whispered confusion. Within 20 minutes all the teenagers were gesturing, looking at maps, laughing, and waving their hands for help when needed.

When we returned to our own room, attitudes had changed. Gone were the groans and protests from the beginning of the hour. Now hands were waving, asking to tell the stories of the people that they had just met. Students taught each other words in Spanish, Polish, and Vietnamese. Everyone wanted to share the journey their interviewee had described. Later, they would tell the class whenever they saw their contact in the lunchroom or on the soccer field. Including other people in the school as part of the lesson gave the learning a different, more realistic quality.

The inspired teacher adapts, enriches, and expands instructional connections for students

A curriculum guideline covering what teachers are expected to teach is a dry document. Technically, one might give notes on information required in each section and claim that all the minimum expectations were met—even if students are unlikely to recall information or be able to apply it to life. Inspired teachers want more for their students.

For an example, let's look further at immigration to the United States. Learning about what happened in the 1890s or 1920s is not very engaging for many students. Yet knowing this part of U.S. history is important to our understanding of immigration today. Enriching instruction to make it engaging is important.

Because several of our staff members had immigrated, I reasoned that students could learn about immigration through a panel discussion. I explained in advance to my colleagues some basic issues that I hoped they would cover and then let them talk to the classes, occasionally adding other questions.

Mrs. Kahn, a mathematician originally from Pakistan, explained the process of waiting years for a U.S. visa and then selling everything and bringing her family with only two suitcases full of possessions. She told about her first job—working in her brother-in-law's veterinary clinic as a receptionist—until she could retake all the coursework required to get a teaching certificate in the United States.

Ms. Tran-Nugyen told how the nuns at her boarding school in Vietnam worked to get her into a U.S. college. When word came, time was so short she had to leave without going back to her home village. She never saw her father again because he died before she was able to return.

Mr. Chan described fleeing the Vietcong alone as a young teen, walking for days to reach the border, and spending years in a refugee camp waiting to be admitted to the United States.

During all the accounts, students listened attentively. The questions they asked corrected many misconceptions and made immigration real to them. By videotaping the panel, I was able to let all my classes hear the information, though later classes could not ask questions of the presenters. After listening to all the speakers, students seemed nearly speechless with amazement at all these teachers and aides had lived through.

One year my resource on immigration was a student in my own class. Mesgun came from Eritrea, formerly part of Ethiopia until civil war caused a split. I suggested he could take 10 minutes the next day to tell us what it was like to be an immigrant if he was comfortable with the idea. He agreed. Because that particular class had many internal divisions, I felt helping students get better acquainted would be a step forward.

The next morning Mesgun described how he began school knowing no English. Every night he worked his way through school assignments he copied down, translating every word using his Arabic-English dictionary. The process took six to seven hours some nights, but he gradually made sense of English, learning to read, write, and speak.

Classmates peppered Mesgun with exclamations and questions, leading to an explanation of the Arabic alphabet and details about his school in Eritrea, his family, his daily life, and his housing. Rather than give a 10-minute presentation, Mesgun held the class enthralled for nearly 50 minutes. Even better, the next day students greeted both Mesgun and other classmates with greater warmth and enthusiasm than ever before.

Each of these different approaches to teaching immigration more deeply had benefits. What they have in common is a focus on listening and asking questions. For students who are too shy to ask questions or who have poor recall of what they hear, follow-up is critical, as are lessons that address different learning styles. An inspired teacher plans subsequent lessons to fill these gaps.

Inspired teachers adapt the curriculum. When they assess student knowledge, they may need to add background information to bring students up-to-date or add new challenges to avoid repeating what most students have already mastered. They may plan lessons that always include two or more avenues for learning, such as movement plus writing or listening plus drawing. They may differentiate expectations, allowing some students to work alone while others work in pairs or letting some write out responses while asking others to type them.

Enriching the curriculum takes many forms. A history teacher may include lessons of science discovered during the era being covered. A physical education teacher may teach the math skills needed to calculate body mass index or the percentage of improvement in weight lifting. Sometimes teachers in various disciplines cooperate to enrich their curricula.

It would be unusual for an inspired teacher to pull out last year's notes and give the same lesson without any adaptation. For one thing, the teacher has grown. For another, this class is different in major and minor ways. The main reason inspired teachers change their lessons is that they teach interactively. Circumstances change; certain options may no longer be possible. Every moment is another opportunity for pulling more from students and giving back more. Every hour is a chance to find out what works best. The job of improving instruction never ends. Nor would inspired teachers want it to. Many confess that they are never satisfied, always looking for a better way, a more interesting assignment, or a more challenging project that will help students succeed at more difficult new tasks.

Great teaching is as much an art as a skill. Inspired teachers know more than facts. They know how to present information so it can be understood, how to provide tools to aid students in recalling and using information and ideas, and when to stop talking and let students think. Inspired teachers use teaching skills the way great painters use oils. The results may look simple and obvious, but they are the fruits of mastery.

Actions to grow by

☐ If you hear yourself saying students always behave a certain way in your classroom, experiment. Change your behaviors and reactions to disrupt the pattern and produce a different result.

☐ List every student's special interests. If you don't know them, spend time getting to know each person better.

☐ During one period of time, a week perhaps, make at least one connection for each person in your class between a personal interest and the topic under consideration.

☐ Read about Howard Gardner's (1983) theory of multiple intelligences. Connect to every one of them at least once during a day's work. Watch for different types of responses from different learners.

☐ Investigate National Board Certification. Measuring your teaching skills with objective standards will help you to grow your expertise.

For Information and Inspiration

Tools for Teachers, www.kk.org/cooltools/archives/001662.php

———

Dyer, W. W. (2006). *Inspiration: Your ultimate calling.* Carlsbad, CA: Hay House.

Gardner, H. (1983). *Frames of mind: The theory of multiple intelligences.* New York: BasicBooks.

Grandin, T., & Johnson, C. (2005). *Animals in translation: Using the mysteries of autism to decode animal behavior.* London: Bloomsbury Publishing.

Hunter, M. C. (1982). *Mastery teaching: Increasing instructional effectiveness in elementary and secondary schools*. Thousand Oaks, CA: Corwin Press, Inc.

Langer, E. J. (1997). *The power of mindful learning*. Reading, MA: Addison-Wesley.

Rackliffe, G. (1998, October). Finding the heart of the lesson [Seminar]. At Fire Up Conference, Grand Rapids, MI.

Silver, H. F., Strong, R. W., & Perini, M. J. (2007). *The strategic teacher: Selecting the right research-based strategy for every lesson*. Alexandria, VA: ASCD.

Teaching to student strengths. (2006, September). *Educational Leadership, 64*(1).

Yelon, S. L. (1996). *Powerful principles of instruction*. White Plains, NY: Longman Publishers USA.

3

Solving Instructional Problems

All teachers face problems regarding curriculum and instruction. Problem solving is difficult. When a situation frustrates us, we want to fix it. Sometimes we try the first thing that comes to mind. Our effort may solve the problem, cause no change at all, or make things worse. Even when we give the matter much thought, we can't be sure we have found the solution until we take action and look at the result. Searching for solutions is one of the reasons that Deborah Meier, in *The Power of Their Ideas* (2002), says that teaching is far more intellectually challenging than she ever expected it to be.

Over time a teacher can build strong problem-solving skills. For example, teachers look for ways to help every student succeed by presenting material differently or adjusting the lesson. Good problem solving usually includes continual reframing of the questions teachers ask themselves, because redefining a problem generally leads to new approaches. This chapter looks at how well instructors accept the intellectual challenge of continually seeking ways to improve their presentation of material.

The Unaware Teacher

The inability to identify an instructional problem is one hallmark of the unaware teacher. Novices usually see only surface issues regarding effective instruction and are less likely to look for underlying causes.

The unaware teacher is blind to most instructional and curricular problems

Teachers give orders or directions with varying levels of effectiveness. Ms. Obadare teaches 4th grade. The bell will ring in 15 minutes and the class has just finished its last lesson of the day. She tells students to put away their books and clean up. They finish in record time. Ms. Obadare decides to prepare the class for tomorrow's lessons. Maybe she wants to keep them busy now or save time tomorrow.

"Class, we will be having art in the morning so I am going to pass out your paper now so you'll be ready. Everyone will get three sheets. Put them in your desk now and we'll use them tomorrow."

Ms. Obadare sees no problem with her decision. She can't yet see how her own choices might create problems rather than prevent them. Other teachers might anticipate that the papers may be lost, crinkled, or used for scribbling or paper airplanes long before art class. Then searching, scolding, and resupplying are necessary before art can begin.

Similarly, a civics teacher who is determined to help this year's class pass the test on the U.S. Constitution may have students memorize the Preamble, overlooking the problem that unfamiliar terms—"insure domestic tranquility," for example—can be memorized without being understood. If he neglects to help his students comprehend, he will likely be disappointed by test scores. His first attempt to solve the problem of poor performance is not likely to be successful.

The unaware teacher takes a chance at solving problems

Unaware teachers do try to solve instructional problems, but their efforts appear random or ill-considered. For instance, a student teacher becomes annoyed with a disruptive student. In frustration, he grabs a spray bottle normally used to water plants and sprays the student. The student erupts and causes a scene. Looking back, the student teacher realizes his own misjudgment. He hasn't yet learned to consider the consequences of each idea before selecting a course of action.

Unaware teachers don't consider or use instructional methods that are highly effective. They assign a group activity without teaching interaction skills, and the activity is unsuccessful. As a result, they are convinced that their students are too immature to work in groups. The same teachers may spend too much time facing the blackboard, never thinking to appoint students as scribes and teach facing the class. Why? Because the teachers are unaware that part of the problem is in the instructional method. Instead, the teachers choose to stop writing on the board and use seatwork only.

Wise teachers find coping methods that reduce or eliminate instructional problems. Better preparation makes the material clearer. Teaching rules for contributing to a group discussion shapes young learners into more effective participants. Unaware teachers are oblivious to these approaches. They act out of instinct, not skill, and they blame students for poor results.

The unaware teacher attempts haphazard solutions

Ms. Obadare's problem is a procedural one regarding the directions she gives. Many other instructional problems are related to content. If Ms. Obadare tries to teach division and none of her students succeed, what will she do? A haphazard solution would be to offer candy to everyone who gets a perfect score on tomorrow's homework. A logical solution would be to check whether the class has mastered the times tables because success in division is related to success in multiplication. Another logical option would be to ask three colleagues how they introduce division and what levels of success their students have with these methods. Ms. Obadare could then try out methods that seem to hold promise. But she isn't aware of her options.

Questions to grow by

☐ Can you list bothersome situations you have encountered during the last month?

☐ Do you recall what you said or did immediately before these annoying situations arose?

☐ Can you identify ways that your own actions may have contributed to student behavior?

☐ Are you able to think of alternative ways of doing activities that don't go smoothly?

☐ Have you asked other teachers how they handle similar situations?

☐ Have you asked other teachers the reasons why they chose their approaches?

The Aware Teacher

Teachers who are just becoming aware of problems in the areas of curriculum and instruction are still limited to surface understanding. They settle for speedy, incomplete solutions.

The aware teacher grasps only the surface of problems

An aware teacher can recognize problems exist, even if the solutions are still hidden. After teaching a course several times, a teacher notices that every class has struggled with the same concept.

"This is hard for them to follow," she whispers to an aide. "It's required, so we can't skip it. But they just don't seem to catch on to it very well."

She is not blaming the students for not studying or not trying. She sees they are making an effort but doesn't know how to make the lesson more accessible to them. She may spend extra time or give more hints, but she can't yet identify what instruction students need from her in this unit, so the problem remains. In time she may be able to try out a variety of approaches to solve this problem, but not yet.

Teachers at this level still have to wrestle with each individual step of a problem because they have not yet learned to "chunk" relevant information. Novices tend to mentally work through each of the steps that make up the problem while experts learn to see problems in clusters and react to them more strategically (Adelson, 1983).

The aware teacher looks for quick fixes

Some teachers are workshop addicts. Every semester they enthusiastically sign up for training and return to the classroom and describe in detail the technique they learned about. They try to put the entire method into action as if they were following a recipe. Unfortunately, things usually don't go as well as the workshop leader described. Disappointment sets in. Eventually the new technique is abandoned, or rarely used, because positive results are not immediate.

Mastering a new technique or approach takes time, often years. Learning a technique requires frequent practice and the ability to reflect on what is working and what is not working and then make adjustments. Workshops can be helpful, but they offer only a starting point for personal change, not a quick fix.

Sometimes the search for a quick fix is a plea for help. Stopping by a colleague's classroom to air frustrations and ask what she would do can be healthy. Sometimes a suggestion gleaned this way is helpful. But a colleague will generally offer only one or two ideas—whatever seems natural to her. To expect a quick comment to cover all the possibilities that might be useful or appropriate is unrealistic. If we don't make a sustained effort and search broadly for solutions, we shortchange ourselves and our students.

● ● ● **TIP** ● ● ●

To see a problem clearly, look at it from many angles:

- What are the facts?
- What are my feelings?
- What are the positives?
- What are the negatives?
- What are the possibilities?
- What are the steps?

Weigh each possible solution using the same questions. (Adapted from DeBono, 1985.)

The aware teacher uses partial solutions

Awareness of an instructional problem usually triggers an attempt to solve it. But few will experience complete success the first time. Consider Mr. Alden. Every week he starts a new chapter in the social studies textbook. He assigns readings and questions to answer. He gives lectures. Before the chapter test, he reviews the material. Week after week he is discouraged when he grades the tests. Some kids earn *A*s and *B*s, but a few routinely earn *F*s. It baffles him that anyone could sit through every class period and fail the test.

Mr. Alden reads that pre-tests help students to be aware of what they don't know and help them to better focus their attention on the material when they start to study it. He decides to use the most basic test provided in the class textbook as a pre-test.

After the pre-test Mr. Alden teaches the chapter as usual. He feels encouraged when he hears student comments: "Oh, I missed that on the test" or "I was wondering what that word meant when I took that pre-test." He is eager to see the test scores when Friday comes. Unfortunately, grades don't improve as much as he hoped. The lowest scores have risen slightly, but he wanted the low-performing students to actually pass. He decides that pre-tests are probably worth the time they take, but he is at a loss about what to do next. He has found a partial solution but will need to keep trying other approaches as well.

Another teacher might decide that the low-performers need tutoring. He might institute a Wednesday club and expect anyone who doesn't pass the quiz or test to come in after school for 30 minutes of concentrated help. The additional help, or even the desire to get out of it, might motivate better test performance. Still, not every student will magically become a great student. A partial solution helps, but the problem is not completely solved.

One year I team taught with Ms. Keller, a special education teacher. We taught 35 students in one room; 8 had special needs. One morning Ms. Keller was teaching a lesson while I moved around the room. Two young men interrupted her several times each, with either silly comments or excessive chatter to their neighbors. She reprimanded them, but they did not settle down. By the end of the lesson, she was tight-lipped with anger over their behavior, threatening to eject them if they continued.

I agreed that they were misbehaving, but I wondered if I could change their perceptions in order to change their behavior. While the class worked on a written assignment, I spent a few minutes with each young man. I knew each had a job. I didn't want them to know where my comments were headed, so I used work as the setting for my imagined scenario.

First I pulled a seat next to Jason and sat down.

"You work down at the convention center, don't you?" I began.

"Yeah, at the concession counter." Jason smiled, happy to stop working and start talking.

"I thought so," I said. "I want to hear how you'd react to something if it happened to you at work, OK?"

"Sure," he said.

"Let's say you got ready, went to work on time, and were all set to start your shift. And let's say another guy was scheduled to work the same time as you. So, it's early and you decide to wipe the counter and the other guy is checking the soft drink dispenser." I paused.

Jason nodded as if he could picture it.

"So here comes the first customer. You look up at the customer, but before you can speak, the other guy leans over the counter in front of you and asks the customer what he wants. So you shrug and check the napkin dispenser. He does the same thing twice more as new customers arrive. Then he starts ordering you around—'Get some ketchup packets,' 'Open a carton of cups'—but you know you are supposed to wait on customers. If that happened to you, how would you react?"

"I'd be mad," Jason said indignantly. "He's keeping me from doing my job."

I nodded sympathetically. "I'd be mad, too. But did you ever think, maybe that's how Ms. Keller feels when she gets ready to teach and someone interrupts her or makes noise every time she tries to explain something?"

The emotions on Jason's face expressed consternation, embarrassment, and contrition. "I never thought of that," he said. "I'm sorry."

"I didn't think you had. That's why I brought it up. I think Ms. Keller would appreciate it if you did things differently."

I went over to the other young man and ran through a similar scenario. Clearly Eric had never considered the implications of his behavior either, and he looked sheepish when I pointed out what he was doing. I hoped my comments made a difference and waited to see what would happen the next time Ms. Keller was in front of the class.

Things went smoothly for the first few minutes. Then Jason and Eric started into their typical pattern.

"Jason, Eric," I said quietly. "Ms. Keller is trying to do her job."

Jason apologized instantly and behaved for the rest of the lesson. Eric remained quiet for less than three minutes. Jason seemed to remember the scenario for the rest of the year. If he started to get out of hand, I could simply say his name and he would redirect his attention to the lesson or assignment. Eric was not much affected by my attempt to change his perspective or by any of Ms. Keller's admonishments. Still, it was a relief to have one of the two behaving better. Although the solution was only partially successful, the improvement was worth the effort. Ms. Keller and I continued to try different ways to change Eric's behavior.

Effective solutions usually take more than one simple step. To believe that if something worked once it will always work is unreasonable. Because students are different, teachers need to be persistent about finding methods to reach a range of needs. Experimenting with a number of partial solutions may be necessary to find a combination that meets all student needs in the classroom. For this reason, a good teacher will need a large body of approaches so he can select a tool, try it, and if necessary select another and then yet another.

Experimenting with partial solutions means that the teacher is building up a repertoire of techniques that he can call on as needed. We can congratulate the aware teacher who has found a partial solution because, as long as he keeps at it, one partial solution at a time, he is growing toward expertise. The day will come when he does not have to settle for a partial solution.

Questions to grow by

☐ As you think of possible solutions, do you ask experienced colleagues whether your solutions seem sound?

☐ Do you ponder what you might be overlooking in a given situation?

☐ After you solve a problem, do you revisit the solution to improve it further?

Self-Development

• Zoom in and out. Electronic maps can zero in on block-by-block detail or back up to look at the global picture. Problems can be examined in the same way. To find new insights, consider both minute details and the larger situation.

• Ask your students. They may also be dealing with the same problem and might be able to offer good suggestions. Encourage student solutions with prompts like, "Here is how I see this problem. How do you see it?" or "Here's the solution I am considering. Does anyone have a different idea?"

Collegial Support

- Speak up objectively. When a colleague describes a problem or solution that seems out of place, calmly state an alternative view. People can easily miss important ideas when they are stressed, emotional, or inexperienced.
- Create problem-solving systems. A regular discussion group, a departmental brainstorming time, or a study group can offer a setting for people to bring up problematic issues and collaborate with others to find workable solutions.

The Capable Teacher

Teachers who are capable at solving curricular and instructional problems find issues not just by hunch, but by looking at data from the class. They also make systematic efforts to find solutions.

The capable teacher uses classroom data to find problems

Earlier Mr. Alden's discouragement about low-scoring students motivated him to try pre-tests; he was beginning to use class data. He looked at test scores before and after the pre-tests to assess how well pre-tests worked for his students. There are some teachers who believe that once they teach something, they have fully discharged their responsibilities for student learning. They do not use student data to assess their own performance. Capable teachers do.

At the capable level, teachers use a sort of educational triage. They look for evidence of who gets it, who doesn't, and who is somewhere in between. When a substantial number of students seem to be lost, capable teachers notice the problem and make adjustments. They give quizzes, not just to record grades but to decide whether reteaching is needed. They ask questions in class, scanning for reactions to assess students' comprehension. Some will ask students to indicate their knowledge with a thumbs-up or thumbs-down response. Capable teachers choose their next action based on formative assessment of learners' progress.

Sometimes the class data are found outside the classroom such as in the testing results related to No Child Left Behind in

U.S. schools. Faculties examine the scores of the whole school and its subgroups in the various subject areas that are tested to assess adequate yearly progress. Teachers look at how subgroups perform—boys and girls, majority and minority—to see if everyone is learning. If some subgroups are stalled, the faculty looks for reasons and tries to stimulate improvement.

The capable teacher searches systematically for solutions

Self-discipline is essential to solving problems effectively. The capable teacher is neither haphazard nor self-indulgent. Every day is a logical search for new ways to improve the performance of the students in his care. This teacher is observant and analytical, assessing how well each of his attempts translates into improvement, stasis, or regression among his students.

Some problems are the teacher's own. For instance, we have to manage internal fears and anxieties. I had been teaching two decades when a lunchtime conversation revealed that most of my colleagues also had September nightmares about the coming year. Many teachers also feel uninformed about developing technology and insecure with students who are increasingly wired into information the teacher is just discovering. They search for solutions to reach students who see old methods as irrelevant. Finding a way to accept insecurities and still be effective is another solution sought by teachers.

The capable teacher finds workable solutions for the entire class

Capable teachers may form the habit of asking direct questions of the class to get feedback, such as "Do you understand this point now?" or "Is this example clearer than the one I showed you yesterday?" They may ask students to write a summary of the day's lesson and then review each response carefully to assess each student's level of understanding. They may routinely stop themselves in the middle of explanations and ask pupils to turn to a neighbor and explain what has been taught, then invite questions from anyone who stumbles. This is a way to discover weaknesses as they occur and reteach if needed.

Teachers may have students physically signal answers to practice questions, perhaps holding up one finger for true and two fingers for false. Teachers can scan the room and see if all, most, or few students know the answer. If someone doesn't signal correctly, the teacher can instruct a person who knew the right answer to tell the class how to reach the correct answer. Feedback like this is not hard to gather and pays off in greater instructional effectiveness. By identifying problems early and often, teachers can use every minute in the classroom more effectively.

Technical methods reveal how well an attempt to solve a problem has actually worked. The teacher may graph the grades on each test he gives to see if students are consistently showing a high level of comprehension. Or he may do an item analysis on test questions. If certain questions are answered incorrectly by a large portion of the class, there is either a problem with the way the question was worded or a weakness in how the teacher taught that particular concept. He may confer with other teachers who have the same students to brainstorm more effective approaches, or turn to other professionals in his school or professional network for advice. He may seek peer coaching by inviting a colleague to observe his teaching to help him identify his own strengths and weaknesses.

In every example here the teachers actively seek solutions to each problem they identify to meet the needs of students. Rather than feel discouraged, capable teachers begin to see the pursuit of excellence as part of the intellectual challenge of teaching.

Questions to grow by

☐ Do you examine the student error rate for test questions or assignments?

☐ Do you attend workshops and professional development opportunities as often as possible?

☐ Are you actively developing a professional network for support and inspiration?

The Inspired Teacher

Inspired problem solvers look everywhere for new information and then adapt ideas to form solutions for curricular or instructional problems. For instance, they might read business management materials in search of new ways to approach teaching or managing students. Inspired teachers also seek solutions for both group and individual problems.

The inspired teacher seeks outside information to grasp problems completely

Beginning teachers use their own instincts and memories of their training or school experiences, supplemented by questions to colleagues, as they seek effective approaches. The day comes, however, when teachers realize that these resources aren't enough. Problems remain and more help is needed. Inspired teachers use methodical searches for better ways to help students master content.

Inspired teachers differ from the workshop addict who attends as a blank slate, expecting to take the advice of the presenter whole. Skilled teachers bring a specific set of needs and questions and sift through everything presented at a workshop, seeking tactics to apply effectively in the context of their own teaching.

A highly skilled teacher may read a book on brain research and adapt its message to enrich her teaching. She may use a news report as a lead-in to tomorrow's lesson. She might apply for a summer internship at a local business, in order to make her teaching more relevant to the working world, or to borrow motivational ideas used in work settings. One teacher might decide to take an advanced college course in his major to update his knowledge of recent developments in the field. Another accomplishes the same goal by subscribing to journals or reading new books in the field.

Inspired teachers also overcome their fears: the fear of asking a stupid question, the fear of revealing insecurity, the fear of being regarded as less than perfect by colleagues, administrators, or students. They are seekers who continually search for new and better information from many sources.

Help is everywhere. Years ago, I took a course on listening from the communication department at a local university. Even though other teachers highly recommended it, I was skeptical. The idea of 14 weeks of discussing listening seemed redundant. However, I look back on that course as a great source of insight into the ways lessons could go wrong as I attempted to teach. Before the course I would have been willing to whine (with legions of other teachers, managers, and parents), "I told them that." After the course I spent more time considering what students heard and what they actually grasped, and then changed my behavior accordingly.

Skilled teachers are always on the lookout for analogies, posters, games, experiments, simulations, news reports, songs, video clips, and educational films to enrich their attempts to impart content knowledge to students. The influence of the outside information is reflected in the lively and engaging flavor of many of the lessons they present. Inspired problem solvers are teachers who constantly grow and are never idle.

Experts cannot always articulate the reasons why they select the effective solutions they use. Their skill in chunking information is so complete, they no longer think of the separate steps they take. Their reactions feel intuitive and may look that way to an outsider. This seeming intuition for what works is probably the result of developing an alert intake system that regards every fact and life experience as a possible resource for teaching.

The inspired teacher addresses problems comprehensively

Many inspirations and sources discovered by teachers seeking outside information don't come in a finished, usable form. An intermediate step is needed to adapt the material to make it better suited to classroom application and to better solve a problem completely.

Some years back, the Billy Joel song "We Didn't Start the Fire" was popular. The song contains a litany of references to historic events and pop icons. Many teachers quickly saw its usefulness in U.S. history courses. Some merely played it to their classes. These were probably aware teachers. Some obtained a printed copy of the lyrics or took time to transcribe them. They passed out copies of the words so students could read the lyrics as they listened. This allowed teachers to discuss each reference in detail as needed. These were probably the capable problem solvers who wanted students to do a better job of remembering and understanding the history of the time covered by the song.

A few teachers went further. I saw teacher-developed versions of the lyrics that contained a breakdown of the events referred to, with the years written in the margin next to each section of the song. The songwriter selected a few people or events to summarize each year, and the teachers wanted students to see this clearly. Including the years allowed the class to critique the songwriter's choices.

"What do you think?" the teacher asked. "Do you agree with his choices? Why did he include this part? What did he leave out? What would you have put in?"

This approach turned into an analysis of important historic events. Some classes were invited to parody the song or create stanzas for years not covered in the original, to deepen and broaden students' understanding of the curriculum.

The inspired teacher finds solutions for the entire class and for individuals

Whether a class contains 12 students or 42, it is a challenge to solve the problems posed by its unique makeup. To recognize and address the particular needs of each subgroup or individual within the class is difficult. The inspired teacher is able to do this and do it effectively.

Dividing a class into groups for instructional reasons is not a new idea. Remember the bluebirds and robins, reading groups working their way through different primers in the 1950s? Students do not have to be divided by ability or skill level in order to be effective.

Daniel Fader, who taught composition at the University of Michigan, used discussion groups within his freshmen composition classes. He wanted groups that included both stronger and weaker writers, so he formed the groups after the first essay had been submitted. Then, for the rest of the semester, three-person teams would read and discuss the essays of each member.

"In any set of 10 groups," he said in a lecture to high school teachers, "I have found that seven groups function quite well with almost no input from me. Two groups will struggle from time to time and need some advice and assistance. One group in 10 will be pretty dysfunctional most of the time."

Fader came to believe he had several roles. The first was to train the whole class in techniques and roles that would work in most cases. After the groups formed he stood by to see which groups were thriving. These groups needed an occasional comment to feel connected to the instructor, but advice was rarely called for.

The other groups got most of his time because they needed it. Two groups would usually need regular checkups and occasional retraining or advice to find their way. The last group needed him so often that he became an ex officio member, sitting with them for short or long periods and offering comments as if he were a group member.

Inspired teachers identify the actual level each student is at. Then they can correctly target instruction. Sometimes a handful of students need the same thing, so a small group works on the same activity or assignment. Other times everyone is at a different point. The teacher considers a range of choices. The teacher or an aide or a volunteer may work with one child. Within the school there may be supplemental services like special education teachers. Behavior problems may be addressed by counselors, social workers, or the principal, while school nurses, speech therapists, and others meet different needs.

Group interaction can increase learning effectively. Some teachers use Fader's example and form trios containing high-performing, low-performing, and middle-performing students. These teachers have found that the low- and middle-performing students benefit from the high-performing students' knowledge and the high-performing students gain practice in communicating clearly and interacting with a variety of classmates. Low-performers' confusion reveals when the "genius" is not being clear and middle-performers learn to translate, giving high-performers the benefit of learning to restate ideas. Understanding difficult ideas is often much easier for students if the ideas are presented by a classmate who just mastered them because the student reveals the way he got past the confusing parts.

Some teachers devise methods to enlist parental aid. Some teachers use a journal that students carry between home and school. In it teachers write notes about behavior, suggestions for parents, practice sheets for skill building, and even enrichment ideas.

Recess, lunch, and before- and after-school times can be used for additional instruction too, not just punishment. Some students have special needs that require quiet, extra time, or teacher involvement to ensure success. Inspired teachers keep seeking solutions for every problem until they find satisfactory answers.

Inspired teachers set up solutions for dozens or even hundreds of instructional problems, one at a time, all year long. These teachers broaden their own knowledge and increase their professionalism. As a result, their students receive the best instruction to master the broadest curriculum possible.

Actions to grow by

☐ When you sense your students "don't get it," write down exactly what they *do* get.

☐ When you implement a solution that works fairly well, come up with three ways to make it even better and give at least one of these options a try.

☐ To learn more about a problem, repeatedly ask "Why?" Ponder what you discover.

☐ When you find a way to solve a problem involving the entire class, ask yourself if any subgroup of the class would benefit from further adaptation.

☐ Pick five students at random and make a brief home visit. Introduce yourself and ask parents or guardians to describe their child's strengths and achievements. Ask what approaches work well with the child.

☐ Ask students about their own strengths and achievements. Ask them to help you brainstorm ways you can help strengthen their weak areas.

☐ Examine procedures and rules that apply to all. Determine if rules fall more heavily on some individuals than others. Consider how they might be adapted.

For Information and Inspiration

Adelson, B. (1983). Structure and strategy in the semantically-rich domains. Unpublished doctoral dissertation, Harvard University, Cambridge.

De Bono, E. (1985). *Six thinking hats*. London: Little, Brown.

Garner, B. K. (2007). *Getting to "got it!": Helping struggling students learn how to learn*. Alexandria, VA: ASCD.

Levine, M. D. (2002). *A mind at a time*. New York: Simon & Schuster.

Meier, D. (2002). *The power of their ideas: Lessons for America from a small school in Harlem*. Boston: Beacon Press.

Root-Bernstein, R. S., & Root-Bernstein, M. M. (1999). *Sparks of genius: The thirteen thinking tools of the world's most creative people*. Boston: Houghton Mifflin.

Sullo, B. (2007). *Activating the desire to learn*. Alexandria, VA: ASCD.

4

Improvising

According to the poet Robert Burns, the best laid plans of mice and men often go astray. Wise teachers plan effectively, but they also face surprises. How well they handle the unexpected is the subject of this chapter.

Despite well-planned explanations, lack of student comprehension is common. Teachers look out at faces full of confusion, consternation, frustration, or defeat. What to do next? The best teachers depart from their preplanned script and respond to the audience. Using knowledge of both students and subject, they try different approaches. Teachers add more examples, act out a procedure, invent an appropriate analogy, or stop to query students step by step: "Do you understand this part? What about this step?" Spontaneously finding appropriate responses to student needs—be it one or many—indicates strong improvisational skills. Those lacking this skill move lockstep through lessons without making adjustments to the needs of listeners.

The Unaware Teacher

Understandably, beginners usually don't improvise well. The topic or challenge is too unfamiliar. They are like parents with their first baby. Once parents learn the basics, they have the confidence to do what seems best without consulting relatives or baby books. But this doesn't occur on day one.

When new teachers begin their careers, the best advice is: have a plan, read and reread, look for good ideas in the curricular materials, estimate the length of lessons, list and assemble supplies, then follow your plan. To have 30 minutes left in a class period and nothing to fill it with can be intimidating. Students will not start a new lesson voluntarily, so a plan is essential.

Inexperienced teachers begin to build knowledge of their subject matter by preparing diligently every day. They learn which methods work by experimenting with new approaches and carefully noting the result of each. Experience accumulates, underpinning future improvisation.

We need to be realistic about how soon useful improvisation will develop in new teachers. There's a difference between valuable improvisation and lack of preparation. Filling a lesson with aimless chatter is not the same as skillfully varying an instructional lesson.

The greater the expertise, the easier the performance looks. Michael Jordan always made sinking the basketball look simple. A great teacher appears to speak spontaneously, pass out a paper or two, write something on the board, and suddenly everyone "gets it." If it looks that simple, you are seeing an inspired teacher at work. Trouble begins when people mistake the result for the process. If the result looks easy, they expect to duplicate it by doing something easy, too. That expectation is unrealistic.

In real life, a plan—detailed, complete, with more content than you are likely to cover—is essential to success in teaching. Most teachers need to master a subject and create a distillation that students can comprehend, using a plan. The greatest teachers can plan spontaneously, with continual adjustments—in other words, they can improvise.

Once beginners make a plan, they become attached to the plan and want to follow it exactly. Their plan was carved carefully from a large body of knowledge that the new teachers are still digesting. Therefore, novices are much more comfortable with the plan (the known) than everything else in the entire field of study that they have not yet planned lessons about (the unknown).

You can expect to see three behaviors among those not skilled in improvisation: Their lessons tend to be front-to-back presentations—more like a highway than a flow chart. They are frustrated by surprises in the classroom. And they resist changes and adaptations.

The unaware teacher uses straightforward plans with no flexibility

Let's suppose that Ms. Thornberg is a new 2nd grade teacher. She is planning to teach how to tell time on an analog clock. She will explain the long hand and the short hand, define half hours and quarter hours, and offer practice for students. She might make clocks from paper plates or draw examples on the board. She will try to identify the things her students need to know and then present the critical information in a way the children will understand. Because she is new, estimating the length of the lesson is hard. If she prepares well, she'll go into class with a clear mental map of what she is going to do.

If this is the first time she has taught youngsters to tell time, she will surely face some surprises. She may see bewildered children who don't recognize clock faces because they live in a digital world. To her surprise, some students report that the substitute teacher taught them how to tell time last month while they were waiting in the hall during a tornado warning. These scenarios, and many others, were not anticipated by Ms. Thornberg while preparing the lesson.

Ms. Thornberg knows that some students still need the lesson, so she will present it anyway. Because she is at the beginning of her career, the planned lesson on how to tell time is the only material she has to keep the students busy until lunchtime. She follows the plan with no adaptation, covering the topic required by the elementary math curriculum.

The unaware teacher is frustrated or confused by the unexpected

Ms. Thornberg looks unhappy as the children leave for lunch. Last night she had planned the way the lesson would go. She hummed as she prepared the individual clock faces and chose examples she would write on the board using colored chalk. Reality was not like her plan.

Ms. Thornberg is annoyed that the substitute teacher informally taught telling time to some of her students. She is shocked that four kids had never seen an analog clock before. She is discouraged by her clumsy attempts to explain the phrase "a quarter till." In the middle of the lesson, Joey yells, "Our substitute showed us how to do this!" Her response is, "Sit down and listen anyway because the rest of the class needs to hear this." Reasons for her frustration are clear, but so are the reasons why Joey might be annoyed by repetition. If she is self-aware, she might be able to identify these feelings. Many people are not. The novice might just mutter, "They didn't behave today" or "That substitute should stick to the lesson plans."

The unaware teacher resists changes in planned instruction

Given Joey's uninvited comment, Ms. Thornberg had an opportunity to change her plan on the spot. She didn't do so. Why?

Thinking of a new approach unexpectedly is difficult. Ms. Thornberg had lots of unhurried time to prepare while she made paper clocks and chose examples last night. But at this moment 24 pairs of eyes are staring at her to see how she will respond to Joey's comment. She had the time to imagine options while preparing, but now she has only a few seconds to react.

Another reason is fear. When lessons go smoothly, we feel confident. When they don't, we begin to worry that they will get even worse. Our minds work poorly when we worry. Faced with Joey's comment, Ms. Thornberg may find that her mind is blank, with no trace of the options she previously considered. Nor do new options emerge quickly. So, Ms. Thornberg is fairly rigid and tells everyone to listen. Her fear may be, *Who is in charge here?* Some teachers feel threatened when a student questions how class will be conducted. Improvising is tough, requiring wide experience and much confidence.

Many people believe there is one right way or a best way to do most things. Virginia Satir (1988), a family therapist, pointed out that she had found over 200 ways to do dishes, and the result of each was clean dishes. In the interest of reducing conflict, she concluded it would be good to let people do things in a way that worked for them as long as the result was adequate. This seems wise, yet it is harder to do than it sounds. Because many people attracted to teaching are very organized and focused, learning to improvise comfortably and accept it in others can be a challenge.

Questions to grow by

☐ Are you able to occasionally insert options into your plans?

☐ Do you consider "what ifs" while planning?

☐ When you're frustrated in the classroom, can you remember that students are not annoying you on purpose?

☐ Have you asked yourself what information students reveal through their unwanted comments or behaviors?

☐ After teaching lessons, do you consider how changes might improve them?

The Aware Teacher

As teachers gain experience, we expect improvisation to improve. With time, subtle shifts occur. Lesson plans remain structured but contain small choices or occasional flex. Sequences are still followed firmly, but sometimes teachers will change the plan during the lesson. Improvisations occur only when a need for change in instruction is absolutely necessary.

The aware teacher plans little flexibility

Let's imagine time has passed. Ms. Thornberg now teaches 3rd grade. She knows that 2nd graders in her school learn the names and locations of all 50 states. She plans to teach the state capitals and important landmarks and then ask students to create travel games and posters to put their knowledge to work.

She bases her planning on the idea that her pupils can label all 50 states when given a blank map. She anticipates that some children won't remember all the states, so she plans some flexibility. After the pre-test to check their recall, she will ask each student to list any 10 states they missed. Anyone with a perfect score can pick any 10. Then she'll ask them to use a U.S. map to find an oddly named city in each state. She believes this exercise will be an amusing way to practice reading maps and will make each state memorable. The planned flexibility is letting students choose which states to investigate.

The aware teacher follows preplanned lessons with little variation

On a typical day Ms. Thornberg will simply follow her plan from beginning to end. Sometimes the plan will allow for some flexibility, as we saw earlier; however, planning for flexibility will not yet be a part of every lesson.

The aware teacher changes plans during lessons if a major need arises

As Ms. Thornberg starts the states unit, the pre-test shows that half the children did not learn the states last year; their teacher, Mrs. Howard, took maternity leave and substitute teachers came and went. Ms. Thornberg realizes that she must change her plan:

"Instead of working on the state capitals, we need to be sure everyone knows the states. I want everyone to trace the U.S. map from our pre-tests onto blank paper. I will pair someone who had Mrs. Howard with a person who learned the state names last year. Use one of your traced maps to label all the states. Point out states on the blank map to quiz your partners. They can peek at the labels if they can't remember the state you point to. If you already know the states, you have a big job now. Can you help your partner learn at least 10 new states before the bell rings for recess?"

On the spot, Ms. Thornberg has improvised a necessary change in the lesson. Her improvisation addresses the immediate need of keeping all the kids involved—those who know the states and those who don't. The adjusted lesson assists those who need to make up the missing knowledge and provides review for the rest. It also builds teamwork skills. Later Ms. Thornberg will have time to rethink her original plan and figure out how to make sure every student not only learns the 3rd grade curriculum but makes up the missing facts from 2nd grade.

At this point in Ms. Thornberg's development, Joey's comment might remind her to invite to the board those who learned how to tell time to draw clock faces, instead of telling them to sit still and listen. This improvisation would turn them into assistants instead of restless detractors. The map activity she invented does the same—those who know the facts participate in the transfer of knowledge, instead of sitting passively. She has developed the ability to react quickly with improved approaches at least part of the time, especially when an unexpected situation is too important to overlook.

Questions to grow by

☐ As you plan, do you consider the range of responses you might receive when you present the lesson?

☐ Do you list possible choices you could make during the presentation based on projected reactions?

☐ Do you listen carefully to students, noticing confusion that might need response?

☐ Do you listen for curiosity, awe, or enthusiasm that may connect to present and future topics you cover?

☐ Are you open to teaching things out of order if a good opportunity arises?

Self-Development

• Improvisation is based on real listening—taking in what is said and not said and the implications thereof—before any response is attempted. If you can find a course on listening or a basic class in communication, sign up for it. Try to remember there is an internal logic in everything students say or do and try to fathom what it might be. This mind-set may greatly improve your responses.

• Imagine your life in the classroom as a documentary you are watching even as you participate in it. What are possible interpretations of actions around you? What alternative endings would you wish for? Imagining will be useful as you scramble for fresh reactions.

Collegial Support

• Ask a colleague if she would repeat a lesson the same way if teaching it again. Encourage her to state several different approaches she might use if repeating the lesson. Stating alternatives after a lesson is good practice for creating them in the moment.

• Have fun with coworkers. Give mock awards at staff meetings and plan enjoyable activities during departmental planning meetings. These activities model improvisation and imply it's also OK to improvise in the classroom.

The Capable Teacher

What will Ms. Thornberg's responses look like as she gains even more experience and confidence? Several new tendencies will occur. Most or all lesson plans will include some flexibility or provide built-in choices. Making some adjustments during the teaching of the lesson becomes common. Maintaining awareness of the general response pattern of the whole class, even subtle responses, and responding with alterations in instruction become natural with practice.

The capable teacher plans for some flexibility

What sort of flexibility or choices might be built into a lesson? At the simplest level, allowing students to choose between two options in a lesson or assignment requires the teacher to improvise in response. She will need to respond to two different patterns of student work as she moves around the room or grades the work. In response to a story from the reading book, Ms. Thornberg might ask her students to list 10 incidents in order of occurrence or to draw a detailed picture of the problem faced by the main character. She believes either assignment will allow her to judge whether the students grasp the main ideas of the story.

The capable teacher makes some instructionally useful changes during lessons

Another style of improvising is making adjustments as the lesson unfolds. Imagine that Ms. Thornberg is reading a story about Laplanders and the word *caribou* comes up.

"What is a caribou?" she asks. Not a hand is raised. Students glance sideways at their neighbors. Ms. Thornberg is a little surprised that no one knows, so she decides to try another approach.

"Then we need to find out about this big animal today," she says emphatically, providing clues in an orienting statement: big, animal.

"Taylor, will you bring the *C* encyclopedia up here? We need to see a picture." This detour wasn't in the original plan, but Ms. Thornberg judges it necessary.

Ms. Thornberg discovers the knowledge gap by paying attention to the reaction of the whole group. She is not directly provoked by a student or situation. Perhaps the story from the reading book would have made some sense without looking at a photo of a caribou, but it will make more sense to everyone after they see the photo.

The capable teacher changes instruction in response to general patterns of reaction

As improvisational skill grows, teachers may begin to constantly weave in enriching detours that were not written into their plans. The detours evolve from steady interaction with students. Improvisation allows Ms. Thornberg to fill gaps she senses and thus strengthens her teaching. To plan for all the contingencies that arise in the classroom would be impossible. Still, as Ms. Thornberg learns to think on her feet, she better meets unanticipated instructional needs.

• • • **TIP** • • •

Improvisational Setting: Knowing the context and background of listeners is a foundation for good improvisation. Learn about your students' music, slang, personal and neighborhood history, and about your school as well. Digest this information and incorporate it into your instruction.

Improvisational Timing: An appropriate pace is essential. Pause before important information and don't rush essential explanations; you can move more briskly through supporting details and peripheral facts.

Improvisational Varying: If you are always loud (or soft), always fast, or always serious, you lose listeners. Save intensity for critical points. Insert ordinary comments in the space before you uncover important information in order to help listeners distinguish relative importance.

Improvisational Ice-berging: Know more information than the lesson requires. Deep knowledge allows for careful selection in the moment of communication. (Adapted from Oida & Marshall, 1997.)

At the high school level, the presence or absence of improvisation is obvious to the observer. If we watch a teacher present the same material to three classes, we see whether the teacher improvised a lot or a little. Improvisational teachers seize on different student comments for further development. They skip a section of the lecture if the class demonstrates quick mastery. They explore students' questions or point out unexpected relationships between students' spontaneous comments and current, past, or future course material.

Improvisation is not to be confused with wandering around the subject area or pursuing trivial tangents. Teachers control their own chattiness and don't try to dominate the class. Behavior is improvisational when it is an unplanned instructional detour resulting from the response of the entire class or an individual. The detour will still reach the original goal of the lesson, or a closely related one, but not in the precise way the teacher had planned.

Only a recording would guarantee that every class gets the same lesson. Real life is unrepeatable. Even a teacher who wanted to repeat every lesson exactly could not. Students' questions and statements, the intercom, and countless things inside and outside the classroom or within the teacher will cause variations in input and output. Wise teachers increase improvisational skills so that the differences from one presentation to the next are recognized as purposeful enrichments, not distractions.

Questions to grow by

☐ Can you design a lesson plan with several options you could pursue based on student responses?

☐ Do you encourage students to ask questions and share comments?

☐ Do you invite student feedback by asking what parts of the lesson were clearest or most confusing?

☐ Do you ever pause and ask students to try explaining concepts to you?

The Inspired Teacher

Inspired teachers know that great teaching is interactive. They are prepared to respond to students' passions, concerns, and questions in a variety of ways. They improvise lessons to preserve and increase student interest in learning. By noting and responding to what students do or say, inspired teachers spontaneously present lessons that are tailored to the needs of their students. They demonstrate that they are inspired by students to react in fresh, useful, or even entertaining ways.

The inspired teacher plans opportunities for unexpected learning

Teachers who learn to improvise have a goal to increase student learning. They frequently make plans that may take two or three different directions depending on student reactions, and all the possible directions are instructionally useful. They also believe that an unplanned detour may be useful to student learning.

Inspired teachers' interactions with students might be humorous, but they might just as easily be serious, subtle, or touching. Great teachers can find the right mood through finely tuned instincts that they use to help students. Great improvisers create learning experiences spontaneously and often. They adjust to what students do and say and weave it into their teaching. They are comfortable making mid-lesson decisions to change the plan.

Spontaneous learning comes in many forms. A spider in the corner inspires discussions of science, nature, or *Charlotte's Web*. Great teachers decide which will best suit this group on this day and improvise accordingly. A confrontation between two students during roll call provides the material for introducing conflict resolution. Based on judgments of class interaction, teachers decide how to effectively guide the lesson. Many metaphors used by teachers to clarify difficult concepts for students are unplanned efforts to meet the needs of the whole class or one struggling individual.

According to Virginia Spolin (1999), spontaneity has seven aspects. Spontaneity has a sense of playfulness. It demonstrates personal freedom, setting aside constant approval or disapproval of actions. Spontaneity is built on the relationship between the presenter and members of the audience. The audience has a genuine reaction and does not feel acted upon. Direct experience of the world and people around us are the only requirements for building improvisational skills. The body, voice, and gestures are the means of spontaneity, rather than intellect alone. Inspired teachers show these attributes in their spontaneous interactions with students.

The inspired teacher adjusts readily and effectively to student responses

The teacher who adjusts easily to what students do or say uses strong observational skills coupled with imagination. Experience gives the teacher a wide set of choices. All the attempts made over the years to teach this or similar material are floating in memory, ready to be reused or adapted. Also present in memory are countless conversations with colleagues and ideas gleaned from training sessions, books, or curriculum materials.

In earlier levels, teachers note the general reaction of the entire class and respond accordingly. More sophisticated is the ability to note the progress and reactions of individuals. We might think it would be counterproductive to spend time worrying about the reaction of 1 student among 30. On the other hand, the teacher's job is to teach all 30, and this is accomplished individually. Further, students may take turns functioning as warning beacons. If one individual misunderstands or is confused, others who don't show it might also need more clarification. Even those who have a general understanding can usually benefit from another example or a reteaching to deepen and broaden their knowledge. A great improviser can quickly reteach using a fresh example or spontaneous activity that doesn't even feel like review. No one is bored and many are helped.

The inspired teacher makes useful adjustments throughout lessons

Imagination and insight are important ingredients for successful improvisation. Teachers need to carefully observe students to determine when more explanations are called for, and then create new examples or analogies. A teacher who can comfortably make mid-lesson decisions and incorporate unplanned but supportive changes is a person who can envision multiple possibilities and choose among them. The teacher can judge in real time how well students comprehend the material and turn on a dime to align with unforeseen student needs. Sometimes a different mood or tone for the class can also be achieved through improvisation.

The type of improvisation needed in teaching involves a departure from the plan in a way that advances learning. Imagine a classroom. At the bell signaling the end of the lunch hour, 15-year-old Hubert arrives, excitable as always. He is often reprimanded in this class and others. In the first 90 seconds of class, he climbs over a table, swipes a paper, trips a classmate, and calls to a passerby in the hallway from his seat in the front row (assigned to reduce his unrestrained behavior).

Ms. McDonough, the teacher, who is having a bad day, is sick of his behavior and snaps at him, "Do you take pest lessons or did you learn that on your own?"

Hubert freezes, stares at her with a baleful and penetrating gaze, and scowls as quiz papers are passed out.

Some might claim that the teacher improvised in an attempt to settle Hubert down. Actually, she indulged her own anger and frustration at Hubert's expense. Because she is experienced and aware, she is able to admit this mistake to herself. After calming down, she considers the cost of her own behavior. Having Hubert as an enemy for the rest of the year is not good for her, for Hubert, or for the rest of the class. She has class rules posted and procedures to follow when rules are violated, but she did not follow them when he acted up. Now, because she erred as grievously as Hubert did, she believes this is not a good time to invoke her rules.

Ms. McDonough considers her options. Discussing the behavior in front of the class will not work. Neither will calling his parents because she recognizes that she must first repair her relationship with Hubert. She and Hubert must be able to work together for their own sakes and for the good of the class. While pondering the problem, she announces the next activity, telling the class to silently read pages 147 and 148. Her original plan was to introduce the section, but she gives precedence to her issue with Hubert over the mini-lesson.

When everyone is occupied, she leans over Hubert's desk and whispers, "I need to talk to you in the hall."

In the hall she pitches her voice low and speaks calmly while Hubert glowers.

"Hubert," she says, "I am not proud of what I said to you earlier, and I think I owe you an apology. I should not have said that. At the same time, I feel discouraged. I know you are intelligent and could help the class, but instead you do things that distract everyone."

She watches Hubert's reaction. He appears startled.

"This is what I think we need to do. I think the two of us need to find a way to work together so you can learn and so other people can, too. I know you could add a lot to our discussion. What do you think about this? Can we work together? I think we need to start over with a fresh slate."

Hubert keeps looking at her.

"Do you think we can work as a team to make the class better instead of worse?" Ms. McDonough asks to prompt a response from Hubert.

As Hubert stares silently, his eyes fill with tears and his lip quivers.

"I'm sorry, Ms. McDonough. I'm having a really bad day. I didn't sleep last night because I had a big fight with my parents."

"I'm sorry to hear that, Hubert," says Ms. McDonough, amazed at his tearful reaction.

Hubert wipes his eyes.

"Do you think we can start over and try to be on the same side?" she asks.

He nods. "I'll try. I really will."

They reenter the classroom.

At no time during this conversation did Ms. McDonough know for certain what to say next; she wasn't sure what she would say until she heard it coming out of her mouth. She was operating from a clear idea that the relationship needed to be healed, but she had to discover how to do so by improvising.

Hubert did not cease being disruptive, because it seemed to be reflexive with him, but he did redirect himself each time he transgressed. This self-correction did not occur in other classes, where he continued to be disruptive. Ms. McDonough alone had gained his cooperation.

Where does one get improvisational skills? There are many contributing factors: experience, knowledge, imagination, observation, willingness to experiment. Desire or intention is probably the strongest aid of all. If teachers want to reach students and assist their learning, they will try everything, until a connection is made.

Before we leave the subject, one more thing needs to be said. Improvisation is the least welcomed skill in many areas of life. Human history is full of examples. Schools are no different from the rest of society. In some schools the requirement that every teacher will teach the same page on the same day in similar fashion is gaining favor. This attempt to improve the least skillful teacher's behavior actually decreases the effectiveness of the most skillful teachers.

A case in point: Mr. Stevens is a second-career teacher. He worked for 27 years in a factory while farming on the side. He served one term on his local school board and volunteered for two decades as an EMT-trained fireman. Then, in his forties, he returned to school to complete his teaching certification and became a 3rd grade teacher.

One day during his third year as a teacher, Mr. Stevens was inspired to go beyond the social studies curriculum and invite a Vietnam veteran into his classroom for the students to interview for Veterans Day. This was not a part of the curriculum but seemed like an interesting and educational offering for his students.

Rather than encourage him, his principal emphatically told him to stick with the curriculum and nothing but the curriculum. She actually said, "I want you to be a Stepford teacher." The principal sought the antithesis of improvisation. Fortunately, some weeks later, she relented and allowed Mr. Stevens to ask his 3rd graders to interview a veteran and write up their findings.

But it's worth remembering that improvisation can arouse discomfort in some people, so the skill may be quite difficult to nurture.

Actions to grow by

☐ If students make suggestions during a presentation, declare an "experimental moment" to try the idea before returning to your planned remarks.

☐ Design your lesson like a flow chart, writing down two alternatives at several points: *If students do A, I will do B; if students say X, I will say Y.*

☐ When presenting difficult concepts, ask students to think of their own analogies to explain the ideas. Discuss which ones are most helpful to classmates.

☐ Set aside five minutes for students or listeners to share ways in which the material relates to their lives or to other courses.

For Information and Inspiration

Brookhart, S. (2008). *How to give effective feedback to your students.* Alexandria, VA: ASCD.

Dyer, W. (2007). *Change your thoughts, change your life: Living the wisdom of the tao.* Carlsbad, CA: Hay House.

Kabat-Zinn, J. (1994). *Wherever you go, there you are: Mindfulness meditation in everyday life.* New York: Hyperion.

Oida, Y., & Marshall, L. (1997). *The invisible actor.* New York: Routledge.

Sarason, S. B. (1999). *Teaching as a performing art.* New York: Teachers College Press.

Satir, V. (1988). *The new peoplemaking.* Mountain View, CA: Science and Behavior Books.

Spolin, V. (1999). *Improvising for the theater: A handbook of teaching and directing techniques* (3rd ed.). Evanston, IL: Northwestern University Press.

Yokoyama, J., & Michelli, J. A. (2004). *When fish fly: Lessons for creating a vital and energized workplace from the world famous Pike Place Fish Market.* New York: Hyperion.

5

Managing a Classroom

Teachers establish norms, expectations, and procedures that form the classroom culture for their students. What teachers do interactively with students builds the classroom environment whether teachers do so consciously or not. Learning environments are most productive when they are free of fear and intimidation. Teachers who are able to positively redirect negative student behaviors toward learning show good classroom management skills. By removing obstacles to learning and encouraging growth, inspired teachers create classrooms that run smoothly.

The Unaware Teacher

A well-managed classroom is no accident. A teacher's actions mold student behavior. Some teachers have no clear vision of what behavior they expect from students or how to reinforce desired actions and interrupt undesirable patterns. Also, students arrive with different notions of what proper behavior is, or no idea at all. If students' previous classrooms were chaotic, they will bring related habits with them. Teachers must retrain students, instilling expectations for the behavior they require from students. The unaware teacher doesn't know how to do so.

The unaware teacher uses muddled directions and procedures

There's an old saying: "If you don't know where you're going, you'll probably end up somewhere else." Unaware teachers don't yet know how to guide their students because they haven't thought clearly about their destination and how to get there. Here's a typical unaware teacher:

"Write your name on your predictions—no, wait. Don't put your names on them because we'll exchange papers and I don't want you to know whose guess you are looking at. Pass them forward—no wait, I don't want you to see anyone else's prediction. Just put them in the box. Hang on a minute; that will be too noisy and take too long. I'll just come around and collect them. Turn your paper face down on your desk until I get to you."

This teacher needs to decide a course of action and then follow through. Students need to know what's expected. Conflicting directions undermine students' confidence in the instructor.

Consistent procedures prevent disorder by creating classroom habits. What is the procedure for passing in papers? One teacher prefers to move around the room to make contact with individual students for a few seconds. Another wants every student to walk up and deposit papers because physical movement will diminish restlessness. Teachers use clearly thought-out procedures to reduce classroom confusion.

When he was a new teacher, Harry Wong, coauthor of *The First Days of School* (Wong & Wong, 2005), asked students to pass papers forward, up the rows. His students swatted classmates' backs to get their attention and called out their names. In response, Wong taught his students to pass papers leftward across the rows so they could make eye contact with the person beside them. The person nearest the wall then took the papers to the assignment box. Passing papers became a quiet and orderly procedure.

The unaware teacher uses procedures in ways that confuse students

Sometimes expectations conflict with one another and teachers must clarify desired behavior. Suppose a teacher prefers that her pupils line up to ask questions, get a drink, and go to gym, lunch, and recess. One day she announces a race to write the correct answers to geography questions on the board. Students lean forward with excitement.

The teacher reads the first question. Four students dash up and scrawl answers on the board. She becomes upset because they didn't line up and reprimands them. There is a conflict between the idea of a race and the teacher's usual expectation for lining up. If she wants lines at the board, students need to know this is expected. There is nothing wrong about her expectation, but it should be made clear in advance to avoid confusion.

The unaware teacher reacts instead of preventing

In the previous example, the teacher reacts after the behavior has occurred. She does not explain her expectations in advance; she reprimands afterward. Unclear expectations waste time and create student misunderstanding.

Harry Wong (Wong & Wong, 2005) makes a clear distinction between rules and procedures. If students break a rule—"no hitting," for example—they face consequences; however, if they fail to follow a procedure, Wong concludes they need more training in that procedure, so he provides more instruction and practice. Wong's goal is to make every procedure habitual and smooth, so time is spent on learning instead of reprimanding.

Unaware teachers reprimand often. Expectations aren't stated in advance, so students learn them only by failing to meet them. Students are scolded because they don't know what the teacher wants and thus do what is unwanted. Some decide that they'll never get it right, so they stop trying.

If students are asked to make models of chemical compounds from toothpicks and miniature marshmallows, what will happen? Many students will be tempted to eat the marshmallows. With no prevention plan, the teacher will soon be admonishing students for eating the supplies. Instead, before passing out materials, the teacher could tell students to eat one marshmallow and use the rest for models to be hung as mobiles in the classroom, or to eat no marshmallows until she has checked their construction. Procedures used as prevention rather than as a reaction make cooperation more common and scolding infrequent.

The unaware teacher deals ineffectively with disruptive students

Knowing when to intervene and how best to do it is an art. At any given moment one or more students in the classroom may be misbehaving. If teachers respond to every transgression, there is time for nothing else. A student folding paper into an airplane is less serious than a student cutting another's hair. Neither is as serious as a physical attack. Each needs a different response.

Making airplanes can be stopped by silently taking the folded paper without interrupting the lesson. The teacher wastes no time discussing it. The "barber" needs to be interrupted, too; however, this act is more invasive and permanent. A strong response can still be done calmly, by asking the culprit to wait in a time-out area until the teacher is ready to discuss punishment.

A physical attack by a student is a genuine emergency that must be stopped immediately. Teachers stop everything to deal with this situation. Until the office has been called, the attack ended, and the perpetrator removed for counseling or expulsion, the planned lesson must be set aside.

In between paper airplanes and assaults is a vast range of behaviors. Good teachers evaluate each behavior and determine appropriate responses. When unaware teachers do not respond at all, classrooms move toward chaos. Teachers must learn to deal with disruptive students quickly and effectively to preserve an atmosphere conducive to learning.

Disruptive behavior is not a character trait. Rather than believing a student is a troublemaker, a lazy student, or a chatterbox, we can rearrange our own thinking. We can choose to believe that a troublemaker is a child who hasn't *yet* learned to be peaceful. A lazy student hasn't *yet* learned organizational skills or the satisfaction of completing a task. The chatterbox hasn't *yet* developed impulse control. Each of them can change recurrent behaviors by creating new habits, with teacher support. The goal is to turn every disrupter into a productive student. Harsh overcorrection wastes as much time as ignoring misbehavior and makes the classroom a fearful place. If we separate students from their errors in judgment, we create a classroom setting that helps all students learn.

Questions to grow by

☐ Do you teach students clear procedures for normal activities in your classroom?

☐ When chaos erupts, do you examine your instructions to see if they contributed to the problem?

☐ Do you frequently scan the classroom to look for disruptions?

☐ Do you attend to the noise level to identify growing disruptions?

☐ Do you distinguish between minor and serious disruptions and respond accordingly?

The Aware Teacher

Aware teachers have figured out that order and organization are important, so they try to create and maintain them. They are so focused on gaining obedience, however, they sometimes use fear, ridicule, or bribery rather than clear, logical guidelines to nurture self-direction. They are unlikely to use prevention techniques and often ignore warning signs, letting problems advance too far before intervening.

The aware teacher provides procedures based on compliance

Classroom management requires that students be taught to follow rules and procedures that advance the goals of the classroom. Some teachers ask for cooperation; others demand complete obedience at all times. Some inspire a desire to please; others use fear of punishment. At the aware level, teachers don't think much about choices for students; they want students to follow guidelines without question: "Be good. Line up. Raise your hand. Don't touch others. Don't throw things. Turn in your homework. Bring your book. Put things away."

If students know the rules and if the teacher consistently enforces them, order will follow. Learning is increased by reducing confusion. But rules don't cover every possibility. For instance, if sixteen 1st graders are lined up at the drinking fountain and Monique suddenly twists out of line, how will the teacher react? She might remind Monique that she broke a rule and has forfeited her chance to get a drink. The teacher might also wonder what prompted Monique's behavior: *Was she stung by a bee? Kicked by a classmate?* Either situation makes enforcing the rule less defensible. Good management includes finding out reasons for atypical behavior and being judicious in reactions.

For instance, if the rule is "stay in your seat," but the class contains a student who is incredibly restless, it might be wise to let him silently pace the back of the room during lectures. Thus, the teacher can reduce the time spent reminding the student to settle down and all students might learn better. The teacher can stipulate that the offer will be revoked if the pupil distracts others. A teacher who demands constant compliance would not think of this coping strategy.

Imagine a situation where an 8th grade teacher is called to the office and leaves a student in charge. There are clear rules: don't touch others, don't take things from the teacher's desk, don't leave the classroom without permission. Suddenly a young man falls to the floor in what appears to be an epileptic seizure. One student opens the teacher's desk drawer and takes out a sweater to use as a pillow. Another goes to the restroom for paper towels because the student has cut his head. Two other students hold their convulsing classmate to prevent further injury. Obviously, violating normal rules during this type of event is better than slavishly following them. Neither the student left in charge nor the ones attempting first aid should be reprimanded for their choices, even though they broke rules that should be followed in most situations.

The aware teacher leaves students unclear about procedures

Although aware teachers know about the importance of regular procedures and attempt to use them, they don't yet do so consistently. When I was inexperienced, I tried to borrow methods from other teachers. Because I hadn't developed the procedures from my own needs, style, and experiences, I often got muddled when I tried to apply them. For instance, I tried recording transgressions on the board with checks and following up with a series of consequences. I found I got distracted trying to decide whether certain annoyances were worthy of being recorded and therefore punished. Eventually I developed my own procedures to prevent, instead of record, infractions.

Inconsistency can result from the teacher's lack of confidence. If students point out reasons why a procedure doesn't work or is illogical, the teacher may make exceptions or stop the practice altogether. When normal procedures erode this way, students remember. Students develop a casual attitude toward procedures when expectations are fluid.

The aware teacher rarely uses preventive strategies

Remember the saying "An ounce of prevention is worth a pound of cure"? The aware teacher hasn't yet learned to stop problems before they start. In the past, I thoughtlessly told students to turn in their papers, line up, or get out materials before I had finished giving instructions. They'd start the action and miss the remaining directions. I'd find myself shouting over a buzz I had triggered myself. Eventually I learned to rearrange the order of my remarks or ask students to wait until I finished my instructions.

Some procedures are so important that we organize preventive measures such as fire drills. Teachers are trained to close the windows, take their roll book, and leave the classroom door unlocked. Students are trained to leave quickly through the door marked on the posted exit plan. One thousand people can exit in two minutes because of clear instructions and regular practice.

During a year, dozens of classroom situations can either go smoothly or not. At the aware level, teachers don't envision all the possible scenarios in advance. Nor do they consistently prepare students to behave appropriately. How are students to proceed to the library, the lunch room, or the bus? How are they expected to act on a field trip or when classmates are giving speeches? Where are supplies stored in the classroom? How are papers turned in or returned? Aware teachers may train students to follow procedures in some areas, but not all.

The aware teacher ignores early signs of disruptive behavior

"That's it, Freddie! That's the third time you've sharpened your pencil since lunch. I see you poking Jessica every time you dance past her. I've had it. You're staying inside for recess!"

Freddie is on the teacher's last nerve. He went to the pencil sharpener, danced down the aisle, and poked Jessica many times. Why did the reaction take so long? This teacher ignores minor infractions and reacts only to major problems. For some teachers, misbehavior is not yet considered a problem, or it has become a big problem and they overreact.

If Freddie is seen poking another student, the wise teacher restates the rule about not touching others. Seeing a student dance down the aisle, distracting others, is addressed with a calm directive: "Walk, Freddie." Trips to the sharpeners are ended with a silent hand gesture, by providing a replacement pencil, or by standing next to Freddie's desk. If Freddie continues to misbehave, an experienced teacher administers consequences. When a teacher doesn't react quickly to misconduct, students are trained to try mischief, knowing they may be free to act with impunity.

Questions to grow by

☐ Can you imagine a series of small steps to interrupt disruptions when they first begin?

☐ Are you able to prevent behavioral problems by changing your management approach?

☐ Have you tried looking for deeper reasons behind student misbehavior?

Self-Development

• Picture students carrying out your directions so you can predict problems and prevent them. Imagine what will happen if you ask students to pick up supplies, what will happen if you pass out supplies, and how it will work if one person from each row does it. There is a place for each method; some days students need to move, some days you don't want them to. By visualizing each activity, you can choose which best advances your behavior management goals.

• Try justifying why you use certain procedures. Stretch your thinking by imagining a different way to achieve that end. Then question the end you have in mind. Does your objective merely prompt compliance, or does it increase learning and provide support?

• Have conversations with students about what helps and what hinders their learning. Their observations offer real insights to new approaches to assist their learning.

Collegial Support

• Help colleagues find ways to prevent problems. If a coworker is focusing on punishment, emphasize the use of prevention and proactive choices. Try asking why they chose a given approach. Invite them to imagine a series of alternatives and predict the results of each possibility.

• Keeping students involved with meaningful, interesting assignments prevents many behavioral problems from developing. Departments can work together to plan novel experiences to help students master important curricular goals. Alternatively, two or three teachers may work together to brainstorm ways to keep students focused.

The Capable Teacher

Rather than valuing exterior obedience only, capable teachers want students to be fully engaged from within; they plan their actions to encourage student involvement, using clearly stated expectations. They have learned to predict or sense some developing problems early. When they catch problems, they use either prevention or early intervention to redirect students toward productivity.

The capable teacher uses procedures that encourage engagement

Good classroom managers use two kinds of procedures: standing orders, which are practices that always apply, and special instructions for the project at hand. Both improve student performance.

At the start of school, effective managers show their students the procedures that will be used all year. A science teacher who requires lab reports provides guidelines and shows examples of good reports. He shows students how to meet his expectations. He wastes no energy complaining that students come to him ill-prepared. He simply teaches them to succeed. This ensures a more productive year.

Similarly, English teachers explain and demonstrate methods they will use for correcting errors and revising papers. Business teachers teach memo writing and ask that class notes be submitted as memos. Art teachers explain procedures for accessing supplies, drying and storing artwork, and displaying finished creations. Wise teachers explain the behaviors they require.

During the first weeks of class, much time is devoted to procedures. Is the time wasted? Not at all. Once procedures are in place, the rest of the school year moves more efficiently, allowing time to cover more material.

Capable teachers also use procedures for specific measures related to the task at hand. It may be simple—an instruction. It may be complex—a time line of due dates to guide students through a seven-week research project. Teachers soon realize that even apparently simple instructions have many interpretations by students. Procedures are designed to help students avoid pitfalls. Teachers establish procedures in advance to assist individuals and maintain a healthy learning environment for all.

The capable teacher consistently communicates expectations

Capable teachers don't assume that everyone knows how to behave or do what they have in mind. No two people carry identical assumptions or memories. When you ask a roommate to buy milk and he or she brings home a half gallon of whole milk instead of the full gallon of 1 percent you had in mind, we're reminded of the many ways the same statement can be interpreted. When a complex project is assigned in the classroom, look at the multiple ways students interpret each section of the instructions. Capable teachers make expectations clear and accessible with discussions, posters, checklists, and models from previous years. Teachers cannot expect desired patterns of behavior from students without clarifying teacher expectations.

Teachers can change or improve their procedures. Adapting an existing rule or procedure or adding one for a good reason is perceived by students as consistency because the expectations are clear both before and after the adjustment. Explaining reasons for changes usually wins students' cooperation. Even if students dislike the rule, they understand what is expected.

The capable teacher sometimes uses preventive strategies to encourage engagement

Capable teachers predict problems based on experience and take action. Ms. Al-Masri, a speech teacher, sees that some students sleep through speeches presented by classmates. Some whisper or pass notes. She tries tapping sleepers to awaken them, but they don't stay awake. Her movements distract speakers and keep her from evaluating speeches well. Frustrated, she decides to involve students.

Ms. Al-Masri gives evaluation forms to students and asks them to evaluate one another. Problems arise. She bases a part of the grade on peer responses, and students and parents claim it is unfair. Providing forms for everyone uses lots of paper and the payoff is small. Students check boxes with little thought and write few comments. She realizes she needs a better way to involve her audience.

Ms. Al-Masri borrows the idea of "glow and grow" from a presentation by Ruth Nathan (1990), coauthor of *Writing to Learn* (Temple, Nathan, Burris, & Temple, 1988). For each speech, students are asked to write down the speaker's greatest strength (a reason to glow) and an area that needs improvement (a way to grow). On speech days students divide a sheet of paper into quarters. As the speakers are announced, listeners write one name at the top of each quarter sheet. After a speech everyone writes down the greatest strength of the speaker and the most important improvement needed. The classroom seems like Valentine's Day as the notes are delivered to the speakers.

This assignment requires more involvement than checking items on a form. Students enjoy writing legitimate notes to one another and speakers enjoy honest, focused feedback. This procedure keeps everyone attentive and increases learning for both speakers and listeners. Ms. Al-Masri eliminates several past problems—sleeping, whispering, and passing notes. Ms. Al-Masri's students report other benefits from the activity. Many are surprised to learn how many strengths their classmates point out. Confidence improves and nervousness subsides.

Finding preventive strategies is a learning process. Each failure is a step toward success if we take a lesson from it. Years of experience can yield an intuitive sense of what any given procedure will elicit from students but only if we pay careful attention and analyze our choices.

The capable teacher addresses and redirects most disruptions

Capable teachers know that ignoring disruptions doesn't work. Intervention is necessary and can be done effectively in a variety of ways. Consider the body language of teachers: an arched eyebrow, a pointing index finger, the director's cut with the hand slicing across the neck, a shake of the head, peering over the top of glasses, waving off, hands on hips, pursed lips, a frown, a look of consternation or dramatic confusion, eyes heavenward, eyes cut to the right or left, eyes tightly closed while shaking the head, mouth tucked to one side, faked look of shock. Capable teachers use such signals to guide students to the task at hand. Students read these messages clearly and usually change their behavior.

Seating charts are a standard tool for changing or controlling behavior. Students who need constant supervision are moved to the front row. Simply standing near a student encourages a return to work, much like the sight of a police cruiser causes a driver to slow down. Clearing the throat or saying a pupil's name can do the same.

These techniques prevent minor infractions from turning into major disruptions. Because capable teachers are highly aware of most actual or potential disruptions, they intervene often enough to keep most students productive most of the time.

Sometimes capable teachers go a step further. After a "don't do that" message, they redirect students with a "do this instead" message. If Mr. Xu walks up the aisle and finds Connor using the eraser of his pencil to outline a race car on the tabletop, Mr. Xu can wordlessly stop him by taking the pencil, turning it around, and returning it. If he follows up with a quiet question, "How many questions have you finished?" the student's attention returns to the assignment and he is likely to continue working after Mr. Xu moves on.

Questions to grow by

☐ Do you critique procedures from students' viewpoints to see if your techniques keep youngsters tuned in?

☐ Do you openly state your vision for student actions before they begin?

☐ Do you have your students practice doing things the right way?

The Inspired Teacher

Inspired teachers make all management decisions based on student learning. Because they believe that every student can understand the material, they arrange their procedures to enable student mastery. These teachers use procedures and prevention strategies so effectively that learners begin to demonstrate self-management. Student disruptions are quickly noticed, and learners are consistently redirected with minimum force.

The inspired teacher uses procedures that focus on student learning

Ms. Lee's third-hour class is the most talkative, distracted, unfocused group she has faced in many years. She uses all her usual approaches with little success. She doesn't want to shift into high-punishment mode, knowing it will make the classroom unpleasant for everyone, but she doesn't plan to ignore the problem.

"We are wasting so much time," she laments to a fellow teacher.

"Time is money," quips her colleague.

The comment gives Ms. Lee an idea. The next day she begins a class discussion.

"How much tax money will be spent on educating you this year?"

"10 bucks?" The guess triggers general laughter.

"No, about $6,700. Now, how many days in the school year?"

"Too many!" Giggles.

"180," says Ms. Lee. "Get out your calculators. How much does it cost per day to educate you?"

Students turn with curiosity toward those with calculators.

"$37.22?"

"Right," says Ms. Lee. "Let's round it off to 37 dollars. Since there are six hours in the school day, what do taxpayers pay for each class you take?"

"$6.16!"

"Yes."

"Hey, I wish they'd just give it to me," calls out a joker.

"They do," says Ms. Lee. "You have to collect it in knowledge, not cash. They must really care about you guys! Now, how many people are in this class?"

Counting starts. "33!"

"Yes. So, what does this class cost?"

"$203.28."

"Good. Let's just say $200. Do I get paid that much?"

"No."

"Where does the money go?" she asks.

"Heat?"

"Janitors."

"Books and furniture."

"People who work here!"

"You're all right," says Ms. Lee, "but think about this: Every day I am responsible for delivering $200 worth of education while you are here. I owe it to taxpayers. It also means you are responsible for learning every day. If you don't learn, you're wasting your $6. If you keep everyone else from learning, you are robbing them. Stealing $200 is pretty serious. We need to get serious about learning."

The class stares.

"I expect you to use every minute you have here. I'm going to try hard to do the same. Don't cheat yourself or anybody else."

Behavior improves. Students realize that they share a mutual goal—learning. Whenever someone slips, they are reminded to get back on track. Interestingly, Ms. Lee doesn't have to do the reminding. Classmates call out, "Stop wasting my $6." Everyone in the class knows exactly what is meant. Students correct themselves without Ms. Lee's intervention.

This mini-lesson shows students a social reality related to their actions and illuminates Ms. Lee's rules and procedures regarding student learning. Students distill the lesson into a new idea: "Stop wasting my $6." This idea redirects students into learning-oriented actions. Ms. Lee's goal was learning, not just rule-following. She imparted this knowledge to students who hadn't grasped it on their own. Rather than force compliance, she designed an activity to increase students' desire to cooperate. Orderly procedures and rule-following emerged, not from compulsion but from a new understanding.

The inspired teacher creates procedures that promote mastery and learning

Inspired teachers know that their goal is not to prevent misbehavior but to increase learning. Boosting learning for a daydreamer, a frustrated student who gives up, or a quick study who gets bored are separate concerns. Skilled teachers understand this. The procedures and expectations they establish are designed to address each student.

Knowing that everyone learns differently, a skilled teacher may adopt the habit of presenting each new concept at least two ways: a lecture and an experiment, a video clip coupled with a hands-on activity, movement or drama followed by a worksheet, a reading assignment plus a discussion, definitions accompanied by three-dimensional objects. Content and management are linked by teachers who use such procedures for their planning. Variety keeps the dreamer focused and gives the frustrated learner multiple entry points for understanding while stimulating the quick learner.

Interaction among students can solve management problems. The quick learner may function well in a group with the daydreamer and the frustrated student. Asking questions and teaching one another change the dynamic for all three. Some protest that the fast learner should not be burdened with helping others, but quick learners benefit by learning to state ideas clearly, understand different viewpoints, and practice team skills.

In many classrooms, procedures are in place to allow students to get extra help when they're stuck or to pursue personal projects if they finish early. Pre-tests, practice sessions, reteaching and retesting, and extra credit or special assignments help students reach their full potential. The skilled teacher creates routines to accommodate all students. Some teachers say "Ask three before me" to encourage students to help one another. Simply teaching students how to access and return reference materials allows them to meet their own needs when the teacher is busy with others. Such practices are designed to keep students learning for more minutes and in more depth.

The inspired teacher uses prevention to promote engagement

The opposite of engagement is inattention and distraction. A wise teacher tries to promote student engagement by making lessons interesting from beginning to end as often as possible. With prior planning, a teacher can prepare lesson openings that grab the attention of students. This effort pays off. Once a teacher gains the attention of an audience, he has a chance to keep students' attention for the entire lesson.

Look closely at students who are not paying attention to the material being presented and you will notice that they are paying attention to something. A comic book? A commotion in the hall? A classmate making funny faces? Whispered conversations? Good observers can sometimes spontaneously tie distractions into the lesson or assign a report or project that connects students' personal interests with the curriculum. Linking student interests to the subject matter at hand helps to keep students involved.

If Jerry is reading a comic book inside his textbook, the teacher can use that observation.

"If we made President Truman a superhero, what would we name him? Budget Man for his cost-cutting during World War II or Atomic Guy for deciding to drop the bomb? What's your opinion, Jerry?"

Preventive strategies are as varied as the circumstances. Teachers who notice students staring at people in the hall often tape a poster over the pane of glass in the classroom door as a basic prevention technique. Also, teachers carefully plan to have the right supplies for a project and consider in advance how to distribute and recover them with minimum confusion. Streamlining instructions, giving guidelines for checking off a series of tasks, showing a model to illustrate the desired result before students begin a construction job—all prevent problems by helping students use their time effectively. When students know what they are supposed to be doing, they can do just that.

Teachers quickly find out whether a class is doing well in self-chosen groups. If successful, engagement is high without teacher intervention. If not, teachers preplan by grouping students with those they cooperate with successfully to be sure time is used productively.

Creating preventive strategies takes imagination. Guesswork is required to predict some or all of the potential distractions or frustrations that students may have with any given task. The wise teacher sets about creating a procedure that will minimize or eliminate as many stumbling blocks as possible. Such guidance helps students climb higher than those without guiding procedures.

The inspired teacher consistently addresses and redirects disruptive students

There are many ways to say "Get back to work." Inspired teachers can walk into a roomful of buzzing students they don't even know and get everyone on task in minutes. They move around, looking at papers to see how much has been written, rotating papers slightly to make them more accessible, or tapping gently at the place to resume work. They start conversations: "Which question are you on? Does it make sense so far? Do you have any questions? Have your read over the directions? Where's your book? Are you having trouble? Do you think you'll be able to finish before the bell rings?" They also make statements and give simple commands: "Here's a pencil. Find chapter 2. Get out some paper. Open your book. The glossary is in the back. You're almost right. Get a dictionary. Check the board for instructions. Time to begin. Try again. Start writing." Each statement redirects a student who is not on task.

By paying attention to each student's level of involvement, the teacher eliminates most serious disruptions—bullying, name calling, fighting. The skilled teacher usually doesn't allow students enough down time to engage in disruptive behavior. The organized classroom makes learning seem attainable to easily frustrated students, so they have less anger to act out. When they do misbehave, more redirecting is in order.

Actions to grow by

☐ Examine procedures and rules that apply to all your students. Ask yourself whether they fall more heavily on some individuals than others. Consider how they might be adapted.

☐ Read books about effective classroom management. Steal good ideas and try them out in your room.

☐ Periodically observe in other classrooms. Don't limit yourself to your own school, your own subject matter, or your own grade level. Watching teachers in assignments different from yours may reveal universal principles that you might otherwise overlook.

For Information and Inspiration

Erwin, J. C. (2004). *The classroom of choice: Giving students what they need and getting what you want.* Alexandria, VA: ASCD.

Kobrin, D. (2004). *In there with the kids: Crafting lessons that connect with students* (2nd ed.). Alexandria, VA: ASCD.

Nathan, R. (1990, May). *Improving writing instruction.* Presentation for Grand Rapids English teachers, Grand Rapids, MI.

Temple, C., Nathan, R., Burris, R. N., & Temple, F. (1988). *Writing to learn.* Newton, MA: Allyn & Bacon.

Wong, H. K. (1987). *How you can be a super successful teacher* [Audiotape]. Mountain View, CA: Harry K. Wong Publications.

Wong, H. K., & Wong, R. T. (2005). *The first days of school: How to be an effective teacher.* Mountain View, CA: Harry K. Wong Publications.

6

Interpreting Events in Progress

Teaching is a lot like controlling air traffic. Teachers and air traffic controllers both deal with many bodies in motion every hour of the day and make continual significant decisions about all these moving objects. Being aware of all the elements of the system at once is an important skill, but beginning teachers usually don't know how to manage this process.

Part of a teacher's job is to observe the actions and reactions of all students under her guidance. She must constantly sort a great deal of information and must distinguish important issues from peripheral ones. Then she must choose effective responses to important matters and disregard minor issues to prevent reacting to trivialities. Inspired teachers are remarkably skilled at interpreting events in progress and finding appropriate responses.

The Unaware Teacher

Each student is aware of his own feelings and reactions. He might laugh at others' jokes, sabotage the teacher's plan, or be fully attentive. But a student's own behavior is the extent of his responsibility. Teachers' responsibilities are much greater.

Teachers are expected to monitor the classroom and react wisely. They cannot merely obey rules and follow instructions. Teachers must attend to everything and decide if each person's behavior, including their own, is benign or problematic, and then decide what action, if any, to take. At first, this seems impossible.

The unaware teacher feels overwhelmed by the complexity of the classroom

Unaware teachers cannot process the volume of details that surround them as they teach. They attend to some details, missing others completely.

Mr. Decker, a student teacher, has organized the background information for his lesson on a chart. As soon as the bell rings he lays a transparency on the overhead projector, and the chart appears on a whiteboard on the back wall. Immediately, he starts explaining information about various groups of immigrants on his chart. Several students squint at the board, but Mr. Decker doesn't notice.

His supervising teacher, who is entering grades into the computer, glances over at the whiteboard. The experienced teacher walks over to erase a diagram left on the board from a previous discussion. Mr. Decker is so focused on presenting his chart that he doesn't notice the interfering marks on the board.

Although the chart can be read from six feet away where Mr. Decker stands, it is very hard to read from the last row. Even as students far from the board crane their necks, Mr. Decker does not consider that the chart might be too small to read.

Later Mr. Decker introduces a film clip covering the immigrant experience at Ellis Island. He starts the clip and drops into the desk chair below the monitor, gazing into space as he listens to the narrator's voice.

The experienced teacher looks up to see how things are going. He stands and pushes the overhead projector against the back wall. Two students whose lines of sight were blocked by the projector settle back in their seats.

During the 10-minute film clip, three students lower their heads to their desks. Two appear to be sleeping. Mr. Decker does not appear to notice this behavior. At this stage in his development, it would be surprising if he noticed everything. In contrast, his supervising teacher is so attuned to the classroom that multiple details attract his attention even when he is otherwise occupied.

The unaware teacher cannot sort relevant from irrelevant perceptions

Enter any classroom in the world. At any given moment, a student is likely to be doing something that bends or breaks a rule. Technically, that person is eligible for a reprimand. But is it wise? Will the reprimand detract more than the infraction itself?

Some teachers may yell at a pupil for rustling papers in an annoying manner—a minor infraction—yet ignore another who is quietly torturing a tablemate with a series of pokes, pinches, and jabs. Unaware teachers cannot determine which events impede learning enough to warrant intervention and which should be ignored.

Instructional issues need to be sorted, too. If one student can answer all the review questions, it does not mean that everyone knows the answers. Better teachers look for widespread signs of understanding.

The unaware teacher makes little or no response to student cues

People frequently send and interpret signals. Yawning suggests that a person is tired or bored. It's a social faux pas to signal boredom, so we often try to suppress a yawn because it's a message we don't want to send.

What cues do students provide? Tears, temper tantrums, and fights are cues writ large; however, many cues are smaller in scope, are shorter in duration, and are therefore overlooked by the unaware practitioner. A frown, a nod, or a look of confusion signals different levels of comprehension. Are hands raised tentatively or wiggled impatiently? Each tells a different story. Small gestures may reinforce or belie a spoken response, providing important cues for the teacher. Tone of voice is also important; some teachers listen to words only and miss the rest of the message.

Unaware teachers plow onward, neither looking for nor making many adjustments because of student cues. Because they don't respond to student cues, their teaching lacks an interactive quality. Their classroom behavior is no different than it would be if a filmed audience were projected on the back wall.

••• TIP •••

The best way to improve your ability to interpret events in progress is to practice interpreting events after a lesson. Enlist a colleague to observe occasional lessons and tell you what he notices and how he interprets it. Or talk through all the details you can recall with a mentor who was not present while you were teaching. Pay special attention to details colleagues mention that you didn't notice or interpreted differently. Work with them to imagine still more ways of interpreting the events under consideration. Starting sentences with "What if ..." will help. In time, this practice will translate to richer, more useful observations and interpretations of your teaching.

Learning to respond to students' cues as they occur is difficult. Consider Ms. Mishra, a student teacher in an urban school. Maintaining order takes a lot of energy. Today she is teaching 8th graders about the slave trade with three planned activities.

When class begins, Ms. Mishra turns on the overhead projector and starts a timer, telling students they have just six minutes to complete a journal entry. They work fairly quietly and most are finished writing when the timer rings, waiting patiently for the next activity.

Ms. Mishra then passes out a reading about the slave trade and asks students to underline key facts. They focus on the text. Then they share important details from the reading, justifying to the class why each point is significant. Ms. Mishra nods approval of several answers. One student's answer impresses her and she praises him, "Good thinking, Jamal. I hadn't thought of that interpretation before."

Next, the young teacher tells her students about a map activity related to the reading. They are to take notes on the map printed on the reverse of the reading. She projects an outline map of the Atlantic Ocean, which includes parts of the surrounding countries, on the whiteboard, gets out her colored markers, and prepares to put notes on the transparency for students to copy on their own maps.

In contrast to the smooth transition when students shifted easily from journal writing to reading, a general murmur is now rising. Suddenly students are looking for markers, sharpening pencils, and consulting with neighbors. Ms. Mishra calls for order but struggles to get students to stay with her as she writes on the transparency. Within five minutes order deteriorates. Talking increases and students are misbehaving, as wadded paper sails through the air. Ms. Mishra is becoming angry but maintains her composure with effort. Desperate to regain control, she tries dimming the lights and demands that they all write reasons why she shouldn't give them double homework because they are not working in class. After several tense minutes, the bell finally rings.

After class, Ms. Mishra sits down with her mentor and hears the traditional "Let's talk about how it went."

Ms. Mishra sags in despair on the tabletop and moans, "They were awful. It was a terrible lesson."

"Before you go there," says the mentor, "tell me what went right."

At first the younger teacher stares in amazement, unable to think of anything that went right. Finally she finds a response.

"Well, they were pretty good at the beginning of the hour."

The mentor nods and waits.

"Actually, the discussion went pretty well, too, I guess. For a while they were better than they had been all week. Jamal had a really great idea."

"That's true. Can you put your finger on exactly when things changed?" the mentor asks.

"Right after we started filling in the map of the Triangular Trade," Ms. Mishra says. "That's when lots of them started misbehaving. Nothing I did made any difference."

"I agree. Do you have any idea why?"

Ms. Mishra shakes her head slowly.

"I have some guesses," says the mentor. "Although they completed the journal entry quickly and seemed to understand the reading, I think the map confused them. When you put the outline map on the board, I too wondered what I was seeing. The outline of Florida helped me figure out that it was the Atlantic Ocean, but it took some time. It probably looked confusing to the kids, too. Confusion often translates into frustration or fear and then misbehavior. How could you try to reduce their confusion?"

"Tell them what it is?"

"That's one way. You might also frame the same section of a world map to show the part-to-whole relationship. If it's a wipe-off map, you could just draw the outline on it."

"I never thought of that."

"You also had trouble getting them back when things began to slip. You were trapped at the overhead, writing in all the answers, because that's what your lesson plan demanded, right?

"Yes."

"If you circulate, the people you are nearest to will behave. You can also interrupt some bad behaviors before they actually happen. How could you free yourself to move around the room?"

"Get a student to write, I guess."

"That's one way. Another is to write it in advance and have a student uncover answers for you. If you aren't stuck in one spot, it will make a difference."

The unaware teacher views events as separate and unrelated

The fact that Ms. Mishra couldn't sort these issues in the midst of a lesson is not surprising. She has the tunnel vision of the beginner. She cannot yet compute and react to incoming data as they happen; she considers events one at a time. Someday she will learn to make instant adjustments in response to multiple student cues, but her multidimensional perception is still immature (Bond et al., 2000, p. 51). Ms. Mishra will come to understand that students who don't understand often fidget or start talking. She will also figure out that even a quiet classroom is not proof that everyone understands. Teachers need to notice and respond to subtle cues for optimal learning to happen.

The novice cannot sense the classroom gestalt—the web of relationships and interactions that affect one another. Misbehavior is seen as the personal failing of a single student. Could poor instructions, a poor relationship with the teacher, learning differences, conflict with a classmate, or a problem at home contribute to misbehavior? These possibilities are invisible to the unaware teacher.

Similarly, failure to learn is blamed on individuals' lack of effort. The teacher does not question whether his assignments were relevant or whether he failed to provide guided practice. He never wonders whether his examples were clear. He does not check whether every test question was actually covered in his lectures or assignments. This teacher does not investigate undercurrents among kids or ask if bullying is causing a child to falter.

Questions to grow by

☐ Do you check for and wait for attention before you begin each new activity?

☐ Do you periodically survey the room to read the body language and behavior of students?

☐ Can you do a mental triage on student actions as they occur in the classroom—very serious, somewhat important, not worth reacting to?

The Aware Teacher

Aware teachers have begun to sense and understand the tenor and reactions of the class as a whole. Selecting important events from a barrage of less important occurrences, however, is still difficult for them. While they have begun to comprehend the verbal and nonverbal cues that students send, they cannot effectively do this on a consistent basis. Because most of their energy is still focused on gaining obedience, they interpret much of what they see only in terms of obedience.

The aware teacher sees classroom events globally

Aware teachers gauge the general reaction of the class. From students' general body language or facial expressions they know if the class as a whole is restive, attentive, or enthusiastic. They think of the group as "my 4th graders" or "my first-hour physics class." Aware teachers notice less about the individual reactions that contribute to class chemistry, and they don't sort by unique response patterns or personal preferences, tendencies, or habits.

Because the aware teacher sees the classroom globally, he may label whole classes as smart, unruly, or apathetic, forgetting that 12 kids are usually quite cooperative, 8 are easily distracted, and 7 students frequently act out. Time and sophistication are needed to learn to interrupt the misbehaviors of the seven chronic offenders and simultaneously show the eight distractible students how to ignore the offenders' misconduct. The aware teacher may believe that the whole class is either for him or against him. He may feel wronged because one or more students are misbehaving at any given time.

The aware teacher struggles to discriminate among perceptions

A barrage of events happens each day in classrooms, hallways, and gyms and on buses, playgrounds, and courts. All events are not equally significant, and determining which are and which aren't is a learned skill.

In the classroom, there are dozens of students and actions to attend and react to. For a new teacher, general advice can help. For instance, when a teacher circulates from desk to desk answering questions, it is wise to keep most of the room in peripheral vision. Major disturbances will be less likely to escalate with the teacher's awareness. Similarly, a teacher who trains himself to briefly scan the classroom just before leaning over each student will better keep track of the pulse of the room. Aware teachers do this occasionally but not yet habitually.

Later in the developmental process, a teacher may grow "eyes in the back of his head," as he learns to better read students and the classroom. He hears changes in his students' voices that tell him a conflict is moving from playful to serious, even though he is involved in a separate conversation. He may react to one student's complaint with a jovial "you'll handle it" and know that another student's plea, though similar, needs an immediate solution. This is not favoritism. The ability to sort a comedic comment from a heartfelt plea, though the two may sound similar to outsiders, is a teacher's skilled perception of his students.

The aware teacher responds inconsistently to cues

Although aware teachers are more attuned to the verbal and nonverbal cues students provide, they still miss some. From an observer's viewpoint, aware teachers' reactions are uneven. They may notice louder voices more often and consistently respond to those situations. Perhaps teachers are multidimensionally aware when teaching familiar material but develop tunnel vision when struggling through new lessons. In short, at the aware level, the teacher can sometimes sort out the relevant from the irrelevant and react appropriately; at other times the activity in the classroom is more of a blur.

The aware teacher focuses on gaining compliance

Teachers sort and respond to events in the classroom with a purpose—or several different purposes. In the beginning, most teachers long for order. They want students to follow rules and do assignments. Gaining cooperation makes classrooms run smoothly and is a necessary first step.

Although schools reward compliance, if a teacher never moves beyond mere obedience, valuable insights may be lost. Students who ask questions, often bothersome ones, contribute immeasurably to classrooms. The aware teacher doesn't recognize purposes beyond compliance.

Telling a student to "stop asking so many questions" may gain obedience but diminish enthusiasm. Punishing a victim without identifying and stopping the bully teaches injustice. Acting as if every question has one, and only one, correct answer narrows thinking. Telling a student that his concerns are not important weakens student interest. Aware teachers can't yet weave the idiosyncrasies of students and settings into a comprehensive whole, so they aim only for order.

Questions to grow by

☐ After you survey the class in general, do you go back and focus on individual responses?

☐ Have you learned to dignify responses and errors and then regularly practice that skill?

☐ Can you catch yourself when your responses are not up to your usual standards?

☐ Are you able to view students' mistakes and misbehavior as cues instead of wrong-headedness?

Self-Development

Observing other teachers instruct is a rich learning activity. At first you will likely pay close attention to what the teacher says or does; this is a good way to gather teaching ideas. After a few observations, however, try to shift your focus to what students are doing. Sit in the back row. Look for movements. Decide who seems to be attentive, thoughtful, confused, or bored. Note the interaction between teacher and students. Compare the teacher's responses to your own hunches and intuitions. How would you have handled things? What other choices are available?

Collegial Support

When you observe other teachers in action, follow up with comments and questions to tease out more details and new meanings. "Did things go as you hoped or planned? What do you think it meant when ...? Did you see ...? Do you think it's important that ...? Would you handle things the same if ...?" Invite a variety of interpretations or add a few of your own. Point out things students did or said that the teacher may not have seen or overheard and talk about the implications.

The Capable Teacher

Capable teachers can usually identify and manage many simultaneous events. They use a well-tuned ability to discriminate the relative significance of various events as those events are occurring. These teachers disregard less important events and prioritize others in order to formulate useful reactions and make effective plans. They have begun to treat events, usually students' actions, as clues for improving instruction at least some of the time, rather than as a series of good or bad behaviors to be corrected or rewarded.

The capable teacher understands simultaneous events

Capable teachers are usually alert. Very little gets past them. They assess simultaneous events and calculate their significance. Capable teachers sort events in their minds while they continue to teach or monitor the class. They ignore some events and respond to others in ways that contribute to their teaching goals.

A bully, no matter how subtle, is likely to get caught by a capable teacher. The teacher directs inquisitive students to books or the Internet for more information, rather than silencing them. Students' connections between the lesson and current events are acknowledged and perhaps redirected, but rarely declared completely irrelevant. The teacher notices when students' reactions suggest that he should speed up, slow down, reteach, or enrich the lesson. Wrong answers are no longer just an individual failing; they are also viewed as cues for the teacher.

The capable teacher distinguishes between relevant and less relevant information

Ms. Padrón, a student teacher, works with 9th graders in a Spanish I classroom. She is under the supervision of Ms. Lewis, who demonstrates to her student teacher how to recognize relevant responses.

Ms. Padrón introduces a new verb form. She explains the new information, writes it on the board, and then has a student choose the right form for the sample sentence.

"Everyone got it now?" she asks.

Heads nod cautiously and one voice murmurs, "Yes."

Ms. Lewis looks up from some papers, glances around, and speaks in Spanish to the younger teacher, "Las cabezas dicen que sí, pero los ojos dicen que no."

This means "Their heads say yes, but their eyes say no." Applying this advice to the situation, Ms. Padrón notices confused facial expressions that she missed before. She reteaches the material, adding more examples and more practice.

Ms. Padrón knows that checking for understanding is important. Unfortunately, weak yes's are not relevant clues as to whether the material has been completely mastered. Ms. Lewis notices relevant cues that Ms. Padrón misses.

The capable teacher consistently responds to cues from students

We can tell that Ms. Lewis makes it a habit to pay attention to the nonverbal responses of the class as well as the verbal ones. She knows that kids sometimes answer yes to please the teacher, but the "aha!" expression is rarely faked. She checks all students' expressions, not just those of star pupils. She keeps alternative lessons in mind so she will be able to reteach one, two, or even three times in response to the students' difficulties with each concept.

She welcomes questions, examples, and comments from students, viewing these as interactions with the material, not interruptions. She treats students who have questions with dignity. Students are therefore not afraid to ask questions or request clarification. The more questions they ask, the more cues Ms. Lewis gets about what they need. The cues provide the communication needed to effectively modify lessons for students.

The capable teacher connects some student behaviors with instruction

Capable teachers use student behaviors to decide how to proceed with instruction. Some have general lesson plans—a few sentences or a short list written in their planning books. If asked about their plans, however, they articulate a number of possibilities they have in mind, ready to use as needed. This mental list results from teaching the material several times and noticing previous student reactions to this or similar material. These factors build a repertoire of possible approaches to use in ways appropriate to student responses in class.

Thus, if Ms. Lewis teaches Spanish I for three hours in a row, her instruction changes each hour. One class sails through the day's lesson, so Ms. Lewis has them sing Spanish songs before the bell. Another class takes the full hour to master the new material. In the third class, Ms. Lewis passes out worksheets that cover the same material she wrote on the board during the two previous hours. Why? This class copies so slowly that they usually don't finish the rest of the day's activities. Even though writing down new vocabulary helps recall in other classes, it wastes time in the third-hour class. Ms. Lewis chooses another approach for this group.

Questions to grow by

☐ Have you ever invited a colleague to transcribe what you say and do during a lesson so you can discuss and analyze it in detail?

☐ Do you ever stop to ask the class, "What just happened here?" to find out how students perceive events in progress?

☐ Do you reflect on your own actions and question the effectiveness of each, considering alternatives you might use in future similar encounters?

The Inspired Teacher

A given class often contains a wide variety of student ability levels and behavior patterns. Inspired teachers successfully interact with each student simultaneously. Such skill is analogous to that of a building contractor who coordinates a complex project. The contractor waves in bulldozers, signals crane operators, initials supply requisitions, and greets entering electricians, plumbers, and delivery drivers. The contractor understands the overall plan and its component parts, and can thus manage the individual workers with ease because he understands what is needed from each one for overall success.

Through intense observation and thoughtful adjustment, inspired teachers mold a functioning whole from a classroom of individuals. From the outside, subtle changes the teacher makes by interpreting events in progress look simple. In fact, the class's good behavior may lead coworkers to dismiss an inspired teacher's suggestions with comments like, "Well, that might work with your kids, but mine just wouldn't cooperate." Students cooperate because of the teachers' efforts, not because of predisposition, and inspired teachers know this. Great teachers use their multidimensional perception to alter classroom dynamics to the benefit of each student.

The inspired teacher maintains focus while noting simultaneous events

Inspired teachers are goal-oriented. Using multidimensional perception, inspired teachers observe while teaching. They focus on the social and academic goals they have for students no matter what hubbub occurs. They notice what others might miss and collect a great deal of data on student behavior that they will use for later action.

The inspired teacher welcomes student comments and questions, yet no matter how far astray the discussion goes, the detour is temporary. This teacher leads students back to the main subject matter. She also provides activities that allow students to work in groups, assume leadership positions, and make choices, but not in a vacuum. The inspired teacher provides feedback to student leaders to improve their skills. She notes cut-ups and daydreamers and appropriately adjusts lessons. This teacher may do something as simple as tap the paper of the daydreamer in passing as if to say "start working" or move near the cut-up to discourage his chatter, while continuing her explanations. If these actions don't change behaviors, the teacher will choose other responses, while still moving on toward her instructional goal.

• • • TIP • • •

For numerous examples of how one man interpreted and reinterpreted events in progress—personal, social, cultural, and musical—read *Moving to Higher Ground* (2008) by Wynton Marsalis.

The inspired teacher consistently sorts the relevant from the less relevant

While the inspired teacher lectures or explains, she has an open focus on the whole room and her mind gathers information. If someone stands up, she mentally notes it. *Pencil? Paper? Boredom? Trouble?* Yet she finishes her sentence without hesitation, continuing until she knows what the behavior signifies. If the student is getting paper, there is no cause for concern. A bored student may need quiet redirection, either now or later.

Real trouble warrants intervention. The inspired teacher will wait long enough to be sure it is trouble and not so long that the trouble escalates. The open focus she maintains may cause her to walk toward boredom or trouble as it develops. Her proximity, a touch on a shoulder, or a quiet shake of her head may quash a potential problem. These actions cause her classes to appear well-behaved but having great classes is often the result of great teaching.

The inspired teacher sees patterns in verbal and nonverbal responses

Unaware teachers see events singly; each act or transgression is a separate issue. For instance, if Maria repeatedly misbehaves, the teacher misses the fact that it happens whenever long division problems are assigned. The inspired teacher scans back over days or weeks and plucks out a handful of responses by a student or group that form a significant pattern. Inspired teachers would suspect Maria is confused by division problems.

Consider Mrs. Starr, a high school French teacher. On the first day of class, she introduces herself and the rules. On the second day she passes out a questionnaire. After a few moments of writing, one student, Harvey, wads up the paper and throws it at the waste basket, muttering, "I ain't doin' this." He changes seats and starts to talk to another boy.

"You can't talk now. People are working," says Mrs. Starr. She stands behind his original seat and pointedly pats the back of it until he shuffles over and sits in it.

The teacher could have made an issue of Harvey's misbehavior. Why didn't she? The noise of the confrontation would have disturbed the other 20 students. Also, it is only the second day of class, and she doesn't have much data with which to decide how to intervene. Like a good lawyer who never asks a question unless the answer is known, she chooses not to begin a confrontation unless she is sure of a useful result. If she chooses to polarize the relationship between herself and this young man, it will set the tone for the rest of the year. She wants to cooperate with him in his learning rather than become enemies in the first week of class.

She uses observation and research. She notices that Harvey listens intently and answers some questions during class. His worst behavior occurs whenever she asks him to copy from the board, write answers on worksheets, or take a quiz. At those times he makes surly, confrontational comments. She checks his

school records. He flunks almost all classes, has severe processing problems that require special education assistance, and is
frequently sent to the office for insubordination.

Her conclusion is that Harvey learns by listening. Either he
cannot write or it takes an effort that overwhelms him with frustration. If she asks for writing, he has an outburst. Her response
is to de-emphasize writing and emphasize listening and speaking with him.

At the beginning of the third week, Mrs. Starr calls Harvey
aside. She tells him she will give him oral quizzes. She will also
give him a copy of what she normally writes on the board and
let him make his notes on the sheet. The rest of the students will
continue to copy information from the board. She later casually
tells the class that Harvey will be using typed notes. They express
no resentment; many have been in class with him for years and
know him well. With this adjustment Harvey's outbursts almost
disappear. His behavior becomes unremarkable, and he partici-
pates regularly in conversational French during class.

Mrs. Starr helped Harvey to become a cooperating and learning member of French class despite his writing difficulties. He
now converses as well as his classmates, even though his scores
on written tests will remain low. The positive outcome she
achieves is a direct result of her inspired abilities and actions.

The inspired teacher links responses to instructional priorities

Mrs. Starr's choices are closely linked to her instructional
priorities. She has no interest in proving who is boss; she wants
to bend student behavior toward learning. She wants students
to learn French and behave with self-control. She patiently collects data and interprets information to find creative responses
to any difficulties that arise.

Her goal is to help Harvey and every other student succeed in
French. She recognizes that Harvey's behavior is directly linked
to his own strengths and weaknesses and doesn't assume his acting up is meant as a challenge to her authority. She won't stop
asking him to learn, but she will decrease the number of times
he faces overwhelming frustration, by adapting her presentation
to bring it within his reach. She makes teaching him look easy,
rewarding, and natural. Teaching is natural to her because she is
an inspired teacher.

Actions to grow by

□ Set up a video camera in your room and run it once or twice a week to catch students' actions in response to your teaching. When busy concentrating on teaching, we miss things that are happening around the classroom. Watching the tape of students while we listen to our own voices allows us to notice details that we can sort out differently when the pressure of teaching is over. The point is not to catch students misbehaving. The point is to become more aware of details that can inform our teaching. Students will show us how to teach them if we remain open to the clues they send through their reactions and behaviors.

□ Do a student analysis of a few individuals. Pay close attention to their actions and comments in class. Observe them in the lunchroom, in other classes, before or after school, or on a team. Or make a brief home visit to get acquainted with family members. Look over their permanent files in the office. Consider how your understanding of the students grows and how this affects your interpretation of those individuals.

□ Join a peer coaching group with your colleagues. After each lesson your peer observes, talk about how you and the observer interpreted various events or actions. Differences in interpretations broaden your own range of reactions and conclusions.

For Information and Inspiration

Anderson, L. H. (1999). *Speak*. New York: Penguin.

Bigelow, B., Christensen, L., Karp, S., Miner, B., & Peterson, B. (Eds.). (1994). *Rethinking our classrooms: Teaching for equity and social justice*. Milwaukee, WI: Rethinking Schools.

Bond, L., Smith, T., Baker, W. K., & Hattie, J. A. (2000). *The certification system of the National Board for Professional Teaching Standards: A construct and consequential validity study*. Greensboro, NC: Center for Educational Research and Evaluation, University of North Carolina.

Delamont, S. (Ed.). (1984). *Readings on interaction in the classroom*. New York: Methuen.

Marsalis, W. (with Ward, G.). (2008). *Moving to higher ground: How jazz can change your life*. New York: Random House.

7

Being Sensitive to Context

Every classroom is a microcosm different from all others. Classrooms may appear similar, but beyond a first impression are many subtleties. Each class is a collection of individuals; each student brings unique experiences, talents, perspectives, and needs. Students have different cultural and familial patterns that shape thinking and behavior. They have different assumptions about meaning and proper behavior. To teachers unaware of context, these varied subtleties are imperceptible.

Classrooms exist within larger contexts—neighborhood, city, state, national, global, social, ecological, political, or technological. Considering these contexts is a large task, but because contextual knowledge is so useful the effort is worth the energy.

The best teachers pay attention to their students and to the classroom environment. They make appropriate adaptations to the specific setting and individuals involved. These teachers do not accept initial reactions or stereotypes without question; rather, they seek alternative explanations after gaining more in-depth knowledge of a particular context. They are not content with their original assumptions and take time to ponder classroom events and look for various interpretations. Being sensitive to context informs teaching practice and increases effectiveness.

The Unaware Teacher

Making incorrect assumptions is the mark of an unaware teacher. Think about a computer literacy class. The curriculum contains projects that require computer homework. In some schools every student has a home computer; in others few have access to computers outside of school. The teacher who is unaware of this context faces frustrations and might conclude that certain students don't care, without considering other interpretations based on true context.

The Power of Context

A common anecdote says that a father enters a subway car with three children. The children pound on the seats, but their father ignores them. They stand on the seats and then jump off to run the length of the car. Passengers are silent but watch with a heightened attention that signals disapproval.

The father speaks to the woman seated across from him. "We just came from the hospital," he says, eyes wet. "My wife died." There is a change in the subway car. An elderly man hands the father a folded handkerchief and other passengers offer condolences to the children.

We sympathize with the annoyed passengers because the family is violating social norms regarding subway behavior. Yet three words—my wife died—change everything. Such is the power of context.

The unaware teacher sees situations and students simplistically

My first teaching assignment was in a middle-class community similar to one I lived in as a teenager. I assumed that the students and their families were similar to my own experience. I learned names and recorded grades, but I viewed students simplistically. I was blind to their personal and cultural peculiarities.

Later I worked as a "roving teacher." I taught 30 homebound adults, former dropouts ranging in age from 20 to 60. I visited homes with various environments. Some homes were silent; others vibrated with a blaring television or screaming babies and toddlers. Some homes smelled of lemony cleaners; others smelled of mildew. The students themselves were diverse. Some were isolated; others were surrounded by an extended family that interrupted every conversation to reveal embarrassing details. They talked about heart failure, adoption, discount coupons, abandonment, lottery tickets, in-laws, shopping, death, and dismemberment. I realized that there are no homes like mine—and no homes like anyone else's either. Every student is one of a kind.

The unaware teacher rarely modifies activities regardless of changing situations

I used self-directed study guides with my homebound students. Each student read the same text and filled out the same workbook; my job was to administer tests at the end of each unit and record grades. Unaware at first, I did not add much to the basic requirements, but as I got to know individuals I talked about additional matters that were related to a specific student—for example, how to register to vote for those who hadn't done so before. I was gradually becoming aware of how to alter activities to better fit the context of each student's life.

We all have deeply held assumptions. Remembering that not everyone shares our positions, especially those outside our usual social set, can be hard. A city teacher who moves to the country or a country-bred teacher in the city will likely run into many conflicting assumptions between himself and students. While neither set of ideas is wrong, difficulties will plague instruction until the teacher recognizes the issues. Sensitivity to context reduces such conflicts.

The unaware teacher uses one-size-fits-all instruction

In the classroom, context makes a difference. The day after the shooting death of a student is an inappropriate time to refer to a bullet leaving a handgun to illustrate trajectories in physics. Teachers who assume that any prepared lesson or script will be appropriate to every situation do not yet understand the power of context.

Many teachers write goals such as, "All students will pass the test on the Civil War" rather than "All students will demonstrate their knowledge of the Civil War." The first goal narrows the options for students of different interests and abilities. The second allows each student to demonstrate his skills and strengths in areas like public speaking, PowerPoint production, film making, or design.

Questions to grow by

☐ Do you make an effort to learn unique facts about each student?

☐ Do you visit students' homes in order to understand and appreciate personal contexts?

☐ Do you casually interview experienced coworkers to learn more about the existing context of the school, neighborhood, or city?

The Aware Teacher

Aware teachers know that students are not identical, and they look for identifying features that will provide points of understanding. Such teachers are aware that some students are more athletic, are slower readers, are from single-parent homes, or fall into various other general categories. This awareness of students' personal contexts leads teachers to begin to make modifications, however weak, in response to their students' situations. Infrequently these teachers are also able to respond to students' individual needs by making adaptations, though this is not yet a constant.

The aware teacher uses categories to describe students and groups

Without awareness of context we have little insight to student diversity, special traits, and backgrounds. Through time or training a teacher defines students differently, but at the aware level, labels abound. Some students are "special ed" or "gifted." Johnny is "not very bright." Mary is "such a little lady." Pam is "hard to control."

Labels can contain some truth, but not the whole truth. Johnny may not appear to be bright, but what are the accompanying factors? Does he need glasses? Is he gifted mechanically rather than verbally? Is he a hands-on learner trapped in a paper-and-pencil world? If Mary is ladylike, what is the reason? Is she painfully shy? Do family duties make her old beyond her years? Pam is hard to control, but why? Do six older brothers encourage her tomboy streak? Is she an athlete with energy to burn in a school that eliminated recess?

Starting with superficial definitions of students can be useful but is ultimately limiting. If we don't consider students beyond their labels, we can't comprehend their distinctive context. The more we learn, the more we see every action in its context, allowing us to react more appropriately.

For instance, if Pam is defined as hard to control, a teacher might try to force her compliance, leading to a battle of wills. What if the teacher sought information about Pam's context and adjusted her own behavior accordingly? If Pam needs an outlet for her athletic energy, send her on errands as the class gopher. Addressing underlying causes eases the pressure on the child and the teacher. Unaware teachers cannot yet do this.

Knowledge of poverty or cultural differences can show teachers the context of some of their students. Describing a person strictly in terms of poverty provides an incomplete picture, yet it is one tool for understanding context (Payne, 1998). Similarly, when teachers learn that their cultural assumptions differ from those of their students, they begin to see patterns that were previously unnoticed (Rothstein-Fisch & Trumbull, 2008). Thereafter many teachers approach students differently.

Some labels are code words that trigger certain assumptions. "Urban school" may be used to imply certain challenges that may not be true. Most people in my city were surprised to learn that the graduates of one of our large urban high schools received thousands more dollars in total scholarship offers than the graduates of the specialty high school, which was labeled as gifted and talented.

The aware teacher weakly modifies in response to students or situations

When a teacher faces 24 students, several of whom act in frustrating ways, the teacher may feel helpless to intervene. If the teacher is told that one student has high-functioning autism, however, he can study the characteristics of autism and perhaps find effective instructional approaches for that student. Buoyed by success, the teacher can develop long-term plans for the autistic student.

If a second student has dyslexia, the teacher can again seek information about effective instructional techniques to effectively teach that student. Other categories—emotional impairment, learning disability, legal blindness, severe hearing loss—provide contexts to better understand individuals. Students are more than their labels, but labels can lead us to whole bodies of knowledge that help.

Most schools have systems to assist pupils with particular needs. Speech therapists, for instance, schedule private meetings with children with delayed speech, a lisp, or a stutter. The therapists can also work with teachers to identify when giving speeches to classmates provides good practice for students and when it aggravates the speech problem. The classroom teacher can modify her expectations accordingly.

Special education teachers can show colleagues alternative methods for students with unusual thought processes or atypical ways of responding. This exchange occurs through informal conversation or a more formal Individualized Education Plan (IEP). An IEP specifies exactly what modifications will be made by law. Modifications emerge from the conference discussion of specialists, teachers, and parents. The group seeks methods that suit the individual student's personal or academic context.

Over time, teachers can learn techniques that work with dyslexic students, emotionally troubled youngsters, and those with other specific learning challenges. Teachers can learn from knowledgeable people outside the classroom who provide specific instructions for individual students or from research conducted by teachers themselves.

Aware teachers may remain blind to individual and cultural differences outside of labeled categories. They are willing to make some instructional modifications, once the need to do so is pointed out, but they aren't practiced in generating modifications. As teachers get better at creating helpful changes, they use more of them more often to reach the capable level.

The aware teacher occasionally adapts to individual needs

In some cases, an aware teacher independently makes individual adaptations. For instance, if a student or a parent asks directly for a change, the teacher may grant permission or devise an accommodation. Similarly, the teacher's past experiences may equip her to effectively deal with certain issues. If the teacher has a deaf sibling or an autistic nephew, students with those particular issues may be readily helped, while other individual needs are not as easily handled. We all bring our own background, or lack of it, with us. We do, however, have a responsibility to keep learning so we can gradually meet more of our challenges well.

Questions to grow by

☐ Do you seek out the exceptional qualities of each student, remaining open to surprises?

☐ Have you implemented suggestions from your students' Individual Educational Plans?

☐ Do you brainstorm ideas with other teachers who have the same students as you?

☐ Have you solicited ideas from parents about what works for their child?

Self-Development

• Rethink what you see. Social psychologists point out that we always judge our own behavior less harshly than we judge that of others. For instance, we rationalize our own ill-tempered shouts at our children because we are tired, believing our own crying children are unreasonable, but mentally berate other parents who scream at their children, suspecting those parents of emotional abuse.

• Seek new interpretations. When you see annoying behaviors or people who are not doing things "right," imagine reasons why that behavior would make sense to the person you are watching. Imagine personal problems, a difficult upbringing, unseen handicaps or illnesses, or other things that may have happened to them just before they entered your line of sight. After some reflection, do you reinterpret the appropriateness of the behaviors you have seen?

Collegial Support

• Create an open environment. Many schools are hard to penetrate. People volunteer to help and may never receive a return call. Parents may feel they are treated as interruptions instead of resources or partners. Work to eliminate barriers between school staff and the community.

• Build bridges. Help the community within your school connect to the larger context in which it exists. Get to know local merchants, residents, parents, service organizations, and corporations. Encourage all faculty and staff members to meet with community members and attend community events; much can be learned about context in this way.

The Capable Teacher

Because teachers are a large part of the classroom context, self-awareness is an aspect of reading the context. If certain student behaviors particularly frustrate teachers, they will need to set procedures that minimize such triggers and learn to minimize overreactions. Personal contexts also change depending on whether teachers are teaching familiar or unfamiliar material. When teaching unfamiliar material, teachers may understandably revert to a more simplistic, controlled lesson design. Teachers need to recognize their limits, without using limits to give themselves permission to stop trying to grow.

In addition, the school itself has a context. Crowded or spacious conditions, ample supplies or none, solo or team teaching—all these contexts affect teaching. Teachers must work effectively within the limits of their environment.

The capable teacher plans for contextual situations and student needs

Capable teachers can generally recognize contextual truths. They read both the students they teach and the settings they teach in. Good context readers recognize the skills and customs individuals bring to school and merge those predispositions with school expectations. As they become increasingly attuned to student needs, some capable teachers consult more frequently with administrators or colleagues, seeking modifications to improve instructional effectiveness. Capable context readers experience few major student tantrums; they can see a student's difficulties and aggravations and make adaptations to prevent most crises. They also note how cultural backgrounds play out at school. For instance, some children learn that looking adults in the eye is rude while others learn that it is a sign of attention and respect.

Many elementary schools have eliminated recess, believing that increased instructional time is more important than play time. Without recess, the classroom context changes and capable teachers plan accordingly. One teacher might add songs with motions to her lesson plans. Another will choose to add a five-minute stretch to the mid-morning and mid-afternoon class routine. A third adds a short exercise period after lunch—ten jumping jacks and a two-minute jog in place—before settling down his students for a reading period. When asked about the reasons for their plans, their responses reveal efforts to work effectively despite classroom demands.

As a teacher builds a large repertoire of methods, units, lessons, and teaching tricks that work, she must decide which method best fits—and that requires reading the classroom context. For instance, capable teachers might stop in the middle of a lesson to observe, "This isn't working, is it?" and then solicit suggestions and questions from students to improve the lesson.

••• TIP •••

All individuals have unique life experiences and contexts. I have been told that if parents are recorded looking at their newborn infant, people who view the recording can tell if the baby is a boy or a girl. This observation suggests we are in different contexts from birth. Similarly, individuals from different cultures experience life differently because of both the treatment they receive and their interpretation of events.

Unless we ask questions and check for feedback at every turn, we will likely misunderstand one another. If we approach interactions with some flexibility, leaving room for questions, learning, and readjusting, we will learn more about each person's context.

The capable teacher modifies activities and instruction for changing needs

I once overheard a colleague, Jay, discussing grade school memories with other staff members. "I couldn't sit still in elementary school," he said, "so I used to get in lots of trouble. But one year I had a teacher who just let me stand up. I would walk all around the desk, writing on the paper as I went. That was a good year."

Jay's teacher accepted that he wasn't faking his difficulty sitting quietly. When this teacher met Jay, she probably observed that her expectations for remaining seated had no effect on him. Perhaps the more she told him to sit, the less he produced and the more problems he caused for himself and others. She may have decided that it was wiser to let Jay work standing up than to waste a whole year scolding him while the class listened. She seems to have established an agreement that if he was working at his desk, he didn't have to sit to do so.

Capable teachers learn from many sources. When a parent explains that her son has dysgraphia, a difficulty capturing his ideas in writing, the teacher learns that giving extra time for test taking or administering the test orally relieves the problem. Parents learn from pediatricians and specialists, and can explain appropriate adjustments to a teacher willing to listen.

Through experience, teachers learn that unalterable assignments and identical instruction are not always equitable. Adolescents with poor handwriting should have permission to use a word processor. What is gained if they are required to turn in scrawls that the teacher cannot read?

In addition to making individual modifications, teachers learn from experience to sense a need for a universal change. If students beg to learn under a tree on the first warm day of spring, teachers recognize whether the class will cooperate or be too distracted to function, and decide accordingly. In the aftermath of a school tragedy, teachers depart from the lesson plan and react to the radically altered context they share with students.

The capable teacher uses responsive instructional practices

Lectures can deliver a lot of information in a short time and are an effective instructional tool. Students who learn best through social interaction or from seeing, touching, or doing, however, are poorly served by a lecture-only approach. Even those who learn well from lectures usually recall even more when other activities reinforce what they have heard. For these reasons capable teachers use many instructional practices.

What sort of practices do capable teachers use? Writing key words on the blackboard as they are introduced in a lecture allows students to see as well as hear. Posters, illustrations, video clips, artwork, and PowerPoint presentations also provide visual contexts for learners.

Whole-class discussions, small-group discussions, debates, and mock trials are examples of learning through interaction. Although there is a clear purpose for the interaction, there is no script or single right way for students to participate. Students activate their knowledge and their personalities as they work together.

Manipulatives are objects that can be used for practice or simulation to teach or review concepts. If kindergarteners use letters cut from sandpaper, tracing each letter as they say its name, they are using manipulatives. Students can learn about fractions by cutting paper plates into thirds or fourths or fifths and physically comparing the size of the pieces. They can use play money during an economics lesson or fake passports during a geography lesson. In each case, kinesthetic experiences help students access a concept or fact. Capable teachers are aware of a whole range of such instructional choices and use them as context demands.

In addition, students' cultural contexts play a significant role. Some cultures value helping, sharing, and supporting group goals. Others value competition and individual effort. Wise teachers recognize such differences in students' contexts.

Questions to grow by

☐ Do you explore the experiences and beliefs of individuals during daily conversations?

☐ Do you research the categories by which your students are labeled?

☐ Have you studied varied ways to deliver instruction to identified categories of learners?

☐ Do you think about difficult students, imagining their experiences, motivations, and viewpoints?

The Inspired Teacher

Inspired teachers might be said to see their students the way an artist sees a box of paints—each different, yet part of the whole. The artist knows that red will always react with blue by creating purple, not orange. If orange is the goal, the artist must combine red with yellow instead. These facts do not diminish red but must be known in order for red to make a contribution. In a similar fashion, inspired teachers are aware of students' needs and plan instruction accordingly. They create specific modifications to address learners' needs and work differently with various individuals, groups, and situations.

The inspired teacher seamlessly interacts with social and cognitive contexts

When skilled in reading layers of context, a teacher is like an orchestra conductor. Well-versed in the range of each instrument and the goals of each musical composition, the conductor notes which players need to play louder and which need to ease up or adjust pitch. A good conductor knows which musicians need encouragement and which respond to a challenge. Through successive rehearsals the conductor brings out the best in each musician to create a successful whole.

Similarly, a skilled teacher knows the framework or context within which he and his students operate. He knows which labels and categories apply to each pupil, but he also knows that a label doesn't define a student; a label merely illuminates one facet of each child. The skilled instructor sees each pupil as a complex individual and accepts both strengths and weaknesses while urging the child forward.

Such teachers know personal circumstances in the child's life and, without excusing unacceptable behavior, interact effectively. Teachers look at thought processes and academic performance, while not overlooking the child's behavior in interactions with others. All aspects are worth considering because all contribute to learning success or failure.

The inspired teacher generates specific modifications that address students' needs

An inspired teacher creates a range of modifications, applying them to individuals, groups, or whole classes. This teacher no longer needs to be prompted to recognize needs or choose ways of addressing her students. Doing so has become automatic. Fred Astaire and Ginger Rogers made people feel that they too could dance well because they made it look so easy. The higher a practitioner's skill level, the easier a job looks.

If we are privileged to see a great teacher in action, her teaching looks simple. She writes something on the board, holds up an example, gives a few instructions, singles out a child or two, moves around the room, murmurs some comments, passes out supplies, collects work, and moves on to the next lesson. Yet if a substitute teacher takes over after lunch, performance deteriorates. Why? Chances are the skilled teacher was seamlessly generating lesson modifications moment by moment. The words casually written on the board were well chosen for effect. The example clarified expectations and met the needs of specific learners. The instructions were given to prevent problems that might emerge. The teacher moved around the room to check on specific individuals and redirect their efforts as needed, her presence silently disciplining students who might be tempted to chat. Supplies were designed to assist the hands-on learners. This teacher wasn't just going through the motions. She planned ahead and actively taught with students' social and academic needs in mind.

Inspired teachers also notice and prevent overt and covert bullying. The context of what has previously passed between two students is critical. These teachers react appropriately, protecting the goat while retraining the bully. Children feel safe when good teachers are in command.

The inspired teacher differentiates instruction for specific individuals, groups, and situations

Highly skilled practitioners systematically differentiate instruction. They establish routines useful for all students and appropriate to the physical and social setting. Then they add on specific patterns of action that address needs peculiar to certain individuals or groups within the class. Such teachers don't apply these systems once in a while—the systems are routine and consistent, designed to meet each student's needs.

My 8th grade English teacher, Mrs. MacFarland, used dozens of approaches to encourage our appreciation of literature, though she didn't state these objectives aloud. Our small farm community had students of many learning levels, including Ellis, a gifted classmate. One day Mrs. MacFarland asked Ellis to memorize a story by Edgar Allen Poe, "A Cask of Amontillado," and present it as a dramatic reading. Years later I still have a vivid memory of the day Ellis acted out the story for us. His voice soared and then dropped to a raspy whisper. His eyes rolled wildly to show the insanity of the character.

Asking Ellis to perform was a way to meet his need for challenge while addressing the needs of the poorest readers who learned more from hearing the story than they would have gained from reading it. Besides the gifted Ellis, our class had some readers who struggled. To address the needs of these students we practiced choral readings, gave impromptu speeches, and read and discussed a range of stories and poems.

We grasp the value of context if we imagine the teacher as a gardener. She plants shade-loving plants in shady spots, knowing that full sun will stunt their growth. She sets sun-loving plants along the driveway, where they bake happily all summer long. She enriches the soil around hungry plants knowing the added nutrients will improve this year's yield and make the soil better for years to come. She accepts that marigolds, irises, and tulips are different and provides the water, mulch, and care to help each one grow and bloom.

Actions to grow by

☐ Choose an unfamiliar area to expand your knowledge and sensitivity. Study a field such as anthropology, city planning, gender studies, intercultural communication, listening skills, sociology, world cultures, or urban studies. As a learner, consider how it feels to approach a new topic. Look for ways that the new information alters your assessment of the context in which you teach.

☐ Purposely frustrate yourself. Choose an experience in which you know you'll be uninformed, unskilled, or confused. Notice how you process difficult information. Pay special attention to your emotions. Do you become depressed, unresponsive, surly, or argumentative? Ponder whether this experience parallels the experience of students you teach.

☐ Learn a new language. Take a class or listen to audio of an unfamiliar language. Learning a language foreign to us is a great way to become aware of our own assumptions and operating principles. We learn that our ways are one way of doing things, but not the only way.

For Information and Inspiration

Comer, J. P. (2004). *Leave no child behind: Preparing today's youth for tomorrow's world.* New Haven: Yale University Press.

Delpit, L. D. (1995). *Other people's children: Cultural conflict in the classroom.* New York: The New Press.

Fleischman, P. (1988). *Joyful noise: Poems for two voices.* New York: Harper & Row.

Freire, P. (1970). *Pedagogy of the oppressed.* New York: Continuum.

Hall, E. T. (1966). *The hidden dimension.* Garden City, NY: Doubleday.

Improving instruction for students with learning needs. (2007, February). *Educational Leadership, 64*(5).

Payne, R. K. (1998). *A framework for understanding poverty.* Baytown, TX: RFT Publishing.

Poverty and learning. (2008, April). *Educational Leadership, 65*(7).

Rich, A. L. (1973). *Interracial communication.* New York: Harper & Row.

Rothstein-Fisch, C., & Trumbull, E. (2008). *Managing diverse classrooms: How to build on students' cultural strengths.* Alexandria, VA: ASCD.

Villa, R. A., & Thousand, J. S. (Eds.). (2005). *Creating an inclusive school* (2nd ed.). Alexandria, VA: ASCD.

Wheatley, M. (2005). *Finding our way: Leadership for an uncertain time.* San Francisco: Berrett-Koehler Publishers, Inc.

Wood, P. (2007). *Lottery.* London: Penguin Books.

8

Monitoring Learning

We cannot make students learn. But we can create circumstances in which learning is more likely—a responsibility expert teachers accept. Teachers can help students learn by taking the time to observe and find out about what students are interested in and then encourage students to connect their interests to the topic under study. Teachers further stimulate student learning by examining what each student says or writes and correcting misperceptions that are revealed. Consistently responding in a supportive manner increases the likelihood that students will learn.

Learning is usually invisible. We cannot see what is in the mind of another, although sometimes we hear it: "Now I get it!" Most of the time, our sense of what students learn is indirect. If we can't see the "aha!" moment, we may simply hope that by teaching we have done our part and that learning will automatically follow. In reality, we must check often to see whether our teaching resulted in learning and take remedial action if it has not. In other words, teachers monitor learning by gathering information about each student's understanding and then using the data to adjust their instruction to effectively increase student learning.

The Unaware Teacher

Unaware teachers believe teaching equals learning, but they do not check to see if their equation balances. These teachers don't know that teaching includes gathering information from student behavior or assessments and using the information to measure whether teaching caused learning. Students' learning problems remain undetected. Thus, teachers cannot take corrective action when necessary.

The unaware teacher ignores lack of engagement

The unaware teacher, busy delivering information, doesn't check whether his listeners are involved. Ignoring lack of student engagement, he misses the most basic clue as to whether learning is taking place. Students who aren't engaging with the subject are not acquiring the knowledge the teacher hopes to impart.

What is the cause of disengagement? Is the material too easy, too hard, or too familiar? Irrelevant to the student? The unaware teacher will not gather this information, so he cannot use it to adjust his plans or style of teaching. Instead, he marches through lessons without modification.

Some teachers say "Pay attention," "Here we go," or "Ready?" yet they don't wait for the attention of the audience or check to see if everyone has found the page or assembled their materials. Nor do they pause in the middle of instruction to call wayward students back to the subject; they plow on.

When unaware teachers check on student involvement, they do so haphazardly. Arbitrary monitoring is confusing to students. If students become accustomed to chatting, daydreaming, or doodling, they will not cooperate when their teacher begins yelling in frustration and demanding silent, focused attention. They haven't been trained to meet this expectation and resent the sudden demand for it. They assume their teacher is having a bad day and they expect it to pass. Intermittent interventions have little enduring effect.

The unaware teacher fails to see student misunderstandings

English contains many synonyms, words with multiple meanings, and words that sound alike. Thus, student misunderstandings are common. If the teacher refers to an apple *core* and a student thinks about his uncle in the U.S. Marine *Corps*, the resulting conversation may be confusing. The teacher may dismiss student comments as irrelevant, never seeing the connection between the two words.

During the second year I taught U.S. history, an exchange student from Poland was in my class. We studied the settlement of the Great Plains and the displacement of the nomadic Native Americans who had depended on buffalo.

At the end of the unit, I tested the class. After the test, the Polish student stopped at my desk.

"Mrs. Steele, there is one thing I am not understanding," she said. "What is this bison?"

Stunned, I pointed to an illustration of the animal. How did I teach the entire unit without students understanding this synonym? I had never checked to see if students knew the two names for the animal. I learned to check the comprehension of listeners more carefully.

The unaware teacher responds inconsistently

Monitoring learning to provide feedback and corrections is essential to increasing learning. The feedback must be useful and the way we respond is important. Sarcasm is of little use in the classroom. For example, a student of mine made an unreasonable request: "Can I leave early so I can get an extra dessert in the lunchroom?" I was amazed at the boldness of the question, assuming everyone in the class knew that I would not agree to such a request.

I looked at her in annoyance, put my hand on my hip, and laid a heavy dose of sarcasm into both my voice and facial expression. "R-r-r-i-i-ght!"

The student smiled happily and stood up to leave!

"Stop!" I said. "Do you know that sometimes people can say a word and mean just the opposite?"

She looked confused.

"It's called sarcasm. Meaning changes with the way words are said," I explained. I demonstrated sarcasm for the student and she understood she wouldn't be leaving, and I understood that all responses are not created equal.

Suppose a teacher cheers and claps with delight at every correct answer on Monday, overacting like mad. On Tuesday she nods morosely after each correct response. On Wednesday every wrong answer gets a snarl and an insult, "What's wrong with you? You should know that by now." On Thursday the class is mute, fearing more insults, so the teacher makes individuals write each correct answer five times on the board. On Friday she brings candy for a review and gleefully tosses mints to brave students who raise their hands.

Were Monday's answers more correct than Tuesday's answers? Monday's received a dramatic cheer; Tuesday's a barely perceptible nod. Wednesday's pattern of humiliating those who made mistakes created fear. Students are hesitant to answer questions in the face of possible ridicule. If the classroom doesn't feel emotionally safe, candy during the Friday review won't repair the damage.

Learners benefit from consistent response patterns that reveal whether information is correct, incomplete, partially right, completely wrong, or not related to the question. Students benefit from knowing they will be treated kindly. While variety may increase interest, self-indulgence and uncontrolled anger are not rational methods for providing helpful feedback.

Questions to grow by

☐ Do you check to see what percentage of the students is listening to you?

☐ Do you ever reflect on the reasoning behind a student's response?

☐ Are you calm and clear when giving feedback to students regarding their answers?

The Aware Teacher

Teachers at the aware level demonstrate some progress in monitoring student learning. Because they believe involved students are more likely to learn, these teachers evaluate the classroom and ask stragglers to start working or pay attention. But because their skills are still elementary, these teachers often fail to notice subtle student errors, omissions, and misunderstandings. They are also likely to simply tell students that answers are right or wrong, offering little correction, clarification, or elaboration.

The aware teacher monitors student engagement to gain compliance

With growing awareness, teachers take note of attention patterns; they know a student who is not involved misses important information. Sleeping students are tapped on the shoulder. Back row whisperers are asked to explain the next math problem. Teachers move around the room as students work to ensure kids are doing the assignment.

The monitoring done at this level is general. Have pupils opened their texts? Do they have pencils? Are they facing forward? Are some covertly reading magazines? Disruptive students are noticed and dealt with.

Aware teachers see student output as a reflection of efforts to learn. Is work being regularly turned in? Are questions answered correctly or at least attempted? Teachers send notes or mention missing work during parent-teacher conferences because doing the work is a clue to whether students are learning. These teachers keep track of students' productivity.

Teachers at this level still have difficulty differentiating between various issues that bring about inattention or unsuccessful assignments. One can spend a year telling an energetic child to sit still and listen but never see any decrease in fidgeting. One can spend a semester reminding a dyslexic student to read only what's written on the page yet see no improvement. Monitoring whether students are engaged with the topic at hand is an important first step, but not a complete solution.

The aware teacher misses small misunderstandings

It's hard to imagine all the ways students can understand or misunderstand what teachers say. Because teachers' mind-sets predispose them to certain interpretations they may overlook other interpretations, including gaps in students' comprehension. For example:

Teacher: "Today we are going to study how stems work in plants."

Mona: "I got to wind my grandpa's watch last night!"

Teacher: "I've warned you about interrupting our lessons."

Mona: "But it's from the plant and ..."

Teacher: "Please stop talking and listen."

Mona shakes her head, folds her arms, and scowls for the entire science lesson.

When Mona hears "stem" and "plant" in the same sentence, it triggers a vivid memory not connected to botany. Her grandfather earned a gold watch when he retired after 42 years working at a fertilizer plant. His watch has a stem for winding and hands that move. Mona is proud that she can read the dial and wants to talk about it. The teacher heard her comment as an unrelated interruption.

Immersed in her science lesson about plants, the teacher misses the connection between watch stems and the stems on plants. She fails to mention that some plants are green and growing while others are factories that manufacture products. Instead of guiding Mona to see a connection and also gaps between her grandfather's watch and today's lesson, Mona is reprimanded. She disengages from the lesson as she glowers at her teacher.

The aware teacher limits feedback to "correct" or "incorrect"

A simplistic approach to student responses places all answers in one of two categories, correct or incorrect. In some cases this is true. But sometimes responses are correct and incorrect at the same time. In a question-and-answer session, a teacher states clearly whether the facts are correct or not. The listeners test their perceptions against the more knowledgeable teacher and learn from the exchange. The only weakness in this approach is that it doesn't go far enough. The teacher is still sorting everything into two categories.

The teacher who gives only yes-or-no feedback misses chances to fine-tune a learner's understanding. Such teachers make arbitrary rulings when partial truths arise. They declare a statement right or wrong, though students may silently sense the ruling is inadequate.

Opportunities to build student faith in the safety and support of the classroom are important. "Dignifying errors" is a technique that redirects students when their comments are off target. Here's a teacher using the technique:

"Matthew, can you name all the states that border the Gulf of Mexico?"

"Florida, Alabama, Texas, and Louisiana."

"Right so far, but there's one more."

"Hmm, let me think."

"It starts with an M."

"Montana?"

"Montana borders Canada. We need a state that borders the Gulf of Mexico."

"Missouri?"

"Missouri starts with the same first syllable as the state on the gulf."

"Oh yeah, Mississippi."

"That's it."

Dignifying Matthew's errors leave his self-esteem intact and coaxes out the correct answer. The teacher verifies the correct parts of answers, then gives the student chances to add more information. Notice the steps. First, she allows thinking time to demonstrate faith that Matthew is capable of getting the answer. The best students are often given several chances because they can usually be relied on to answer correctly. Weak students may get only one chance to answer, because they are often wrong. The teacher's experiences with various students become self-fulfilling prophecies. We can strengthen the performance of weaker students by giving them more time and support to answer.

The teacher also offers a hint—the first letter of the state. A hint helps students connect with what they know and leads to learning. Matthew guesses wrong, but the teacher continues to aid him.

Her next response is the strongest part. When Matthew says "Montana," the teacher tells him what he has answered: a state that borders Canada. Matthew will probably remember this new fact about Montana. Her response preserves his dignity and disarms the snickers of classmates.

His next guess is closer. Again, the teacher points out the correct part of his answer—the first syllable. Then Matthew remembers "Mississippi"—he has named all five states that border the Gulf of Mexico. If he had not, the teacher had one more planned step. She would have offered Matthew a lifeline—the chance to pick a student to name the state he couldn't recall.

Some might argue this method wastes time. While it might take 20 seconds longer, there's a hidden benefit. This exchange sends a strong message about classroom culture. Everyone sees that the teacher is patient, kind, and interested in assisting everyone in meeting expectations. She doesn't heap scorn on incorrect answers. Students who see teachers accepting and correcting errors are more willing to take risks because students know they are safe. Others who are struggling like Matthew will hear the thinking process out loud so they can integrate it into their own thinking.

Unfortunately aware teachers haven't yet reached this level of sophistication. Calmly saying "correct" or "incorrect" offers consistent feedback and helps students. Discriminating responses that lead students to complete understanding would be even better.

Questions to grow by

☐ Do you attempt to keep all students focused on the lesson?

☐ Are you collecting a list of possible approaches you could use to redirect students?

☐ When a student seems off topic, do you ask, "Is that connected to our lesson?" rather than immediately ask for silence?

☐ Do you ask yourself, "Is any part of this student's response correct?" If part of the response is right, do you say so?

Self-Development

Test your knowledge of students by reviewing the class list and noting details about every individual and their learning. You may realize some individuals are largely unknown to you. Make a conscious effort to get better acquainted with those students, watching for their patterns of response.

Collegial Support

Encourage colleagues to be more investigative. Use the 5 Ws—who, what, where, when, why—plus how. Formulate questions that help tease out information that your colleague is only slightly aware of and hasn't yet used.

- Who did the work? Who had questions? Who seemed distracted? Who needs more help?
- What was going on just before the problem began? What happened afterward?
- Where did the problem begin? Where were you?
- When were they attentive? When did they start to misbehave?
- Why do you think that happened? Why would he react that way?
- How do you explain that? How could you do things differently? How will you change that lesson?

The Capable Teacher

Capable teachers are not content for students to simply look busy; instead, they pay attention to whether students are actually interacting with ideas and completing tasks. These teachers are careful observers who attentively listen to monitor students' level of understanding. They have developed a more sophisticated way of questioning students; when announcing whether answers are right or wrong, they give detailed feedback to increase student understanding.

The capable teacher observes and listens to monitor understanding

A capable teacher wants all students to participate fully, so he is observant. When he assigns a worksheet, he doesn't sit down to grade papers. He scans the classroom to note the behavior of individuals and considers the implications of what he sees. If young Forrest erases the same answer three times, then slumps back in his chair in defeat, the teacher notices and wanders over to Forrest's desk, pondering the student's difficulties. Does this youngster have reading, processing, or handwriting problems? Is he struggling with unfamiliar information because his previous school did not cover this material?

The teacher chooses an effective way to intervene. His goal is to get the student reengaged, but he does not bark, "Get back to work." Because of the frustration that Forrest has demonstrated, the teacher chooses a supportive approach.

"Looks like number two is giving you some problems, Forrest," he says. "Let's look at it together."

The capable teacher reads between the lines—or the words— when students talk to him or to one another. The capable teacher would probably react differently to Mona's comment about watches. Because he is listening openly, he might see the connection. Even if he doesn't see the connection, he would show less frustration than an aware teacher. He might ask Mona why she mentioned watches and allow her a moment to explain. This approach averts angry exchanges and impulsive punishments. A capable teacher sees classroom events as chances to gather information rather than as challenges to his authority, so he is less confrontational.

The capable teacher is aware of relationships between his students. He listens carefully, hearing the snide comments about a student and reproaching the guilty party. He knows which pupils excel at restating new information. He asks them to tutor classmates, lead groups, or share with the class. These activities keep all students focused.

The capable teacher also begins to enlist students in the job of monitoring learning, whether it is their own or that of a partner or small group. By teaching students to observe their own understanding or performance, and to push themselves to ask questions or try again, the teacher multiplies his effectiveness.

In the small rural school I attended as a child there were only about seven students at each grade level. I know of some private schools that limit class sizes to 10 or 12 students, but most publicly funded schools have class sizes ranging from 17 up to the high 30s and beyond. As class sizes grow, individual attention becomes more infrequent, so helping students build habits of self-awareness and self-analysis, and helping them help one another, is essential to their success.

The capable teacher focuses on learning and task completion when monitoring

With increased awareness comes the ability to listen more precisely. Suppose a teacher asks a question and a student guesses correctly. Earlier, the teacher would have been satisfied to get the right answer, knowing the whole class had heard it. Now, however, the teacher notices the upward inflection of the student's voice, which indicates her uncertainty. So he pauses.

"Melinda, you're right, but you don't sound very sure. How did you figure this out?"

"I guessed."

"OK, how do we know this is the right answer? Who can give us some clues about how we can think this through?"

This kind of probing allows various students to unpack their thinking and share pertinent information. Each person gains a clearer idea of how to apply knowledge to reach a conclusion. The strategy isn't used with every question, but the teacher can use it when appropriate.

An observant teacher also catches small errors or misunderstandings and corrects them as they occur. Once he has taught the same lesson a few times, he builds up a sense of what is easy and what is troublesome to the average class and listens for problems. Students' responses determine whether he adds more details or asks kids to repeat important information aloud to a partner. He has developed the ability to watch for evidence of learning and take action when it's absent.

The capable teacher reports correctness and adds feedback

Capable teachers consistently inform students when their answers are correct. Every paper collected receives feedback. Oral responses get a nod or a statement that informs the student about their accuracy. Sometimes capable teachers simply state the right answer. Other times they call on students and clearly inform the class when the right answer is given, making certain all can hear. If the issue is complicated, capable teachers expand upon the student's response, clarifying fine points.

Pointing out controversies and disagreements about issues is a part of feedback. If a student shares one side of an argument, a capable teacher points out the other side of the issue. Students learn that people may have strongly held ideas that are diametrically opposed. This dialogue introduces divergent thinking and may increase respect for differing ideas.

Effective teaching encompasses more than statements about factual content. Capable teachers congratulate shy students for taking risks. They point out when a student who struggled with a concept demonstrates mastery, or thank the class for sticking to a project or rising to a challenge. Feedback is sometimes negative, as in, "I see six people with no pencils in their hands and no answers written down, so let's get going." In each case, teachers are gathering and then using information to increase student learning.

Questions to grow by

☐ Do you pay attention to each student's reactions and performance?

☐ Do you have preferred patterns for intervening when kids are stuck or lost?

☐ Do you expand on students' answers in order to increase their understanding?

The Inspired Teacher

Inspired teachers have a broad repertoire of methods for reengaging students with the learning process. They consistently check understanding through questioning, observing, and listening, as well as through analyzing students' oral and written responses. They can direct students to higher levels of understanding by regularly using many kinds of feedback, all designed to correct errors and increase learning.

The inspired teacher uses strategies for reengagement

The greater a person's skill, the more effortless the job appears. If we see a great cellist or guitar player, we think, "Gee, that would be fun." We don't consider the hours of effort and years of practice that precede the performance, and we fantasize about being immediately proficient.

A teacher who is an expert in monitoring learning makes the task look easy. The teacher has created a setting where staying involved is irresistible, not just because of students' innate desire but as a result of the teacher's effectiveness.

Keeping students engaged in productive effort starts the first day of school. Every fall each teacher creates, or fails to create, a culture of learning for this class, this hour, this year. She establishes behavioral rules that are simple and few, and she makes sure that everyone understands them. Perhaps more important than rules are the daily procedures that she teaches and reteaches until they are automatic.

Procedures usefully shape the classroom environment and support student learning. Students know where to put completed work so it won't get lost. They know where to get supplies and where to return them after each use. These measures teach students how to use their time if they finish early so others aren't distracted. Procedures allow youngsters to make a simple transition from one activity to another. Such actions also demonstrate social relationships—how to respond to a bully or an unfair ruling without resorting to fights or fits. Procedures create a setting where students are naturally and continually engaged.

No matter how clear the procedures are, they will sometimes be disregarded. The skilled teacher doesn't ignore incipient problems; she responds before they escalate. If the teacher senses that Jenny is agitated, she moves in that direction while talking. She pauses briefly to touch Jenny's forearm or ask a quiet question to help reduce the child's frustration. If the back row is disruptive, the teacher appoints a student to write on the board and directs the discussion from the back of the room, inches from offenders, who fall silent. Observers might not realize that subtle interventions have occurred.

If infractions are more severe, they too are dealt with. Students may be called by name and asked to pay attention, but only if the teacher feels it is appropriate. She starts by simply standing near the offenders. If that works, she will not have to waste time scolding them and breaking the concentration of the rest of the class. If a first request doesn't work, a student may be asked to stand in the hall until the teacher finishes the lesson. Then a private conversation may effectively redirect the student.

A student waiting in the hall or a time-out location is not distracting others. The class doesn't see how offenders are dealt with, but they know that distracting others is not permitted. In a private conversation, the student cannot play to an audience. Privacy also allows the student to be more honest about actual problems that prevent learning. Students learn from inspired teachers that inattention isn't an option. These teachers always redirect students.

The inspired teacher assesses student understanding

This teacher is a detective who is always looking for clues. He is alert during discussions to see if everyone is involved. He may ask students to simultaneously signal the answer to a question by holding up the right number of fingers for a math answer or signaling a thumbs-up or thumbs-down for yes-or-no questions. Such evaluation allows the teacher to survey the room and sense if anyone is confused.

An inspired teacher listens for the nuances in answers to correct each small misunderstanding. He pays attention to tone of voice and body language to determine who is uncertain or unconvinced. He welcomes honest errors as clues for further learning.

If he gives a pre-test or test, a skilled teacher may use item analysis. Every question is evaluated to see how many students missed it. When several students miss a given question, the teacher gains useful information. Maybe the concept was not well taught or the test question was poorly written. If so, the teacher will teach differently next time or rewrite the question so students know exactly what is being asked. The skilled teacher uses the information from the item analysis to alter his own actions so students can learn more.

Some teachers ask students to jot down a brief summary or reaction to the lesson nearly every day, or to list questions that remain in their minds. Scanning these journal entries or scraps of paper gives teachers a glimpse into the thinking process of each student. The gathered information can be used to redirect both teachers and students toward expanded understanding.

The inspired teacher guides students to higher levels of understanding

Inspired teachers often have personal standards that exceed curriculum guidelines or state minimums. Though they know that there are limits on time and energy, they rarely accept poor or even average results. They monitor learning because they enjoy watching students' eyes light up with comprehension. Gathering information provides the data needed to light up more eyes, more often.

This teacher begins with a clear understanding of what needs to be taught and what needs to be learned. She knows that teaching doesn't guarantee learning; she is constantly on the lookout, checking to see how much learning her teaching is actually triggering. She makes as many adjustments as needed to increase her students' understanding. Achieving the goal of the lesson isn't her only objective. She often says, "By the way, another interesting thing about this is ..." or "This won't be on the test but ..." or "Wow, your comment makes me think of something else interesting that you'll enjoy." When students grasp a concept, she presses on, taking them a few steps further in comprehension.

Inspired teachers are mentors. They develop a clear and detailed picture of what each individual under their tutelage knows. They use that information in a variety of ways to constantly nurture students' growth and development.

Actions to grow by

☐ Some teachers ask for feedback from students at the end of the course. Regular feedback is more useful and can be applied while students are still in our classroom. If we ask a few simple questions after each unit or test, we gain valuable information:

"What new things did you learn in this unit? What did I do that helped you understand a hard part? Did a classmate help you understand something difficult? If so, explain. What concepts are still unclear or confusing to you?"

You can choose whether to simply read the answers, have a class discussion, or privately talk with individuals who admit to confusion.

☐ Investigate metacognition, the study of how we learn and become aware of the thinking process as it occurs. Knowing about this higher-level thinking skill will permit you to monitor your own learning more effectively and thus encourage your growth as a teacher.

☐ Combine the two previous suggestions. Teach your students about metacognition so they can ask themselves how they are doing. They will become more aware of their own learning processes. As they begin to assess their own learning throughout each lesson and unit and to identify where they need more help, the monitoring of learning in your classroom will be multiplied.

For Information and Inspiration

Assessment to promote learning. (2005, November). *Educational Leadership, 63*(3).

Charlton, B. C. (2005). *Informal assessment strategies: Asking questions, observing students and planning lessons that promote successful interaction with text.* Markham, Ontario: Pembroke Publishers.

Informative assessment. (2007, December–2008, January). *Educational Leadership, 65*(4).

Popham, W. J. (2003). *Test better, teach better: The instructional role of assessment.* Alexandria, VA: ASCD.

Stiggins, R. J. (1997). *Student-centered classroom assessment* (2nd ed.). Upper Saddle River, NJ: Prentice-Hall.

9

Testing Hypotheses

Novices tend to believe things should have worked, if not for circumstances or students beyond their control. Experts ask themselves whether their experiments did work and what might be done thereafter to sustain or increase the progress made by students. Inspired teachers make educated guesses about many things—what might motivate a certain individual or class, what barriers to learning might exist, or what emotions might cloud the thinking of individuals or groups. They evaluate their results when they try out their hypotheses. Inspired teachers are those who do the best job of using the scientific method to question the predictions and assumptions of their own teaching.

The scientific method is composed of five steps. First, we must name the problem or identify the question. What we identify will mold the rest of our research. Perhaps the problem is that students are not engaged in math class. Developing teachers often ask broad questions such as "How can I make my students behave?" More reflective teachers develop more focused questions such as "Which types of math lessons best maintain students' interest and increase their participation?"

Second, we make an educated guess—a hypothesis—about the cause of the problem and make predictions based on the hypothesis. The developing teacher might hypothesize that students need a review of the rules or a harsher punishment. The more reflective teacher may guess that more paired practice or real-life examples would better hold student interest and result in more learning.

Third, we test our hypothesis by doing an experiment or study using proper controls. We implement the experiment and carefully observe what happens, gathering useful data. One teacher might videotape the class throughout a lesson and replay the recording several times to analyze and interpret details. Another teacher may examine each student's test results. Setting up formal control groups in a single lesson or course may be challenging or impossible. Instead, teachers can compare responses from previous units or among separate classes.

Fourth, we check and interpret the results of the experiment. Discussing results with a trusted colleague is helpful; another colleague usually offers additional interpretations that aid the experimenter in gaining a richer understanding.

Fifth, we report results to the scientific community. The first community to share with is our own school or district. In addition, results can be presented at conferences or submitted to educational publications. In any case, sharing results helps both listeners and presenters to question more assumptions and build expertise.

••• TIP •••

Sarah Capitelli reports in a draft paper on the Carnegie Foundation Web site that the first year she taught English to a classroom full of Spanish-speaking students, she demanded only English be spoken; her hypothesis was that using only English when speaking was an unquestionable necessity. That year students were usually silent and unresponsive, knowing too little English for effective use. The second year she tested a new approach. She still spoke exclusively in English but permitted students to question her or their fellow students in either language. She found that students asked and learned by using their command of Spanish to make sense of English. She *disproved* her original hypothesis to improve her instruction and student learning.

The Unaware Teacher

Unaware teachers have not yet realized that a variety of guesses and assumptions motivate their thinking and decision making. They do not question most of their choices or attempt to formulate new hypotheses about classroom events.

The unaware teacher rarely thinks about ways to enhance learning

Teachers who don't evaluate information are like blind archers; they keep shooting, never knowing how close they are to the bull's-eye. Any improvement is the result of random chance, not the evaluation of results. Unaware teachers lack the skills to improve their own teaching.

Unaware teachers wonder why students sometimes get it and sometimes don't. They don't compare the differences in learning after various activities, so they don't know which activities help students understand and which don't. They never evaluate classroom data; they just teach. The idea of trying a different strategy and then checking to see if it improves learning doesn't occur to them.

Some teachers confuse their own hypotheses with facts: *He can't learn this. She only does that to annoy me. These kids don't care about learning.* Because they never test their hypotheses, these theories are likely to become self-fulfilling prophecies. Evaluating classroom data is important if we want to enhance student learning.

Sarah Capitelli (2002), mentioned in this chapter's tip, reports her assumption that "oral language development through listening and speaking tasks was antithetical to the instruction of English grammar and structure.... Including instruction around grammar and structure might discourage students from taking risks with oral language and might ultimately be counterproductive." She eventually challenged this assumption and framed new questions: "What is the relationship between oral language development and the learning of English language grammar and structure? How can student conversations impact English language grammar and structure development?"

The unaware teacher uses incomplete, superficial solutions

When problems arise, unaware teachers react hastily. Imagine a teacher who receives a report of the reading levels of her students from the district office. Twenty of her students are described as reading below grade level.

"Look at that," she says to a colleague. "This class needs lots more practice."

"Starting today," she announces in class, "when it's your turn to read aloud from our English or social studies book, I want you to read two paragraphs, not one. We need to practice more so everyone learns better reading skills."

Longer reading is the only solution this teacher considers. Effective problem solvers generate many possible approaches and then evaluate them to determine which are most promising. Unaware teachers do not seek multiple ways to solve problems.

This teacher assumes that more practice will yield better readers. If the time allotted for reading aloud is not expanded, students may read two paragraphs at one time but wait longer to read again—no gain in practice time at all. Also, there is no evidence that simply reading aloud more, by itself, will improve reading. New approaches to comprehension, inference, and recall are also needed. This teacher does not evaluate her own assumptions or their results, so she is unlikely to seek outside information either.

A person accustomed to questioning hypotheses might ask a series of questions: *Can these students easily sound out words? Do they find meaning in what they read? Does reading aloud really improve comprehension? Can my students recall details they have read? What approaches help students read better?*

Asking such questions leads to complete and comprehensive solutions, but unaware teachers don't consider these questions. Because unaware teachers cannot think deeply about various aspects of a problem, or consider the implications of their chosen responses, they are capable of only superficial responses. They don't identify the whole problem.

The unaware teacher rarely tests any solutions

The unaware teacher has an unreasonable confidence in his own solutions. Habits and practices are regarded as unchangeable. The teacher doesn't question his own actions and blames others for poor results. Cause and effect are not used to evaluate solutions.

Testing a solution requires carefully looking at results. If results are not satisfactory, skilled teachers try different approaches. Unaware teachers miss the messages inherent in negative classroom events. Each incident is an invitation to test a new method, but unaware teachers do not respond.

The most powerful question to ask is "Why?" In my first years of teaching, I was flummoxed when students asked why I was assigning a certain task or using a certain procedure. I tended to assign the questions at the end of the chapter and thought no more of it, so I found it hard to give reasons for my assignments.

Years later I taught a student named Vic who often asked why. By then I knew the purpose behind my choices. I could readily answer when Vic asked questions like "Why do we have to work in groups? I'd rather do it by myself."

"Vic, some people are shy and won't ask questions in class, but they do in groups. I know that employers are looking for people who function well in teams, so I need to give you some practice. Also, because you've just listened to me lecture for two days, I decided you needed a change. If it doesn't work out, we'll do it differently next time."

Jaws dropped as students realized I had logical reasons for assignments. Although Vic questioned nearly everything I did during September, by October he didn't bother to ask anymore. He saw that I tested solutions and made adjustments as needed during the first month of school. I was incapable of such continual adjustments in my first years as a teacher.

Questions to grow by

☐ Write down information you believe about your students and curriculum. Pretend these are guesses and think of ways to prove or disprove your assumptions.

☐ Poll several colleagues, asking what processes they use to identify successful instructional methods and then evaluate their processes.

☐ Talk through a planned lesson with an experienced teacher, asking him to predict problems he thinks might arise if you teach the lesson as planned.

The Aware Teacher

As awareness dawns, teachers try to achieve congruence among the various aspects of their plans and the demands made on them as instructors. If the school has adopted schoolwide goals or practices, teachers will use these goals as a basis for planning lessons.

The aware teacher modifies goals based on curriculum guidelines

Suppose that Ms. Patel specializes in science at Carver Elementary. If the Carver staff is concentrating on improving students' writing skills, Ms. Patel will look for writing-related assignments for her science classes. Many textbooks provide teacher materials that include a variety of suggested lesson activities. If the textbook lists three options for a lesson on cell division—acting out a play, drawing a diagram, or writing a journal entry—Ms. Patel is likely to direct her students to write a journal entry of a dividing cell to help them meet schoolwide goals for writing. Drama and art don't appear to fit the schoolwide initiative, so she skips them. If her students never experience these other types of assignments, they will miss something important, but we can understand why Ms. Patel focuses on journal writing.

The aware teacher seeks one quick solution, not several possibilities

The aware teacher still suffers from tunnel vision. In the previous example, Ms. Patel quickly decides to assign the individual journal entry. Acting out cell division might also be a group writing activity. She could easily assign small groups and ask each to write a script to be acted out, thus turning drama into writing plus drama. These recorded presentations could even be shown to parents during parent-teacher conferences, but this possibility does not enter Ms. Patel's mind.

The aware teacher tries solutions in general, intuitive ways

The motto of the aware teacher is *This ought to work.* The sense that something ought to work is a form of intuition and not to be entirely discounted. In many cases the ideas and approaches that come to a teacher this way are helpful. Those that work are a useful part of a teacher's repertoire.

Nonetheless, aware teachers have no methodical checking system for the approaches they use. Years back, in a training session for effective teaching techniques, I learned new terminology for many habits and interactions that I had tried, usually intuitively, during a decade of teaching. The presenter described numerous techniques, explained the supporting research, and gave examples. As I listened, I recognized parallel examples from my own teaching. Analyzing my personal examples, I recall thinking, *Oh, now I know why that lesson always works so well.*

Once I could name procedures and understand the educational research that explained their effectiveness, I could better use them in the classroom. Instead of accidentally using a technique, I could appropriately modify and apply it to new situations. Techniques I once used to introduce specific grammar lessons, I could now slightly alter and use for a psychology experiment, a history unit, or a communications activity.

I moved from intuitive or general testing of my solutions to a more ordered and logical way of examining the projected and actual results. I saw new applications and became more scientific in analyzing my work with students.

Questions to grow by

☐ Do you carefully read curriculum outlines to identify all the curricular goals and then consider which approaches might best help your students reach those goals?

☐ Do you brainstorm with colleagues to develop hypotheses to guide your teaching choices?

☐ Do you talk about the results of your teaching with other teachers?

Self-Development

A friend described to me a boss who had one standing instruction for all employees: "Don't come telling me about a problem until you have thought up 10 possible solutions, at least one requiring no money."

Thinking up many possible approaches is good advice for teachers. Each possibility is a hypothesis; we don't yet know if it will work. By thinking of a whole range of possibilities we guarantee many options to choose from. Having many possibilities to choose from will usually yield high-quality hypotheses because the best idea is rarely the first that springs to mind.

Collegial Support

Most of us are quick to jump to conclusions. If we feel certain that we know what events or data mean, we no longer treat our idea as a hypothesis, open to testing and evaluation. Therefore, when talking with a colleague, ask questions that promote broader thinking for both yourself and the other person. For example:

• Are there other factors that might contribute to this situation?

• What are some other ways a person could handle that?

- What approaches have you considered?
- Can you predict any likely reactions?
- How else might you present this material?
- What methods have you experimented with so far?
- Why did you select that method?
- Why did you discard the other ideas?
- Is there a way to combine some of these ideas?

The Capable Teacher

At the capable level, teachers incorporate a scientific approach to improving their work. They use this approach on a fairly regular basis. They operate from the assumption that they will need to regularly question and modify their own approaches and test for effectiveness.

The capable teacher uses guidelines to enhance learning in top areas of need

Wise teachers recognize that it is rarely possible to cover every item listed in the curriculum. These teachers emphasize the most important curricular pieces.

Although I could summarize Watergate, the Boston Tea Party, or the Teapot Dome scandal in a single, factually correct sentence, listeners would not gain full understanding of each complex event. More information is available in every subject area than could ever be taught in one class; teachers must decide where to put the most time and energy.

There are many reasonable ways to decide what to emphasize. One priority is preparing students for state tests, the ACT, or the SAT. Another is utility—what is most essential for daily life. Other approaches include preparing students for productive citizenship, instilling a love of learning, or promoting a commitment to lifelong learning. Effective teachers consistently make decisions based on chosen priorities. Finding out what students most need to learn and how they will best master it motivates each teaching decision.

In order to form useful hypotheses, teachers must continually advance their own content and pedagogical knowledge. Unless we learn new things, challenging our habits and questioning our thinking are difficult. Good teachers read the research and investigate new developments. Then they ponder how they might apply the new information to their own teaching life. Trying new thought processes may be challenging, but it is essential to enhancing student learning.

The capable teacher reflects on lessons using general hypotheses

Knowing general guidelines for teaching can be helpful. General hypotheses allow us to frequently check our work in a variety of simple ways. One such guideline is the law of requisite variety, mentioned in Chapter 2.

How does the law of requisite variety operate in the classroom? The law reminds us that instruction needs to be familiar enough for comfort yet novel enough to maintain interest. Because events are rarely novel and familiar at the same time, we must move between routine and novelty with some frequency. Knowing this law helps us determine what action is needed next.

The law of requisite variety is easy to apply. Looking across a sea of bored faces, a teacher can label the class as apathetic or can instead decide, *I need to spice this lesson up right now!* The second hypothesis will yield a better result. Later, if the class complains as they attempt their assignment, the teacher may criticize them for acting immature or may choose to emphasize the familiar part of the lesson. Again, the second choice is more beneficial. Both of the stronger approaches move the class along the variety continuum, in the direction they need at the moment. Using this general guideline as a way to generate a hypothesis, the teacher sees the students' needs as reasonable needs that she has the power to fill. Even when classroom situations go badly, she can examine what happened and plan for a better result tomorrow.

Teachers learn hundreds of general hypotheses over time. Many become so familiar that they are almost unconsciously applied, which shows the teachers' growing expertise.

The capable teacher modifies instruction based on general reflection

Capable teachers ponder whether the class as a whole seems to follow the presentation, whether their questions reveal growing understanding, and whether most students remain involved and successfully apply the new skill. Teachers then determine what actions to take next. Is review or reteaching needed? Do students know information well enough to move forward to a new challenge?

Hypotheses are also built from year to year. By recalling how well most students understood topics last year, teachers predict how to structure future lessons. Experience reveals that certain topics require more instructional time and energy before student mastery occurs. Teachers develop new activities, analogies, and presentations to attempt to address expected difficulties. Using the new ideas and checking results will either prove or disprove teachers' assumptions.

Remember the teacher who learned that nearly all of her students needed to improve their reading? Her first reaction was to ask students to read longer passages aloud. The capable teacher generates a wider range of ideas to work on improving reading and probably emphasizes reading in every subject.

The capable teacher might consider that reading has two components: decoding the words so they can be pronounced and comprehending the author's meaning. Her actions are based on this two-part understanding of decoding and comprehension. She continually checks whether her students can recognize or say the words and whether they understand the meaning of each passage.

Using this information she modifies her instruction. First she designs ways to check decoding skills and offers support when needed. If her pupils stumble over scientific terms, she slows down and helps them with decoding. She reminds them of the meanings of scientific prefixes and suffixes, relating the information to a recent lesson on roots and prefixes covered in English class. She asks the class to say difficult words aloud as a group to practice pronunciation.

She also spends time in every subject helping students tease meaning from the written word, asking: "What does that mean? Can you summarize this in your own words? What three points do we need to remember from this definition? Would this author agree or disagree with the person whose opinion we read yesterday?" As she notices the specific weaknesses of her pupils, she concentrates on their areas of greatest need. She gradually addresses the needs that first came to her attention when the reading scores arrived from the district office.

Questions to grow by

☐ Do you consider the relative importance of various topics within each unit and allot time accordingly?

☐ Are you able to think critically about the effectiveness of each lesson?

☐ Have you made lesson adaptations based on the comprehension or confusion level of students?

The Inspired Teacher

Inspired teachers continually seek specific information from students and use it to improve their teaching. They constantly formulate educated guesses about virtually everything, testing their assumptions and deciding what has worked and what has not. They are also likely to be connected with the educational community in their own school and elsewhere in order to share and adopt successful ideas.

The inspired teacher analyzes information to form specific hypotheses for improving instruction

Inspired teachers demonstrate even more independence than capable teachers. These skilled teachers would have already determined the capabilities of each of their students long before the reading scores arrived. How? They note the reactions of the group and of individuals and seek more information as needed.

In hula dances, every movement is said to have its own meaning. Similarly, everything that happens in the classroom has meaning if we are alert. Who never volunteers to read? Who stumbles over pronunciations? Who reads for pleasure when assignments are done? Whose hand goes up to answer every question and whose hand never does? Who writes one-word answers when sentences are called for? Clues to improve instruction are everywhere.

A great teacher is a researcher. He investigates new techniques reported in educational publications. He reviews his students' cumulative files. He signs up for workshops and then tries new methods, not just once, but often enough to feel comfortable with the techniques. In every case, his mind responds with a new hypothesis: *I'll bet if I try X, Y will probably result.*

The inspired teacher tests hypotheses during lessons and makes adjustments

Having formed a new hypothesis, the teacher tests it while teaching. He may compare the scores on literature tests in three successive units, one where students discussed the reading in small groups with guide questions, one in which he led a whole-class discussion, and one where students worked individually with worksheets. He checks to see which method prompts the most students to answer the most questions correctly and which students depend most heavily on each approach. If the best results come from small-group discussions, he will suspect this is the best approach for his students to use while reading fiction. As a scientific thinker he will also consider whether the story related to the small-group discussions was easier and continue to evaluate the approaches for effectiveness. He will also think of ways to strengthen the performance of groups. Great teachers test their assumptions every day, with every lesson they plan.

Hypothesis testing is not applied only to the class as a whole. Skilled teachers check how instruction affects individual performance: *If I do X, how does Jessica respond? What is Justin's score? Does Caleb get it? What happens if I do Y instead? What if I do Z?*

The skilled teacher notes the progress of each student as he moves through lessons. This allows him to test which methods work best with individuals as well as with the class. He also examines other data—tests, quizzes, and written responses—to learn more about what works with whom.

The inspired teacher uses the results of hypotheses testing to alter priorities for curriculum and instruction

Data are gathered not for mere curiosity, but to be used for improvement. Olympic athletes work on continuous improvement. Athletes look at tapes of their own performances, of competitors, and of past greats with a trained eye. They evaluate their own performance to determine which additions to their training regimen increase speed, endurance, or strength. The quest for improvement is ongoing.

The same is true for inspired teachers. They try out methods, concepts, procedures, discipline plans, and additional resources, and then carefully judge the results. They begin with a hypothesis about which approach might yield good results. This guess is subjected to scrutiny in the classroom. Methods that work are continually fine-tuned to maximize their usefulness. Techniques that are unsuccessful are radically altered or abandoned. What teachers learn through testing each hypothesis helps them decide how to reprioritize and alter their original ideas for curriculum and instruction.

Gifted teachers don't teach according to a script. Last year's lesson plans, procedures, and assumptions, while useful, are reconsidered and usually changed. No matter how well-planned a curriculum unit, skilled teachers are open to new information. If necessary, they insert a two-day detour when they sense students need to learn about something not originally anticipated. Sensitive to the folly of teaching what students already know, they may decide to skip a section if students demonstrate existing knowledge of the topic. These teachers don't capriciously add or skip material. They make changes based on information gained about students, their prior knowledge, their needs, and their reactions to the material. Inspired teachers move scientifically though their days, checking and then adjusting according to their informed professional assessment of experiments and of each situation.

Actions to grow by

☐ Take a course on statistical analysis in education. Apply your findings to learn how to reach your students most effectively.

☐ Become a teacher-researcher in your own class by identifying topics you want to investigate, forming your own hypotheses, and testing their validity. Some professors welcome independent-study students, so you may get the credits required for maintaining your teaching certificate in this manner.

☐ Spend a day, or even an hour, pretending that "obvious" things might not be true. What if the confident student is afraid of something? What if the slowest student is gifted in some way? What if my students' complaints offer me valuable information?

For Information and Inspiration

Brown, C. T., & Keller, P. W. (1979). *Monologue to dialogue: An exploration of interpersonal communication.* Englewood Cliffs, NJ: Prentice-Hall.

Capitelli, S. (2002, April). *Teaching, classroom, and personal context.* Paper presented at the American Educational Research Association, New Orleans, LA. Available: http://gallery.carnegiefoundation.org/ collections/castl_k12/scapitelli/scap_aera.pdf

Claxton, G. (2000). The anatomy of intuition. In T. Atkinson & G. Claxton (Eds.), *The intuitive practitioner: On the value of not always knowing what one is doing* (pp. 35–52). Philadelphia: Open University Press.

Cunningham, D. (2000). Action research: Asking and answering questions about practice. In G. O. Martin-Kniep (Ed.), *Becoming a better teacher: Eight innovations that work* (pp. 89–98). Alexandria, VA: ASCD.

Marzano, R. J. (2003). *What works in schools: Translating research into action.* Alexandria, VA: ASCD.

Wheatley, M. (2005). *Turning to each other.* San Francisco: Berrett-Koehler Publishers, Inc.

10

Demonstrating Respect

Ralph Waldo Emerson believed that "the secret of education lies in respecting the pupil." Great teachers care about each student as a learner and as a person (Bond et al., 2000, p. 57). Their high regard for students is evident in their words, tone of voice, and actions, all of which demonstrate their belief in students' intrinsic value as people. Not-so-great teachers either fail to show respect or are openly disrespectful.

When I was in 11th grade, my social studies teacher, let's call him Mr. Jones, gave us nicknames he used every day with a booming, condescending voice. I had just moved from a small Kansas town to a large suburban high school. Mr. Jones came striding into class on the first day, put one foot on the stool by the desk, and leaned on his knee to take roll. A short boy scurried in with shoulders tipped forward, carrying a large satchel-style briefcase. He sat across from me, avoiding eye contact with anyone.

"Joe Farch," called Mr. Jones, looking up to see who would respond.

"Here," said the boy across the aisle.

Mr. Jones paused and stared.

"Hey, what's in the bag?" Mr. Jones demanded.

Joe looked confused. He shrugged.

"You don't know what's in the bag?" questioned Mr. Jones. "Whose bag is it?"

"Mine," Joe muttered.

"Then you ought to know what's in it," said Mr. Jones derisively. He took his foot down from the stool and walked next to Joe. He peered dramatically into the briefcase, shaking his head.

"That's what I'll call you," he said. "What's-in-the-Bag."

Mr. Jones kept his word. Every day thereafter he hollered, "Hey, What's-in-the-Bag!" the instant Joe walked into class.

When Mr. Jones learned that Wendy Kwalls had recently transferred from a school in West Virginia, she became "Hillbilly Kwalls." Because I was from Kansas, I became "Farmer Frederick." Mr. Jones also gave other students monikers, and none was kind. Sadly, I remember nothing from that class now except those nicknames and the uncomfortable feeling I experienced watching classmates squirm under Mr. Jones's banter.

Mr. Jones thought he was funny. "Can't you take a joke?" he'd retort. But humor is tricky. Any "joke" that points out weaknesses is suspect because it invites listeners to laugh at classmates rather than laugh with them. Mr. Jones's names highlighted student differences and weaknesses that undermined the classroom environment.

Mr. Jones, who was in his 40s, may have been making up nicknames for years. Apparently, no one—a colleague, an administrator, or a parent—ever objected, so Mr. Jones continued, stuck in a pattern of disrespect for his students. For me, he represents the lowest level of respect for students.

The Unaware Teacher

Although unaware teachers may often talk about respect, they usually emphasize only the respect due to them. These teachers don't give students the respect they deserve. Teachers' lack of respect for students is reflected in the psychological and physical distance they maintain from students. Unaware teachers never invite student input about learning and are likely to reject all student suggestions as irrelevant, or even impertinent.

The unaware teacher demonstrates lack of respect

At the lowest level, people are unaware of the meaning or application of respect. Or, if they are aware, their respect is rarely demonstrated. Their behavior often shows a need to have an unnecessary power over others. Some teachers exhibit nervousness, tension, or lack of self-control that inhibits their ability to display respect to others.

Disrespect occurs in school settings in many ways. For example, calling out "Young lady!" in an annoyed and commanding tone to catch the attention of a passing student. The tone suggests that the student addressed is inferior to the speaker. A student we respect would receive a conversational "Excuse me" in a more neutral tone of voice.

••• **TIP** •••

Behavior that increases the vulnerability of others is seen as disrespect.

Behavior that reduces the vulnerability of others, especially those with less power in a relationship, is interpreted as respect. (Adapted from Bryk & Schneider, 2002.)

Disrespect can be shown with body language. A dismissively raised hand with the palm near a student's face is disrespectful. Rather, a teacher who respects students would gently raise an index finger and say, "Let me finish this, please."

We can use a simple guideline to assure respect toward students. Any tone, gesture, or comment that is inappropriate if directed toward a colleague, the principal, or a parent is also not respectful toward a student. If we catch ourselves in error, we can make mid-conversation corrections.

The unaware teacher maintains physical and psychological distance

Mr. Jones occasionally left the podium to move physically closer to students, but his actions continued to emphasize the power he held over us. When he stood close to us, he maintained a psychological distance.

Maintaining physical distance from students may send a nonverbal message that the teacher does not care for students. I remember students scornfully saying of a particular teacher, "She never gets out of her chair!" After that, I noticed that every time I passed by that teacher's class, she was barricaded behind her desk. Students notice those who don't care enough to walk down the aisle to check progress, correct work, or answer questions. Loudly calling orders to a child across the room instead of having a face-to-face conversation also broadcasts disrespect.

In our touch-phobic culture, many teachers fear being reprimanded for inappropriate touching, but teachers have acceptable options. Shaking a student's hand is respectful. So are high fives in celebration of achievements. Gently moving students by guiding their elbows is also appropriate.

The unaware teacher owns all access to learning

Some teachers disdain all comments, questions, or challenges during instruction. Nor do they accept students' suggestions for changes, improvements, or adjustments. These teachers rarely plan student-led activities or presentations. They do not ask for personal examples related to the topic under discussion. The attitude of such instructors seems to be "It's my job to dish it out and your job to take it," as if learners have nothing to offer to the classroom dialogue. Absent from their instruction is the polite deference that we give to those we care for and admire.

Questions to grow by

☐ Do I treat students as politely as I treat colleagues and friends?

☐ Are my words, my tone of voice, and my gestures friendly?

☐ Do I mingle with students when appropriate, rather than remain aloof and separate?

☐ Do I honor students' comments and questions and seek their input?

☐ Have I occasionally incorporated ideas and suggestions from students?

The Aware Teacher

Although aware teachers avoid disrespect, they show respect for students inconsistently. Some students are treated with more respect than others. Sometimes these teachers trust students with their own learning, permitting student input; however, they control most learning opportunities and are suspicious of student suggestions.

The aware teacher unevenly applies respect

The issue of a student as a teacher's pet can occur with teachers who are slightly higher on the respect scale than Mr. Jones. Teachers with favorites grasp the idea of respecting at least some students. They avoid disrespect but are not yet skilled in demonstrating respect for all. They may encourage all pupils to offer examples and treat all students pleasantly, but the same few students are called on and picked for special privileges. These teachers reward those who are most responsive or who seem the most deserving. They are capable of high regard, but respect is focused on one student, or a few, not equally on all. Perhaps they forget that all students deserve civility and fairness.

In addition to teacher's pets, there can be school's pets. High school students readily identify this syndrome.

"The football players can do no wrong and it isn't fair," students say. "The security guards don't ask them for passes. The teachers let them leave early. Why are they so special? The same rules should apply to everyone."

In self-defense the football players—or the cheerleaders, the student government members, or the float committee members— say, "We're working hard for the school. We deserve a break."

This situation is hard to address. Some students earn special treatment, but rewarding some students can easily get out of hand. Deference to some reveals a lack of deference toward the rest. When one person glides by without any challenge and the next person is rudely barked at, a problem exists. Every person deserves polite treatment, if for no other reason than to serve as a model of respect. Students who are disrespected tend to be surly and less cooperative. Thus, if adults are not courteous, they may themselves contribute to a negative school culture.

Sometimes a student can be a teacher's nemesis. By this I mean a student who is repugnant to the teacher—for reasons of personal hygiene, disruptive behavior, or learning barriers that seem insurmountable. In such cases the teacher may treat most students respectfully but act dismissively, impatiently, or rudely to the nemesis.

There is a story of a 3rd grade teacher who had a nemesis named Teddy. He was unhygienic, inattentive, and a chronic low-performer. The teacher was grateful for his absences and enjoyed scrawling an *F* at the top of his papers. She was surprised to learn that Teddy's school performance in 1st grade had been good, before his mother died.

At Christmas, Teddy gave his teacher an awkwardly wrapped, half-empty bottle of perfume. When classmates laughed, she effusively thanked Teddy and dabbed some on. After class, he confided to her that she smelled just like his mother.

The teacher began to respect Teddy's needs and struggles. As her attitude shifted, Teddy did better. In time he succeeded in school, graduated with advanced degrees, and years later invited her to attend his wedding.

One event—receiving an awkward Christmas present—allowed this teacher to move past her antipathy for a student. Some teachers never give equal respect to all their charges, but outstanding ones manage to do so, hard though it may be.

Teachers sometimes have their own problems that interfere with attempts to be fair and respectful. One year a certain student nearly drove me wild. He was often annoying and undisciplined, but I had dealt with these issues in dozens of students. I repeatedly talked the situation over with a trusted advisor, complaining and describing the physical symptoms his behavior triggered—pressure in my head and a rising anger that I fought to control.

Because the advisor knew about my personal life, she finally asked if the student reminded me of my ex-husband. He did! From that instant on, I reacted to the student exactly as I did to any other teenager. Several years later he saw me and stopped to talk, reminiscing fondly about my class. At first I felt like a fraud, recalling the antipathy I once felt. Then I decided to give myself credit for moving past my negative feelings and giving him the respect he deserved.

The aware teacher maintains primary control over learning

Some teachers hold on to all responsibility for student learning. This may seem like the mark of a hard worker, but good teachers are able to delegate responsibility for learning to students because they respect their students.

In my years as a grade school student, all students completed the same worksheets at the same time. Teachers explained lessons to us and sometimes answered a few questions before we began. Teachers held almost all of the responsibility for learning; students had little or none.

Many elementary classrooms today contain various learning stations around the room. Students explore subjects like science or math by doing a series of activities, working fairly independently. The teacher shows children how to manage the process of visiting several work stations and how to do an experiment or create a product at each stop. In secondary classrooms students are asked to create podcasts, develop PowerPoint presentations, or even teach assigned concepts. In such settings, the teacher has given some responsibility for learning to students.

Like worksheets, the lecture has received a bad reputation as an instructional technique. Although lectures are efficient for delivering facts and can be used to good advantage, they are also inflexible. All students get the same information in the same way at the same time, with no respect for what level of knowledge or confusion they bring to the experience. Using lectures exclusively provides the teacher almost no feedback to indicate if students are learning. Using a variety of teaching styles to meet the needs of all students is a more respectful approach.

The aware teacher trusts students with some of their own learning

People—parents, bosses, or teachers—sometimes believe no one can do a job better than they can. In reality, there are numerous ways to do any job. When a job is completed, it is best to celebrate, not nitpick. At the very least, congratulate the strongest part of a solution before suggesting improvements.

What does it look like when a teacher trusts students with their own learning? Instead of listening to a lecture about water and erosion, every child gets a plastic tray containing a pile of soil and a pile of rocks. Every student is asked to pour one, then two, then three tablespoons of water on each pile. Afterward they write what happened. This teacher doesn't control every action or spell out every answer. The students make discoveries instead of merely parroting answers, thus learning on their own. The teacher looks at students' written notes to find out what knowledge they have mastered and what they need more help to learn.

Instruction might appear more efficient if teachers give detailed instructions and ask students to take notes. With this practice, however, teachers can assess only the students' ability to take dictation. Better learning happens when students participate.

Questions to grow by

□ Can you find some admirable qualities in each student, even the most challenging pupils?

□ Do you check yourself to observe whether you unevenly grant privileges?

□ Do you ask students to explain how they figured out difficult concepts?

□ Do you plan at least one lesson every day that requires students to take action or work together?

Self-Development

• Arrange for individual interactions with students. Set up private writing conferences, short oral quizzes, brief tutoring sessions, and time for students to summarize a project or discuss their own learning. Getting to know individuals outside of group pressures usually leads to increased empathy and respect.

• During six years as an adult educator, I spent one month every fall knocking on doors in low-income neighborhoods to invite residents to complete their high school educations. After my initial fears, I found that nearly everyone was cordial. Ever since, my advice to teachers has been to find a way to visit families.

• Institute a Visit of the Week for one selected student. Stop by a house one day each week for a brief visit. Keep the visit positive by mentioning a student's recent achievement or progress. Ask about the child's interests, hobbies, or past accomplishments. Ask what helps the student learn. If visits are impossible, ask similar questions during a phone call or invite parents and guardians to school.

Collegial Support

• With tact, share your reactions to colleagues' behaviors that are less than fully respectful. Then invite changes. For instance, "You may not have meant to be, but you sounded pretty harsh with Group Two. Can you think of another approach to take?"

• Create an atmosphere free of put-downs. Agree with a partner or group that you will point out one another's disrespectful comments. Then make a habit of adjusting your comments to be more neutral or more positive.

The Capable Teacher

Capable teachers have reached the point where respect is inherent in their interaction with students. They show respect for students through encouraging words and the often-stated belief that students can overcome obstacles. They encourage students to actively participate in their own learning, and they structure activities in ways that make such participation possible.

The capable teacher encourages students to overcome obstacles

During his second year of teaching, Mr. Peterson notices that the spelling pre-tests aren't helpful to his students. Most show little improvement between the pre-test and the final test.

"Let's try an experiment this week," announces Mr. Peterson. "Instead of pre-testing, we will have a group rehearsal for Friday's test. Get into groups of three."

After students move he says, "Look up your scores from the last spelling test. The person in your group who had the highest spelling score will be the reader.

"Readers, say each word and have one of your study buddies spell it aloud. Have the second person vote on whether it sounds right. Look at the word, write it correctly, and think of clues for remembering it—outline the shape, make up a rhyme or a sound clue—you decide."

By turning over practice for the spelling test to students, Mr. Peterson shows his belief that students can successfully study spelling together—and he will check this assumption against their scores. Because the traditional pre-test doesn't seem to help students, he reasons that another approach will be at least as successful. Instead of grading pre-tests, he will look at the methods that students develop and announce clever techniques to the class.

In spite of low spelling scores, Mr. Peterson does not scornfully proclaim, "They never study" or "They aren't trying." He has faith in his students. His new approach encourages students to overcome obstacles by providing their own helpful methods. Mr. Peterson's behavior demonstrates respect in action. He guides students to find errors and overcome difficulties.

He may hear protests when he introduces this new plan. Students may find the new approach hard or confusing at first. He would be wise to acknowledge students' reluctance or frustration, while affirming that he believes they can succeed.

Respect is founded on honesty. Admit to students the difficulty presented by tasks in the classroom or in life. Claiming tasks are easy can minimize learners' accomplishments. What sense of achievement does a student feel when he masters assignments that he imagines any normal person would instantly understand? Instead of congratulating himself for conquering a challenge, he will be ashamed because he found it difficult. Acknowledge students when they say, "This is hard." Recognize that new skills are often hard and then work with students to make them doable.

The capable teacher interacts with students in supportive ways

Ms. Redding was a government teacher perceived to be so tough and outspoken that some students took government in summer school to avoid her. Ms. Redding gave frequent quizzes, and her rules were strict. Under no circumstances did she allow students to make up tests if they missed class for a school-sponsored activity. Tests were taken prior to the first bell on the scheduled day, before students left the building—no exceptions. Yet many of her students spoke very positively of Ms. Redding.

For example, a student named Amie explained to me that tests were hard for her. Anxiety often kept her from recalling information she had known the night before. Ms. Redding noticed her strong answers in class discussions and her low test scores and pulled her aside one day to privately discuss the problem. Ms. Redding told her to come in early the next morning to take the quiz.

When Amie arrived, Ms. Redding yanked a desk out of line and seated Amie with her back to the clock.

"Don't worry about time," said Ms. Redding. "Take an hour if you want. Don't look at that clock. I can tell you are studying just from listening to you in class. Write what you know."

When Amie finished she had earned a *B+* instead of the near-failing marks she usually received.

"From now on, you'll take your tests before school. In class I'll pass out a test to you, just like everyone else, but I will give you the grade you earn before school."

Amie had struggled with testing for years, but Ms. Redding made tests easier for her without violating rules or embarrassing her.

The capable teacher trusts students with their own learning

When Mr. Peterson first decided to find a new way to teach spelling, he did so believing his students could do better if he used a new approach. In all likelihood, his first try did not go smoothly. It usually doesn't. At that point he could keep trying until he found a way to make it successful or give up. Mr. Peterson decided to keep trying.

By the next year, Mr. Peterson knew that group study worked well for most, but a small group of kids were still not spelling well. Mr. Peterson organized a Thursday lunch group for spelling. Strugglers exchanged notes and clues from their respective groups and chanted the correct spelling in rhythm into a recorder. Rehearsal for the spelling test was encouraged before school or at recess. Mr. Peterson let nobody off the hook; instead, he addressed their difficulties.

Having turned spelling practice over to students, Mr. Peterson may decide to share responsibility for learning in other curriculum areas. Over time he could seek structures to support student learning in other curricula. Power sharing must be designed to enable kids to overcome obstacles; cutting them loose with no support system is ineffective. A Chinese proverb says, "The teacher and the learner together create the learning." This adage captures the mutual respect that underlies good teacher-student relationships, including the teacher's duty to offer assistance.

By his fourth year of teaching, Mr. Peterson sets up learning stations. While he still gives short lectures on important facts and uses worksheets when necessary, he broadens his repertoire of teaching techniques. He uses learn-by-doing activities: experiments, constructions, interactions, investigations. After acquiring the needed materials, he develops directions for each learning station, expecting students to record what they discover. Before turning the class loose, he teaches them self-control, believing students capable of monitoring their own actions toward a productive end. After training, he trusts them to do experiments, record data, and draw conclusions, turning over appropriate tasks to them.

Mr. Peterson shows enough respect for students to share responsibility for learning. He also respects himself enough to try new techniques. New skills take months or years to learn; Mr. Peterson practices until he is effective.

Respect is based on caring, affection, or regard; all are positive emotional connections. Some people argue that you don't have to like your students to teach them. But there is a kind of caring that occurs outside the boundaries of liking, and great teachers always seem to possess that kind of care for their students. They care for students beyond misbehavior and difficulties to find their students' potential.

Certain strict teachers seem to expect the impossible from their students. Yet in some cases, students sense an underlying respect that suggests that this stern teacher believes they can do something that seems difficult. Such teachers usually manage to attack the problem, not the child. They instill in their students the idea that student effort will pay off, even though they say that the first draft is "abominable" or the experiment "failed in every way possible." This type of vocabulary is different from the name calling used by Mr. Jones.

Ways to show regard widely vary, but the results are remarkably similar. Capable teachers respect, appreciate, and encourage all their students. For instance, they may respond to children who say they're not good at a task, "You can be; let me show you how." They are likely to demand action and not settle for passivity.

Youngsters are unique and have an inner compass that sorts out what works for them and what doesn't. Certain lessons or instructions trigger rebellion for some students. When students do not fall in with our plans right away, their behavior is not an indictment of the plan, the teacher, or the student; the approach may not be the right method for the right person. No teacher will hit the target every time, and no student will enthusiastically embrace every lesson. When lessons don't go smoothly, change is needed, but we can treat students well as we make adaptations.

Thomas Edison was "addle-pated," or so said the headmaster of his school. Offended, his mother took Thomas out of school and taught him herself. He also educated himself with wild experiments like jumping out of the barn loft. But Mrs. Edison respected her boy for his unique qualities. Without her backing, would Edison have been the innovator he turned out to be? Perhaps his strong will would have helped him ignore eight years of being called addle-brained. But perhaps his confidence would have eroded. The confidence of many students is needlessly diminished by teachers who do not respect them.

Questions to grow by

☐ Do you regularly ask students what helps them to learn?

☐ Can you design lessons in which students participate in teaching and learning?

☐ Do you share your own feelings, memories, and ideas when they are directly related to content?

☐ Are students aware that you trust them?

☐ Do your actions show that you have high regard for each student?

☐ Have you ever asked parents about their child's strengths and accomplishments?

The Inspired Teacher

Respect is demonstrated by a teacher's ability to believe in and affirm every student. Mr. Peterson's efforts to help his kids spell better contained two parts: first he changed the way they studied in class, and then he added a Thursday session for kids who still didn't conquer spelling. If he later tried a third and fourth step in his efforts to reach every student, he would demonstrate even greater respect for them. Caring deeply for his students and being absolutely committed to helping them learn, he acts as if failure is a temporary condition, not a permanent one. He thinks so highly of his students that he notices that they simply haven't learned *yet* and redoubles efforts to help them do what he believes they can do.

• • • TIP • • •

Teaching Tolerance magazine is filled with contributions from teachers who describe lessons and approaches they have successfully used to increase tolerance, mutual respect, and peace. Use it to gather ideas you might try in your own classroom or school. *Teaching Tolerance*, published twice a year, is free to educators who request it. An online version is also available at www.tolerance.org/teach/magazine/index.jsp.

The inspired teacher commits to overcoming barriers

No two youngsters ever face identical challenges, either academically or personally. Objective but caring teachers help identify students' challenges and formulate plans to meet them. Overactive children are pulled aside to help redirect behavior or given squeeze balls to keep their hands busy so they can listen.

If the challenge is a huge student project, inspired teachers make tasks manageable with time lines or flow charts that anticipate the difficulties students will face, providing a road map to guide them past challenges. To expect a lot but provide no guidance abandons those who need support systems. If the project requires primary and secondary sources, teachers explain and demonstrate each, showing how to record information. If note cards are required, students are taught how to use them. Inspired teachers examine student work in order to judge whether each child grasps the research process. Such teachers may decide to award points for completing steps of the process to motivate students and recognize their efforts.

After the note cards are done, the same teachers may say, "I have no idea whether you have enough cards. Figure it out by asking yourself what other questions you still need to answer with research. Don't stop until you get there." Reminding young people that the true measure of successful learning is not satisfying teachers, but satisfying themselves, offers guidance without limitations.

The inspired teacher demonstrates openness and trust

Respectful teachers close distances, both physically and psychologically. They circulate. They make eye contact. Body language reveals genuine interest, and focused attention indicates real involvement. Comments from "Well done" to "I do not permit put-downs here" are said with tact and sincerity. Such teachers admit their own problems and those of students, but always work to overcome them, and delight in the success of all.

What does openness look like in a teacher? Honesty might be saying "I don't remember that, so we'll have to look it up together" instead of "Never mind that, it's not on the test." Candidness might be saying "If I spell words wrong on the board, tell me so I can correct them."

Mr. Spaar, a 3rd grade teacher, reads aloud daily to his students. At the end of *Where the Red Fern Grows*, his voice breaks and tears moisten his eyes.

"Mr. Spaar, are you crying?" asks Myra.

"Yes," he answers.

"But men don't cry," she says.

"Sure they do," he replies, "especially when they feel sad."

Openness shows the teacher to be a real person, not a robot or drill sergeant. Watching a genuine, healthy adult in action is beneficial to students.

Trusting teachers expect the best. A few clear rules are good, but long lists of punishable offenses send the wrong message. Why expect students to do wrong? Expect them to do right, show them how, catch them at it, and offer praise for specific achievements.

One teacher I know spends a whole class period during the first week of school discussing what actions help students learn. She asks her pupils to list things that past teachers have done that helped them or that have hindered them. She asks for lists of actions other students have taken to help them learn and what students have done to block their learning. Four lists are compiled and each is explored. If a student writes "Made a joke to cheer me up," the class spends time discussing examples of when this would help and when it might not.

Every student gains a clear idea of how to help themselves and others, and what behavior is expected in the classroom. This hour-long discussion demonstrates more trust in students than merely posting a list of rules. The teacher shows students that she thinks they can offer good suggestions, gain deeper understanding, control their own behavior, and help their classmates. By asking students to also discuss teacher actions, both positive and negative, she shows that she knows she has responsibilities to them that she intends to fulfill.

The inspired teacher shows high regard and high expectations

During the previous discussion, trust is not the only value modeled for students. Students watch this teacher, whom they met just four days earlier, respond to them. She asks questions about their ideas, calling for examples or reasons for their choices. She plays the devil's advocate so students can defend their positions. She amplifies some responses, clarifies, or takes exceptions to others. No one is ignored or put down. One student's harsh comment is corrected: The teacher suggests a different approach for him to use the next time. Closeness develops as students experience both high regard and high expectations, communicated by the way their teacher leads the discussion. She doesn't settle for the first thing that pops into their minds. She encourages them to dig deeper because she knows they can. This kind of affection and esteem—in other words, respect—helps students grow.

The author bell hooks (2000) describes genuine love as a combination of care, commitment, trust, knowledge, responsibility, and respect. Using this definition, it's safe to say that inspired teachers show genuine love for students.

Actions to grow by

☐ Read a book about listening and apply the ideas to your classroom interactions.

☐ Sign up for a class in a field about which you are ignorant. Observe the level of respect demonstrated when you ask questions or interact. Notice how you feel when you are lost or confused.

☐ Sit through a speech or presentation in a foreign language and note gestures, tone of voice, and facial expressions to see how powerful they are in conveying meaning and feelings. Try the same thing while viewing a TV show in a language you do not speak. Note your feelings as you attempt to understand, as well as the meanings you take from the broadcast.

☐ Watch people around you. Look for behaviors that seem either respectful or disrespectful. Consider how you might apply what you learn through this observation.

For Information and Inspiration

Aronson, E. (2000). *Nobody left to hate: Teaching compassion after Columbine*. New York: W. H. Freeman.

Bluestein, J. (2001). *Creating emotionally safe schools: A guide for educators and parents*. Deerfield Beach, FL: Health Communications, Inc.

Bond, L., Smith, T., Baker, W. K., & Hattie, J. A. (2000). *The certification system of the National Board for Professional Teaching Standards: A construct and consequential validity study*. Greensboro, NC: Center for Educational Research and Evaluation, University of North Carolina.

Bryk, A. S., & Schneider, B. (2002). *Trust in schools: A core resource for improvement*. New York: Russell Sage Foundation.

Building classroom relationships. (2003, September). *Educational Leadership, 61*(1).

Codell, E. R. (1999). *Educating Esme: Diary of a teacher's first year*. Chapel Hill, NC: Algonquin Books.

Creating caring schools. (2003, March). *Educational Leadership, 60*(6).

The Freedom Writers, & Gruwell, E. (1999). *The Freedom Writers diary: How a teacher and 150 teens used writing to change themselves and the world around them*. New York: Broadway Books.

Goleman, D. (1995). *Emotional intelligence.* New York: Bantam Books.

hooks, b. (2000). *All about love: New visions.* New York: William Morrow.

McCourt, F. (2005). *Teacher man: A memoir.* New York: Scribner.

Robins, K. N., Lindsey, R. B., Lindsey, D. B., & Terrell, R. D. (2002). *Culturally proficient instruction: A guide for people who teach.* Thousand Oaks, CA: Corwin Press.

Showing Passion for Teaching and Learning

When asked to recall a special teacher, most people readily answer. A smile or a look of wonder appears on their faces as they reminisce. Decades later they still express gratitude or affection for that teacher.

Memorable teachers are usually passionate, dedicated individuals; they are the type of teachers that we wish every young person could be inspired by. While some teachers do educate without overt passion, all students can benefit from the power of passionate teaching.

Passion for teaching is not mysterious. We can identify the level of enthusiasm each teacher shows. Passion doesn't include manic behavior, rages, or inappropriate attachments; it consists of commitment to students, to learning, and to teaching itself. Listening to teachers talk about their work reveals their enthusiasm, whether expressed quietly or with great animation.

The Unaware Teacher

Unaware teachers do not have a positive attitude regarding their subject, their students, or their careers, nor do they feel responsibility for student learning. In fact, they actively discourage any ambient excitement about learning, setting a poor example for students.

The unaware teacher rarely shows a positive attitude toward teaching or learning

Unaware teachers show no passion because they see little to be enthusiastic about. Watch their classroom interactions.

Students who enter their classrooms are not recognized as special individuals. These teachers are inattentive or focused on something else—a newspaper, a to-do list, a phone call—demonstrating no interest in the class. While last-minute preparations are sometimes necessary, unaware teachers aren't preparing, they're passing time until the bell rings.

These teachers show little interest in teaching. They depart from the planned lesson, idly chatting. Other than complaints, they say little to colleagues. Enthusiasm is directed toward things unrelated to work—a football game or a vacation—not toward teaching.

As a college freshman, I enrolled in introductory sociology because it sounded interesting. The first day, a tall man in a suit and tie entered the classroom, carrying the assigned text. He opened the book, removed some papers with handwritten notes, and began to lecture.

He followed the same routine every day. He walked in, put the book on the podium, took out some notes, and started to talk. Nothing changed except his tie. Looking at his daily notes, I noticed that the pages were yellowed. I wondered if he used the same notes since the first year he selected the text. Not once did he initiate a discussion or solicit questions from students. He cured me of any further interest in sociology courses, even though the subject fascinated me.

Such a teacher has no enthusiasm for teaching. He demonstrated a robotic and uninvolved style of teaching. No hint of love for the subject matter, no interest in his lessons, no constant search for new knowledge, no interaction with students. He created a passion-free classroom, unmoved by the idea of helping learners or making their eyes light up with comprehension.

The unaware teacher discourages excitement about learning

The unaware teacher dampens student enthusiasm. She presents lessons as bitter prescriptions, not as engaging opportunities. Students see no smiling face or vibrant voice. She warns, "You better know this for the state test" or "This is hard, but I don't want to hear any complaining." Naturally, students dread the instruction that follows. Admitting that something is hard is honest; however, impassioned teachers will add comments that create a more positive impression: "Because the whole class did so well on the last set of equations, I have a feeling you'll figure this out in no time" or "I know you can handle it."

When presentations lack variety, enthusiasm is muted. The unaware teacher uses words and actions that take the fun out of learning. "Stop laughing. It's time to do Chapter 11" is a deadening transition from recess to the exports of Peru. Playing panpipe music from the Peruvian mountains for 30 seconds would intrigue students, quelling laughter but not enthusiasm.

How teachers react to students' passion is telling. If Moses comes to class overflowing with information about dinosaurs, electricity, or antique cars, some teachers welcome it, working his interests into lessons. The unaware teacher can't be bothered. Her responses range from "That's nice, go sit down" to "Moses, we've heard enough of that, so don't bring it up again." The student's passion is viewed as an interruption, not a useful glimpse into his interests.

The unaware teacher rarely assumes responsibility for student learning

An unimpassioned teacher might say:

"Hey, I went over it; I can't help it if they didn't get it."

"Why knock myself out? It's covered in the book. Let them read it themselves."

"It's not brain surgery. Nobody dies if they don't know this stuff."

"They don't pay me enough to do more."

These statements reveal a lack of commitment to teaching and learning. The teacher is unaware of the excitement of creating great lessons and misses the chance to enjoy watching students make progress. He is not excited about the subject matter, and he imparts no passion for learning to students. He shows low personal standards or expectations, and he's unaware that problems with his teaching exist.

We want to say to him, "Wake up! Look lively! You are affecting children who will be in 2nd or 7th or 11th grade only once. Care about them; they need you. Care about the subject; it's fascinating. Care about yourself; you could be great."

Questions to grow by

☐ Do you look for interesting facts and odd information to whet your interest in your subject matter?

☐ Do you pay attention to or record your own word choice and tone of voice to see if you sound positive and inviting?

☐ Have you accepted the idea that your job is not just providing information to students but triggering their enthusiasm for learning?

The Aware Teacher

Aware teachers usually approach learning with a neutral attitude. They encourage enjoyment of learning only on rare occasions. At times they display enthusiasm for learning or for teaching, but not consistently. They do sense that students cannot learn alone and thus understand that they share responsibility for helping to trigger the learning process.

The aware teacher sometimes shows positive feelings toward teaching or learning

By accident or design, aware teachers show enthusiasm at least part of the time. When the curriculum overlaps teachers' own interests, their passion shows. When a pedantic biology teacher gives a lesson on tropical plants, she displays a sudden eloquence. She passes around photos of unusual orchids and explains their growing habits. Her students learn that she has a small greenhouse behind her house with a dozen varieties. Students are intrigued and ask question after question.

This orchid seminar carries into a second day of discussion, surprising the teacher and students alike. Delighted, she arranges a field trip to a local conservatory. An 82-year-old volunteer captivates them by sharing a lifetime of orchid knowledge. Several students develop a new interest in biology. Although the rest of the year settles into a duller routine, here is a teacher who, at least once, taught passionately.

Aware teachers sense that enthusiasm is important and try to use it, but their enthusiasm is intermittent. Some days they are enthusiastic. Some days they fake it, hoping to rouse students' interest. These teachers acknowledge the power of passion but use it imperfectly and irregularly. The biology teacher above may talk about the orchid field trip for years, recalling it as a bright moment. She may even make it a yearly tradition, but she isn't impassioned daily.

The aware teacher rarely encourages enjoyment of learning

When a person is not yet passionate about the teaching profession or the subject matter he is presenting, his work has a pedestrian quality. He presents the lesson but doesn't try to make the experience memorable. If students enjoy instruction, it is accidental.

Students' enjoyment is not an aware teacher's priority, as in the case of the biology teacher. The class had fun when she took them deep into the world of orchids, but she doesn't try to enrich other lessons.

Almost anything can contain an element of fun or a refreshing quality. Mastering a new skill can be enjoyable. Trying to beat your own time as you practice can be fun. Seeing a teacher's hobbies and interests intersect with the curriculum is refreshing. At the aware level, such delightful moments occur, but infrequently.

The aware teacher takes limited responsibility for student learning

Aware teachers show involvement in their teaching roles. They believe it's their responsibility to find ways to reach pupils, and they act on this belief at least part of the time. Instead of simply reciting facts and grading papers, these teachers chart student progress or arrange individual conferences. They create learning aids and posters to reteach difficult concepts when students are baffled. They aren't satisfied with merely presenting information; they sometimes check for comprehension, too. When they remember, they try to improve student understanding in a more engaging way. The satisfaction derived from success fuels further enthusiasm and involvement.

These teachers show some enthusiasm; it matters to them that students absorb what they need to know. Most teachers-in-training enter with this positive attitude. When the complexities and frustrations of teaching hit them, some regress because of hopelessness, to a less passionate level. Burnout can also reduce teachers' passion. If schools provide more mentoring, assistance, and support for teachers facing instructional difficulties, hope and enthusiasm are preserved.

Questions to grow by

☐ When you have an exciting day of teaching, do you ponder how to make similar days occur more often?

☐ Do you stop yourself from mentioning negative comments about topics being studied?

☐ Are you able to notice and dwell on positive events and achievements every day?

☐ Do you rejoice when students conquer new material or make original observations?

Self-Development

• We unconsciously express our attitudes. The words we use carry only about 7 percent of our spoken message. Tone of voice accounts for 38 percent and body language provides 55 percent of the total message listeners receive. Whenever words, tone of voice, and body language contradict one another, listeners are more influenced by the messages sent through tone and body language rather than through words (Mehrabian, 1971). Therefore, building positive attitudes is important because our attitudes are sensed by students.

• Videotape yourself and watch with the volume off. What do your movements, gestures, and expressions say? Put a tape recorder in a desk drawer where it will pick up your tone of voice but not your words. Listen for attitudes and emotions in the sounds of your words. Do you sound animated or bored? Calm or angry? Eager or reluctant? Caring or cold? Students take in all of this.

• Make physical changes in your classroom or yourself. Consider the furniture arrangement, the items posted on the walls, and the state of your desktop. What messages do these elements send? Consider apparel and hygiene, facial expressions, and tone of voice. Are the messages positive? Behaving like a person who cares deeply can help you to become more enthusiastic.

• Try reading inspirational books or attending workshops; they may help you love teaching again. Join a support group or short-term therapy; it may help you overcome a negative mind-set.

Collegial Support

- Encourage enthusiasm by sharing positive experiences with coworkers. Noticing good things seems to increase their frequency. Negative attitudes are weakened by actively searching for things to celebrate.

- Give feedback to help colleagues understand problems invisible to them. Point out alternative approaches and invite your colleagues into your classroom to give you advice.

- Negative attitudes are poisonous. Interrupt openly harmful statements with counterstatements. Try instituting a gripe jar; for every complaint or disparaging comment, participants chip in a quarter.

The Capable Teacher

Teachers at the capable level are enthusiastic most of the time. They are committed to teaching and take obvious satisfaction from helping students learn. Capable teachers understand that helping students enjoy education results in more learning, so they do so often. They also know that their actions shape the experience of their students, so they usually assume responsibility for creating positive learning conditions.

The capable teacher shows enthusiasm for student learning and teaching

At this level, teachers really care about teaching and learning. Capable teachers show delight when students learn, even if their enthusiasm is subtle. A sensitive observer might see a teacher wink across the room, silently signaling to a student that an answer is correct. The wink's purpose is to reassure the student, who has struggled in class this week; that student knows the teacher cares. Other students sense the teacher's enthusiasm whether they see the wink or not.

While any teacher may express frustration over difficulties, teachers with passion shake off disappointment and return to the challenge the next day. They rarely whine or wallow in self-pity. They would choose a teaching career again, even knowing its challenges. They express pride in their work and share memories about teaching moments that brought them satisfaction.

The capable teacher sometimes encourages enjoyment of learning

Capable teachers encourage the enjoyment of learning, partly as an extension of their growing knowledge. Teaching a subject for the first time can be so stressful that teachers must play catch-up, preparing nightly for the challenge of the next morning. Even if the material interests teachers, making it comprehensible for students feels overwhelming at first, so helping students enjoy the lesson is a secondary concern.

As teachers relax into a topic, they have energy to spare. Understanding their topics more completely, they are more able to sense student reactions. As they come to appreciate the subject, they are also likely to share their growing enthusiasm with students. They now have time and energy to make the material more interactive for students through film clips, dimensional models, games, and special events.

Helping students enjoy learning is a part of the methodology of capable teachers. One teacher invites speakers on Veterans Day, Arbor Day, or Earth Day. Another opens lessons with a riddle or puzzle. Some ask algebra students to interview adults about ways they have actually used algebra. They may teach the U.S. Constitution through songs or explain nutrition wearing a banana costume. Something interesting, entertaining, or enlightening frequently occurs in their classes, and students appreciate these inventive instructional approaches.

The capable teacher generally assumes responsibility for student learning

Enthusiasm for teaching and learning leads the capable teacher to make steady efforts to teach effectively. This teacher feels a substantial interest in the process of teaching. He cares about whether his pupils get it. He is rewarded internally when his efforts pay off and encouraged to try again and again.

He knows that helping students enjoy classroom challenges will result in increased retention of information, so he tries to add effective approaches to every unit, if not every lesson. His efforts are the difference between success and failure for his students, and he knows it. Expanding his repertoire of methods to assist student learning is enjoyable and deeply satisfying to him.

If we were to eavesdrop in the teachers lounge, we would hear evidence of his sense of responsibility for student learning.

"I despise this new math text," says his colleague. "It covers fractions in September. What a pain."

"It's not so bad," he reassures. "There's a good idea in the teacher handbook that helped me a lot. Cut two paper plates into pieces and tell the kids you are studying pie for math class. My students thought that was funny. Then we wrote out the fractions as I moved the slices around on the overhead projector. They even caught on to mixed fractions better this year. I bet if you try the pie approach, you'll find your students will start to really understand."

Questions to grow by

☐ Have you made a file of encouraging remarks like thank-you notes or comments to encourage yourself on difficult days?

☐ Do you share success stories and teaching ideas with colleagues?

☐ Is it your habit to ask other teachers for interesting approaches to assist students with specific concepts or problem areas?

The Inspired Teacher

Inspired teachers are driven to improve their own teaching and are dedicated to their students' continuous improvement. Because of their abiding passion for teaching and learning, they share their enthusiasm in all their lessons, helping students enjoy learning. These teachers are firmly convinced that they are responsible for student learning and consistently bend their efforts toward doing a better job every day.

The inspired teacher shows passion and dedication for teaching and student learning

The passion demonstrated by teachers at this level of expertise is multifaceted. They love the subject matter they are teaching; their deep appreciation is based on great familiarity. As they learn more, they find more to love. Even a quiet teacher with a controlled manner will exude this positive feeling in every presentation.

Enthusiasm develops in different ways. Some teachers choose a field of study early on and never falter, while some stray far from their original major. Some teach a course in their minor field and become fascinated with that area, eventually specializing in it. Others develop a new interest mid-career and earn a new certification. Some move through many fields or teach at many grade levels because they delight in trying new things.

Inspired teachers constantly seek better ways to teach their students. Figuring out how to motivate learners, how to present difficult concepts, how to choose analogies that lead to understanding, or how to reach a student who constantly struggles—these are of deep interest to passionate teachers. They do not tire of the pursuit of excellent instruction.

Picture the wine lover. He collects wine, reads about it, visits vineyards, and experiments with making his own. He belongs to a wine tasting group. Every glass is a new discovery. He is driven to talk about wine with everyone he meets. No matter how mysterious this passion is to others, there is no mistaking his enthusiasm.

So it is with the passionate teacher. He doesn't force himself to learn about the subject matter; he is drawn to it. He doesn't attend workshops about teaching techniques because they are required; he'd willingly go on a Saturday and pay for it himself. And he doesn't pore over journal entries, worksheets, and test scores to keep his job; he does it because he can't wait to see if his students really understand.

Enthusiasm for subject and teaching includes a passion for student learning. When everyone passes the first quiz, the teacher celebrates as much as the students. He rethinks his lessons while showering at 6:00 a.m. or while driving. He never teaches a lesson exactly the same two years in a row. He buys books during the summer and greets his new classes eagerly in the fall. He wants to reach every single student he meets.

The inspired teacher actively promotes student enjoyment of learning

A passionate teacher wants to share the joy of learning. She cannot believe that anyone would not be equally eager to learn. Enthusiasm like this is contagious. This teacher deliberately tries to present information in an absorbing and engaging manner. The positive feelings she has for the subject are thus transferred to her students.

In college, I had a botany teacher who had this kind of zeal for plant life. Our class met at 8:00 a.m. We were still groggy when he hurried down the aisle of the lecture hall. He was so eager to start that with each step he seemed to roll up onto his toes. At first I could barely suppress a groan, but before long I appreciated his pure delight in botany.

He talked, he showed slides, he diagrammed on the chalkboard. Somehow he held my attention for every minute of that early class. In the lab he displayed a deep fondness for the topics he taught. One day, we peered into our microscopes as he described an organism's characteristic of reversing the flow of its protoplasm every 100 seconds. With controlled excitement in his voice, he consulted his stopwatch. Sure enough, exactly on time, the reversal occurred in front of my eyes; I too felt awed by the mystery of it.

The passionate teacher fully believes that learning is fun, satisfying, and self-reinforcing. He believes that how he talks about this specific topic and the ways he leads students to experience it can make each lesson more engaging. He builds lessons that are intrinsically rewarding. Students learn almost without noticing. "We had fun in Mr. Conklyn's class today!" is just another way of saying, "I learned something new in a way that made it painless."

The inspired teacher personally assumes responsibility for student learning

An inspired teacher has learned that her actions and emotional reactions are her own, not the result of accident or the power of another person. She no longer believes others make her mad; she believes that anger (or any emotion) is her own response and only she decides how to act on it.

The passionate teacher owns her power to affect student learning and constantly uses it. Her interest in teaching and learning leads to continual efforts to create a supportive learning environment. While no one can make another learn, this teacher creates situations in which learning becomes more and more likely, even irresistible. This is a responsibility that passionate teachers happily take on.

Some argue that it's the child's job to learn. That's true. But learning is easier when passionate teachers create classrooms where enthusiasm and support abound. Dedicated teachers show delight when their students learn, and that pleasure urges children onward. These teachers forgive themselves for falling short, yet immediately ponder a new approach for the next try.

Inspired teachers see teaching not as a job but as a personal mission. Despite discouraging moments, they regroup and start again the next day with renewed determination to make a difference.

Actions to grow by

☐ If you feel down or stressed much of the time, investigate the concept of burnout and see if it applies to you. Refer to the book *Career Burnout: Causes and Cures* (Pines & Aronson, 1988) for suggested steps you can take to counter burnout. You may also need to look for symptoms of depression and talk to your doctor if it seems likely that you are depressed.

☐ Another way to rediscover your sense of mission or purpose is to join a circle of trust or a similar support group. This approach is used by Parker Palmer and described at length in his book *A Hidden Wholeness* (2004). Two organizations that use this approach are the Fetzer Institute and the Center for Teacher Formation.

☐ There are eight measures of nonverbal communication that indicate the type of respect that teachers exhibit (Clarridge as cited in Bond et al., 2000, p. 57):

1. Affection—liking or attraction
2. Arousal—nervousness, tension, or lack of self-control
3. Dominance—control, influence, or dominance over others
4. Immediacy—psychological and/or physical closeness
5. Involvement—focused attention paid toward others
6. Receptivity—openness and trust toward others
7. Similarity—identification with others, either verbal or nonverbal
8. Task/Social Orientation—work oriented versus sociable or people oriented

Spend time considering these types of reactions. Ask whether each is appropriate to the situation at hand and the goals you have in mind.

For Information and Inspiration

Bond, L., Smith, T., Baker, W. K., & Hattie, J. A. (2000). *The certification system of the National Board for Professional Teaching Standards: A construct and consequential validity study.* Greensboro, NC: Center for Educational Research and Evaluation, University of North Carolina.

Esquith, R. (2007). *Teach like your hair's on fire*. New York: Viking.

Fried, R. L. (1995). *The passionate teacher: A practical guide*. Boston: Beacon Press.

Keeping teaching fresh. (2000, May). *Educational Leadership, 57*(8).

Mandoki, L. (Director). (1993). *Born yesterday* [Motion picture]. United States: Hollywood Pictures.

Marshall, L. (2002). *The body speaks*. New York: Palgrave Macmillan.

Mehrabian, A. (1971). *Silent messages*. Belmont, CA: Wadsworth.

Palmer, P. J. (1998). *The courage to teach: Exploring the inner landscape of a teacher's life*. San Francisco: Jossey-Bass.

Palmer, P. J. (2004). *A hidden wholeness: The journey toward an undivided life*. San Francisco: Jossey-Bass.

Pines, A., & Aronson, E. (1988). *Career burnout: Causes and cures*. New York: Free Press.

Wolk, S. (2008, September). Joy in school. *Educational Leadership, 66*(1), 8–15.

12

Helping Students Reach Higher Levels of Achievement

This chapter addresses teachers' success in challenging their students to reach higher levels of achievement. Some teachers name learning goals or assign projects. Better teachers arrange for experiences that help students successfully reach those goals and feel satisfaction from their intellectual efforts. Many teachers challenge part of the class part of the time. Inspired teachers design engaging activities to help all students succeed.

The Unaware Teacher

Unaware teachers are not global thinkers—they consider only this lesson, this test, this project. Because they don't see the connection between incremental learning and students' lives outside the classroom, they ask students to do only what is necessary for this moment. They rarely challenge students to think broadly or deeply. They do not use their own expertise to help students succeed; they simply believe students will understand the concepts or they won't.

The unaware teacher rarely challenges students to think

Some people compare schools to assembly lines. This metaphor fits only teachers who haven't learned to challenge students. Such teachers treat schoolwork as a production quota: give the kids 20 problems, correct them, record the scores, assign

20 more problems. They ask students to regurgitate information, not to analyze or synthesize it.

My niece, who became conversant in French while living in Canada, decided to continue studying the language when she entered college. After the first semester I asked her how the term had gone.

"I got a *B* in French," she said with a disgusted look.

"What happened?" I asked.

"We had to memorize 500 vocabulary words for the final, and I didn't get them all right. The test brought down my average," she explained.

There are many other ways to evaluate mastery of French: a conversation with the instructor, an extemporaneous speech, a scripted play with classmates. These varied challenges are lively and interesting and resemble the way we actually use language. Admittedly, memorizing 500 words is one kind of challenge, but other methods create more flexible and involved speakers.

The zone of proximal development (ZPD) is the area where we work to master new concepts and processes; it's the area just beyond what we already know, in which we have the potential to learn provided we are guided by teachers or allowed to collaborate with more capable peers (Vygotsky, 1978). We are working in our ZPD when we have to try hard to keep up but don't get completely lost. We can deal with the challenge if there are social supports to assist our development. Finding the ZPD for students is difficult but worth it. Unfortunately unaware teachers don't even look for the ZPD.

Unaware teachers are inclined to squelch original thinking or deep questioning. Precocious children may propose interesting alternatives or provide tangential information that intrigues them and might appeal to other students. Unaware teachers are likely to say, "That's not on the test" or "You're getting off the subject." When this happens all students miss an opportunity to extend their learning, and gifted children are particularly underserved.

If I polled the students in my niece's French class, they probably wouldn't find the memorization assignment engaging or provocative. I imagine the teacher used an introduction like this: "You might need to know these words someday, so memorize them now. You have to because I'm putting them on the final." The memorization exercise does not teach a new process for assembling French sentences. The only challenge for students is to perform a somewhat tedious task in the time available.

We can challenge language learners in different ways. Many foreign language teachers can teach seven new words during an engaging 20-minute story. In this approach, called Total Physical Response-Stories (TPR-S), students immediately use new words within the context of a story and try to make sense of the story. Students repeat what they are told to and dream up responses using the new words; they rise to the teacher's challenge. At the end of a semester, they too know hundreds of words, probably with higher levels of recall and proficiency than rote memorization yields.

The unaware teacher promotes the idea that lessons are tedious and time-consuming

Some lessons are unglamorous but necessary. Such lessons are made even duller by teachers who state that the material is "not exciting but has to be done." There are strategies to enliven all lessons. Mentioning the usefulness of a skill is encouraging to learners. Promising to help students get through difficult exercises cheers them onward. Math teachers who rap the times tables and history teachers who sing the amendments have mastered the art of challenging students in a more motivating and memorable way.

Unaware teachers expect students to suffer through assignments. These teachers believe that the material, not teachers' attitudes, is at fault. Because material seems dull to them, unaware teachers talk about material in a way that also makes it dull for students.

The unaware teacher believes learners will sink or swim

Unaware teachers believe that learners either get it or they don't. They believe that some students are "good at math" or "excellent writers" and the rest will never be. These teachers present the material once and move on. They don't reach out to kids who didn't get it the first time because they have already taught that material.

A now-or-never attitude toward student learning is unrealistic. Housepainters spend months learning to perfectly cut in the edges. Edison tried thousands of experiments. Students need time to master new material or skills. They are better served by mentors who say, "I think you can do it and I'll stand by you until you do."

A sink-or-swim mentality often triggers fear in learners. Part of the fear is immediate, the feeling of, *Oh no, I will look foolish!* slows the brain. The learner feels incompetent when new material doesn't make sense. Gaps in understanding lead to confusion and then to resignation. If learners say to themselves, *I'll never get this,* the belief becomes true.

Teachers with a sink-or-swim attitude are unlikely to use peer-to-peer tutoring to allow students to help each other. They are not likely to provide those who pass the test with an enrichment activity while they reteach the rest of the class. Reteaching and retesting waste time, they believe, because they are unaware that students learn at different speeds through different channels. Kids who don't comprehend the information the first time are ignored.

Questions to grow by

☐ Do you consciously create engaging introductions for lessons?

☐ When you see a student struggling or failing, do you think of ways to help him succeed?

☐ As you teach facts, do you point out their implications and applications, in other words, why they are interesting and useful?

The Aware Teacher

Aware teachers believe that assignments are necessary but not exciting. They have awakened to the possibility that students can improve their comprehension and performance if given support. The idea is unevenly applied, however, because these teachers are not yet practiced in effectively challenging all pupils.

The aware teacher encourages some students to think some of the time

Teachers are often inspired by a subset of the class. Some might call this group the teacher's pets. An alternative explanation is that some students are easier for certain teachers to understand or relate to. Perhaps the teacher and some students share a similar upbringing. Perhaps a teacher is trained to handle certain groups—special education students or gifted and talented students, for instance. For whatever reason, teachers may have an affinity for certain students and encourage them more.

A teacher may linger longer at certain desks because personalized instruction yields positive improvement with those students. A teacher may wait longer after posing a question so a particular student can collect his thoughts. The teacher believes that this student can rise to the challenge. The teacher is correct, but the teacher is not yet capable of deeply believing in every student.

Uneven attention also occurs in the types of challenges teachers offer. Teachers who enjoy competition hold frequent competitions in the classroom. These are effective with the subset of the class that enjoys competition as much as the teacher. Individuals who don't enjoy competition won't benefit as greatly. Some cultural groups think that standing out from the group is rude, and students from those cultures are likely to feel uncomfortable with activities that require strong individuality. Shy students or slow workers feel diminished if they cannot shout answers as rapidly as the competition demands. Gifted students may correctly answer many questions, but they may not be challenged at all.

A teacher who loves word games or word play may challenge kids with puzzles or similar activities. These offerings are a natural fit for some students but of little interest to others. Some kids are challenged while some are annoyed, bored, or simply not reached, although the teacher intends to include everyone.

Another problem lies in differing individual response to challenges. One 17-year-old told his father he wanted to enlist in the military, probably the U.S. Marine Corps.

"You'll never make it as a marine!" his father scoffed.

"That's when I decided I had to prove him wrong," he said. By the age of 20 he was a Marine sergeant. A different boy might have wilted at the father's comment and abandoned the idea of enlisting.

Predicting student reactions is difficult. Some people love a challenge, convinced they will succeed. Certain students love to prove teachers wrong. If an instructor tells them they cannot do something, they exert great effort to complete the task. Other students resist challenges because they believe failure is a personal indictment; they accept the teacher's assessment and quickly give up. Blanket challenges do not equally test all students.

We should not abandon any specific approach; rotating through a series of approaches is more effective. This way, all class members eventually meet the sort of challenge that best suits their style and personality.

The aware teacher promotes the idea that lessons are necessary, though not exciting

Aware teachers believe that lessons are essential, but because they rarely consider the day's lesson interesting, students probably won't either. Positive emotion is a great tool for improving learning, so excluding it from the learning process wastes valuable opportunities. Laughter, engagement, delight at mastery—these emotional states burn information into the brain. If teachers never provide memorable presentations, should they be surprised if kids don't love learning or recall much information? Research on workplace behavior suggests that positive emotions and well-being translate to greater productivity (Harter, Schmidt, & Keyes, 2003). The same is true in the classroom.

Simply stating the day's objective and explaining why the skill or knowledge is useful help students think positively about challenges. Goals and rewards are often used, but they may not appeal to all students. For instance, if teachers tell students that they can go to recess as soon as they finish a task, some students might be more motivated to complete the task, but slow workers cannot work any faster and still learn well.

A reward for finishing is an external matter. Many teachers use reward systems, believing these make students try harder. Surprisingly, research suggests that when students work for extrinsic rewards like candy they like the subject less. Similarly, students who are frequently rewarded are less generous and cooperative than those who aren't rewarded (Kohn, 2006). Enthusiasm is gradually linked only to the reward rather than the experience itself, and kids no longer find learning intrinsically satisfying.

Intrinsic rewards are more productive for student learning. A teacher who high-fives learners in celebration of a triumph or intermittently points out achievements with handwritten notes is keeping the reward close to the learning experience. If a teacher allows time at the end of the day to encourage pupils to name their day's accomplishments, this reminds students they can successfully meet challenges. External, tangible rewards can obscure the importance of the learning itself.

The aware teacher offers little support to students who try to meet challenges

When a challenge is given, aware teachers have few support systems in place to ensure student success. In 4th grade, my teacher Mrs. Williams planned a personal health and hygiene unit complete with a wall chart from a toothpaste company. Every day for a month we recorded whether we had brushed our teeth, combed our hair, and so forth. Mrs. Williams probably believed that filling in the chart would challenge us to neaten up. I brushed my teeth at bedtime but forgot in the morning, so I had blank spaces where stars belonged. I was quite embarrassed because my shortcomings were so visible. Looking back, my behavior might have changed if Mrs. Williams had sent a letter to my parents explaining what was expected or sent home a checklist. Mrs. Williams offered no support for student success.

"Why didn't you just do what was expected?" some might ask. "You were 10 years old! Why should a teacher coddle kids?"

While student independence is the ultimate goal, kids need teachers' assistance to achieve this objective. By the end of week two, the chart made it clear who was meeting the hygiene goals and who wasn't. Mrs. Williams simply pointed out who was not meeting the goal instead of taking steps to change the behavior of those who were struggling. To get students to change, a teacher must intervene. Helping students succeed is not cheating or coddling; assistance provides learning opportunities. All children start out unaware, and they need support and help to learn and change.

Questions to grow by

☐ Can you look for ways to help more students stretch their thinking more often?

☐ Do you try to find something interesting in every topic and mention it to students?

☐ When you ask students to attempt challenging tasks, do you provide tips or steps to assist their progress?

☐ Do you have an enrichment plan for students who instantly understand each new concept?

Self-Development

• In order to challenge every student, we need to determine what each student already knows. Assessing prior knowledge is essential to designing lessons and activities that cause each learner to stretch. Evaluation of existing comprehension can be done by the teacher or by the student himself. Toward that end, the KWL strategy (what do we Know, what do we Want to know, and later, what have we Learned) can be adapted in many ways. Use KWL as a whole-class introduction and you will get a sense of what various individuals know and what excites a given student or the whole class. Students will work harder to learn things that they have helped to choose.

• Use part or all of the KWL strategy as a frequent student journal entry to find out who needs help and with what. The "what do we want to know" question also provides an invitation for quick learners to help design their own enrichment activities.

• More informally, you can apply KWL in conversations with students as you move up and down the rows. Asking what they understand and what they still need to learn will allow you to better focus your assistance. Ask students who have mastered the basics what they find interesting, desirable, or fun. Then ask them to investigate those options to pursue as a tangential learning challenge.

Collegial Support

• Confidence improves work-related performance. Encourage colleagues to enumerate their accomplishments in order to help them improve their own confidence and performance. Suggest that they teach the same habit to their students.

• Hope is a combination of goal-oriented energy and planned pathways to reach those goals. Talk with colleagues to help them formulate a series of intermediate goals that will guide them to the hoped-for outcome.

• Optimism views bad events as temporary and attributes good outcomes to effort and focused talent. Redirect conversations to help colleagues view bad events as fleeting. Help them to list the attributes and actions that will lead to solutions and good outcomes. Suggest that they share these thought processes with their students.

• Resilience is a combination of an acceptance of reality, the belief that what we do means something, and the ability to adapt and improvise. If you help colleagues to reframe experiences in the light of these three attributes, they—and their students—can reach extraordinary heights. (Adapted from Luthans, Youssef, & Avolio, 2007.)

The Capable Teacher

Capable teachers have a positive attitude toward challenges. They devise general support systems to help students reach objectives that are tough to master. They assist students in thinking deeply or broadly at least part of the time, though these teachers' approaches are still uneven or inconsistent at times. Capable teachers invite students to learn by indicating that at least some assignments are interesting to some or all pupils.

The capable teacher often encourages thinking, but in inconsistent ways

A true challenge is stretching to learn and use something new, difficult, or complex. The best teachers frequently offer such challenges. Capable teachers do this part of the time. To effectively challenge students, teachers must work at the edge of students' understanding, encouraging them to weather some confusion in order to eventually reach new understandings. Because students work at different levels of understanding, simultaneously succeeding with every learner is not easy.

Competent teachers organize their teaching to create a steady, forward momentum. They know what they will teach today and what they will teach next week. They have clear expectations for students and create a setting where students move toward meeting them. These teachers may find it difficult, however, to challenge gifted or accelerated students who already possess a large body of knowledge.

For instance, a kindergarten teacher is charged with teaching the alphabet, some phonics, and basic sight words to her students—the beginnings of reading. What happens when a bright child enters her class reading at the 4th grade level? Her lesson plans challenge nonreaders, but not advanced readers. In desperation, she puts the gifted student in the corner with a basket of books at the 4th grade reading level and continues.

Sometimes grade-level expectations create a glass ceiling for certain students who have the ability to exceed them, but whose teachers have dozens of other students to guide toward those expectations. Structuring assignments to provide boundaries but no limits is one solution to address gifted students. "Illustrate your understanding of photosynthesis" is an assignment that can be met in cut-and-paste fashion by one student and with a three-dimensional wall mural by another. Both have provided an assessment tool. And both can perform to the level of their ability and interest.

The capable teacher promotes some lessons as interesting to some students

"I am so excited," says Mrs. Hopkins to her Spanish class. "Today we're learning reflexive verbs. I have been looking forward to this since September. You'll love them because we can do so many fun things with them in the stories we act out. Reflexive verbs cover all the things we do for ourselves—comb our hair, brush our teeth, things like that. You'll wonder how we got this far without them."

After an introduction like that, who wouldn't pay attention? Good teachers entice students to learn. They believe lessons are interesting at least part of the time. Mrs. Hopkins cares so much about reflexive verbs that she thinks students will also.

● ● ● **TIP** ● ● ●

Read W. Edwards Deming's 14 Points for principles of management at www.lii.net/deming.html. Ponder how his business philosophy, which revolutionized industry, could revolutionize a classroom or a school. Adapt them for use in your classroom and see what happens.

Capable teachers link students' interests with the subject at hand. They show at least part of the class how they can apply knowledge, thus challenging students to master topics. When a geometry teacher mentions the arc of a football in flight, football lovers tune in, though chess players and musicians may not.

Still, grabbing the attention of some students is more desirable than promoting the idea that lessons are merely to be endured.

The capable teacher offers general support for meeting challenges

Capable teachers direct general support toward the whole class or a large portion of the class. Words of encouragement, even rough-edged comments from teachers expressing that everyone can improve, offer student support. Sometimes encouragement may be focused on a group:

> "OK, as we get back into our groups today, I am going to meet with the two groups who haven't been able to agree on their topics," the teacher announces. "I will help you brainstorm so you are prepared for the skits on Monday. All the groups can finish step one today, I think. Ready? Let's go!"

A challenge is clearly stated for all: Complete step one today. The two struggling groups know they will get extra assistance to meet this goal.

The second kind of support is suggested by the teacher's reference to "step one." She refers to a structure for success that has been previously explained: a description or checklist of tasks each group must complete. She teaches this process before she assigns the product. Structures guide students who cannot imagine how to complete their tasks. Teachers who offer challenges along with scaffolding like this improve student achievement. With experience, students will gradually develop the ability to plan on their own.

Outlines of a process to follow can take many forms, such as graphic organizers, Venn diagrams, charts, some homework questions, mock trials, debates, and general habits of mind that the teacher reviews and then repeatedly refers to.

If an English teacher always uses the same set of questions to help students analyze literature, she provides general support for success. For instance: Who is the protagonist? What problem does he face? How is it resolved? As students create mental checklists of information to learn, they meet the challenges inherent in each story or novel.

For difficult, complex, or long-term assignments, more support is needed to guide students to success. In the case of a six-week research project, the guidance about when and how to complete the important steps and finish the assignment will be quite specific. New researchers need an assignment time line to set mileposts on the road to completion. Some teachers set a series of interim deadlines and give points or completion credit for each major step. Students are spared much difficulty when teachers take this approach; they are less likely to procrastinate and find themselves in a crisis on the day before the project is due. In industry, this approach is called project management, so students are also learning a real-world skill.

Some students panic when a large challenge is placed before them. Focusing on and completing minor tasks along the way help manage fear. As each step is completed, what seemed like an impossible challenge becomes possible. When students prove to themselves that they can meet a challenge, they are encouraged to try again and again.

Setting appropriate goals with and for students is a powerful tool (Locke & Latham, 1990). Goals encourage students to direct effort, over a period of time, toward a valued objective. The combination of effort, persistence, and direction carries us measurably further than we go without goals. Goal setting is a valuable tool that capable teachers use to help students reach goals they might otherwise not achieve.

Questions to grow by

☐ Do you think about the level of challenge in each of your lessons and make sure each lesson slightly stretches students' thinking?

☐ After thinking about the characteristics of your lessons, can you alter less interesting aspects to make them more appealing to you and to students?

☐ Have you built options into lessons so students can work at different levels?

☐ Do you provide processes and methods to help students conquer each new challenge you give them?

The Inspired Teacher

Inspired teachers develop reliable systems that help students deeply and broadly think about a wide variety of matters. These teachers consistently plan engaging and varied assignments. Students are eager to learn, not because of gimmicks, bribes, or flash, but because the lessons are demanding and well suited to students' needs. Learning activities are structured so that success is likely, no matter how difficult the challenge. Thanks to such teachers, students build true self-esteem by performing difficult tasks well.

The inspired teacher consistently and systematically challenges students to think

Once teachers know material well, they notice which students do and do not understand the material. Teachers use their experience to improve the next delivery of the material. Capable students usually grasp material on the first presentation and thus find much of school repetitive; therefore, inspired teachers incorporate new challenges into every lesson.

If a teacher with five years of experience knows that half of the students won't know the names and locations of all the U.S. states in September, she plans accordingly. She is also aware that the other half of the class will know the states. How can she challenge one group without boring the other? By systematically varying approaches, she won't duplicate learners' previous experiences. In all likelihood, the students' previous teacher asked them to fill in blank maps, so this teacher plans something different.

First she combines map skills with communication skills in the form of a guessing game. She provides blank maps to pairs of students and asks them to give verbal clues that describe the state without pointing to it. Oklahoma might be described as a cooking pot or as a shape with a long, skinny rectangle on the left side. Describing the shape of the state challenges the student who knows Oklahoma's location; locating the state on the map challenges the student who doesn't. Both students are challenged.

She may also plan a learning-by-moving experience for identifying the locations of states. She buys a large cardboard puzzle map, randomly hands out pieces, and lines students along the back wall.

"When I say 'start,' go to the center table and assemble the map without talking. You can point or gesture but do not talk or guide someone's hand. Let's see how long it takes."

Creating a new experience to learn the states, other than labeling them on a blank map, involves a different pathway of learning.

"You did it! It took 3 minutes and 42 seconds," she announces. "Do you think you could do it any faster if you tried again?"

"Yes!" the class clamors.

She slides the state shapes back into the box, stirs, and redistributes them. She doesn't give learners the same puzzle pieces they used before.

"OK, start." The class strives to beat the clock. Minutes later everyone has learned something about maps and about cooperation, knocking 70 seconds off their time. Then, she asks students to consider the relative locations of the states.

"What state is east of Kansas? Which states are neighbors to Kentucky?"

Perhaps the teacher combines a math lesson on scale with an art activity and map learning. She assigns pairs to draw two states to scale. After a mini-lesson, partners draw a grid and then sketch the states as accurately as possible.

For the art activity, students add symbols—cattle or oil derricks for Texas, and skis and poles for Vermont or Colorado. Then the map, drawn to scale, can be assembled. The class examines all states and discusses the meaning of their symbols while they are learning the shape, location, and name of every state.

Wise teachers constantly challenge students to learn new things and in new ways. They stretch the thinking of those who already know the data, while teaching the data to those who don't. As a part of encouraging students to reach, great teachers enlist them in assessing the quality of their work, not just the quantity. If students ask how long an essay must be, teachers explain that the purpose is to express their ideas clearly but succinctly; the paper should be long enough to convey their meaning with cogent examples, but not wordy or repetitive. Such a statement challenges students to use criteria beyond word count. Such guidelines also require the teacher to judge content rather than overemphasizing length. In a research project a teacher might require 100 note cards but remind students that they may actually have to use more to capture all the information needed to fully develop the project. Inviting students to determine such issues themselves and allowing them to practice making decisions is another way to help students reach new goals.

Questions in the Classroom

In her book *"The Having of Wonderful Ideas" and Other Essays on Teaching and Learning* (1996), Eleanor Duckworth writes about questions in the classroom:

"First, the right question at the right time can move students to peaks in their own thinking that result in significant steps forward and real intellectual excitement; and second, although it is almost impossible for any adult to know exactly the right time to ask a specific question of a specific child—especially for a teacher who is concerned with 30 or more children— children can raise the right question for themselves if the setting is right. Once the question is raised, they are moved to tax themselves to the fullest to find an answer.... Having confidence in one's ideas does not mean 'I know my ideas are right'; it means 'I am willing to try out my ideas.'"

This commentary suggests that teachers should bend great effort into creating an environment where students are likely to challenge themselves with curiosity, questions, and investigations; such an environment is no accident.

The inspired teacher varies lessons to make them engaging, appropriate, and challenging

Let's say that an economics teacher wants to teach how the Great Depression affected businesses. She resists the impulse to lecture every day. Instead she designs a series of experiences that convey the concepts she wants the class to understand.

As an introduction she hands out and explains graphs of unemployment rates, housing starts, and incomes for the years 1929–1939. The next day each student is asked to imagine a store or business that might have existed during the Depression and to sketch it on paper, including stick figures to represent the number of employees the business might have employed. The teacher distributes Monopoly money. Students go through three cycles of purchasing and layoffs. As they cross out employees and see profits dwindle, students grasp the Depression in a different way from yesterday's graphs.

On the third day, students view a clip from the movie *It's a Wonderful Life*. Jimmy Stewart's character discusses a run on the bank and how savings and loans invest their money in the community. Students also learn about inflation and deflation.

Then the teacher introduces real people, using biographic data from the Internet to show individual farmers, shop owners, workers, and students. Each student reads the challenges one person faced during the decade of the Depression and writes a narrative or journal about that individual. Students study the textbook, with an eye for how each event or trend would affect the life of the individual they have been assigned to write about. With such varied and challenging assignments, students are persuaded to comprehend and care about the material.

If the teacher announces a goal for every student to understand mixed fractions before recess, she employs a different kind of challenge. Pairs can quiz each other or individuals might be invited up to the front of the room to explain the concept until everyone grasps the new idea. When teachers and students work together to monitor whether the class meets the needs of every individual, the challenge makes old material feel new.

Still, mastery is the goal, not speed. Some students take more time than others, and teachers must respect their learning pace. Learning faster doesn't predict future success. For an amazing exploration of the power of learning steadily but not speedily, read Jon Franklin's Pulitzer Prize–winning article "The Ballad of Old Man Peters" from his book *Writing for Story* (1986).

Using technology can make many lessons more engaging. Creating a podcast, interacting via the Internet with learners in another nation, and evaluating the reliability of data from multiple sources make a lesson seem real and important, partly because classroom walls disappear. Similarly, walking to a nearby location and interviewing people with pertinent information is engaging and challenging, yet possible for students at any level to complete.

Part of offering appropriate challenges is encouraging students to be themselves. In the book *Now, Discover Your Strengths* (Buckingham & Clifton, 2001), the authors emphasize developing our strengths and talents, rather than shoring up our weaknesses. Improving weaknesses may bring about average performance in that area, but building on strengths allows outstanding, one-of-a-kind contributions.

Teachers don't always recognize their students' strengths. A so-called weakness may be an unrecognized strength. A speaker once told our staff, "Your greatest weakness and your greatest strength can be the very same thing. All through school I was always in trouble for my big mouth, and now, how do I make my living? With my big mouth!" Sometimes the behaviors we see in misbehaving children are the very traits that will make successful adults.

The inspired teacher structures activities to ensure students can meet challenges

Inspired teachers create scaffolding or support for every challenge they give pupils. They don't just assign tasks; they provide road maps students can use to perform well. Part of a road map includes well-known techniques for effective instruction.

A skillful math teacher who presents something new—say, quadratic equations—begins with an overview to help students see the point of the lesson, perhaps mentioning how the skill is applied in real-life situations. Then he explains the process, demonstrating problems on the projector. When students seem to catch on, he asks them to do a different sample problem either alone or with a partner, and then he checks to see whether they did it correctly. He may go back to the board for more explanation if necessary. Then he assigns a few practice problems for students to complete in class, so he can check again that each student understands. Only then does he allow unsupervised students to do a set of quadratic equations for homework. This structure is chosen to ensure that students succeed. We usually expect a math teacher to demonstrate to his students how to solve each new type of algebra problem. In other courses, demonstrations are equally helpful, though they may be rare.

Skilled teachers use another method, too—individualizing. This technique ensures that every single learner has access to, or can create within the space the teacher provides, the structure that will most help the student. Thus, one student receives extra time during recess or reading time to continue working. Another is tutored during lunch or recess by the teacher. Parent or senior volunteers coach several more. Other students use special tools—tactile letters, a Braille translation of the book, a taped version of the lesson. A hyperactive student has permission to pace along the back wall when sitting becomes impossible. The test-phobic child may be quizzed orally, and the dyslexic student may take tests before school when they can be read aloud with the teacher. Some students just need time and space to ponder. Identical instruction is not always fair and equitable. As time and energy permit, inspired teachers attempt to guarantee success for all learners at all times.

When I was in 7th grade, our English teacher provided a private challenge to gifted students. She encouraged various students to learn stories by memory and act them out for speech contests that were held by organizations in our area. We spent time after school rehearsing and presenting our dramatic readings to small assemblies of younger students. Then we competed for lapel pins and certificates at the contests. This challenge enriched our language arts experience beyond what was offered in the classroom.

Tim Russert, late host of *Meet the Press*, credited his 8th grade teacher, Sister Mary Lucille, with providing a life-changing experience for him. He told an interviewer that he was spending most of his time in the back row, shooting paper clips and spit wads, when Sister Mary Lucille appointed him editor of the school paper. Decades later his voice still conveyed a warm amazement at the level of pride and accomplishment that responsibility had given him.

Teachers do not encourage students to reach by assigning more of the same. A gifted student who finishes early should not be assigned 10 additional questions for extra credit. Such students need to be introduced to more challenging assignments that will fully engage them.

Inspired teachers consistently call forth the best from students. Jaime Escalante, who was portrayed in the 1988 movie *Stand and Deliver*, is a perfect example. Escalante challenged inner-city students to master calculus, something most people thought was impossible. Precisely because of the structures he gave to his students, they were able to meet the goals he proposed. Challenges that seem impossible to students can be met if they have a skilled teacher who offers varied, demanding lessons with the kind of encouragement and support systems that bring about success. The best classrooms have boundaries but no limits on student learning.

Actions to grow by

☐ We often assume students don't know what we are about to present. Challenge your own assumptions by pre-testing the class. Pre-tests reveal which students will need to be challenged by deeper or more extensive material, allowing you to make sure everyone is exploring new territory.

☐ Experiment with assignments and assessments that ask students to try unusual activities or reorganize their own knowledge. Such techniques require students to reach while hardly aware they are doing so. For instance, if you ask groups to act out cell division, they will need to assign the roles of cell parts and convert static charts from their text into live action and movement, leading to deeper understanding.

☐ Respect the peculiar interests of individuals rather than dismissing them as irrelevant to the topic at hand. When you link students' skills and interests to classroom learning, you see them reach far beyond what you would have imagined.

For Information and Inspiration

Edutopia, www.edutopia.org

National Association of Gifted Children, www.nagc.org

Buckingham, M., & Clifton, D. O. (2001). *Now, discover your strengths.* New York: Free Press.

Carolan, J., & Guinn, A. (2007, February). Differentiation: Lessons from master teachers. *Educational Leadership, 64*(5), 44–47.

Closing achievement gaps. (2004, November). *Educational Leadership, 62*(3).

Collins, M., & Tamarkin, C. (1990). *Marva Collins' way.* Los Angeles: J. P. Tarcher.

Duckworth, E. (1996). *"The having of wonderful ideas" and other essays on teaching and learning* (2nd ed.). New York: Teachers College Press.

Franklin, J. (1986). *Writing for story: Craft secrets of dramatic nonfiction by a two-time Pulitzer Prize winner.* New York: Atheneum.

Harter, J. K., Schmidt, F. L., & Keyes, C. L. (2003). Well-being in the workplace and its relationship to business outcomes: A review of the Gallup studies. In C. L. Keyes & J. Haidt (Eds.), *Flourishing: The positive person and the good life* (pp. 205–224). Washington, DC: American Psychological Association.

Kohn, A. (2006). *Beyond discipline: From compliance to community, 10th anniversary edition.* Alexandria, VA: ASCD.

Liker, J. K. (2004). *The Toyota way: 14 management principles from the world's greatest manufacturer.* New York: McGraw-Hill.

Locke, E. A., & Latham, G. P. (1990). *A theory of goal setting and task performance.* Englewood Cliffs, NJ: Prentice Hall.

Luthans, F., Youssef, C. M., & Avolio, B. J. (2007). *Psychological capital: Developing the human competitive edge.* New York: Oxford University Press.

Musca, C. (Producer), & Menéndez, R. (Director). (1988). *Stand and deliver* [Motion picture]. United States: Warner Bros.

Reaching the reluctant learner. (2008, March). *Educational Leadership, 65*(6).

Vygotsky, L. S. (1978). *Mind in society: The development of higher psychological processes*. Cambridge, MA: Harvard University Press.

Weinstein, R. S. (2002). *Reaching higher: The power of expectations in schooling*. Cambridge, MA: Harvard University Press.

13

Helping Students Understand Complexity

Complexity is so, well, complex. If an issue has two or three or many sides, then we must investigate details to come to a conclusion. Short and sweet answers are easier to convey to students than detailed and accurate answers. Helping students understand complexity is a difficult challenge for teachers. Beginning teachers provide students with simplified polarities rather than rich continuums.

In education, shared assumptions underlie most types of tests. Multiple-choice tests are designed around the belief that there is one right answer to each question and that the rest are all wrong, and equally so. Yet I have read hundreds of test questions over the years that could easily be interpreted in many different ways. Essay questions also may have many interpretations. Once my 15-year-old son came home complaining that in order to answer an essay question on the state social studies test, he had to write from a viewpoint demonstrating patriotism. He felt demonstrating patriotism was a separate issue from proving he could write a cogent essay using social studies content. He spent the test period writing an essay critiquing the question itself and earned a score of zero. The next year, he told me he planned to answer without critiquing the question. That year he earned a high score.

In general, education emphasizes convergent thinking, such as multiple-choice test questions. Students are asked to master the facts of conventional wisdom so they can take their place in society. Yet invention and creativity demand something else—divergent thinking. This is the ability to think of different possibilities and alternatives outside the well-worn path of conventional thinking. Divergent thinking is what powered Edison, Einstein, and many entrepreneurs.

In addition to divergent and convergent thinking, a distinction must be made between surface learning and deep learning. Surface learning includes no deep involvement with the task. A student may focus on memorization or follow procedures without much thought simply to learn the basics and move on. In contrast, deep learning occurs when someone strives to thoroughly understand and finds meaning and satisfaction in the task at hand. The learner actually sees information in a new way after deep learning (Bond et al., 2000, p. 61).

Teachers' actions have a profound influence on which type of learning students pursue. If teachers always present facts or concepts one at a time, never showing relationships among topics, students will probably experience surface learning. Teachers who connect various aspects of a subject into an integrated whole, however, show the complex relationships to students at a more abstract level, prompting learners to alter their outlook. Teachers who strive to explain complexities help students achieve deep learning.

The Unaware Teacher

Unaware teachers often assume many ideas are too hard for their students to comprehend. Their instinct is to simplify information for learners in order to provide an entry point. This is often a necessary first step; however, learning mustn't end there. Students need to glimpse the fascinating and tangled nature of complex issues for themselves.

Three Levels of Knowing

Simplicity. Children and uninformed adults see the world this way. They simply live their experiences, happily unaware of what lies beneath the surface of immediate reality.

Complexity. This is the ordinary adult worldview. People are aware of complex systems in nature and reality, but do not discern or attend to patterns that relate various systems to one another.

Informed Simplicity. This is an enlightened view of reality. It is based upon the ability to discern or create clarifying patterns within or among complex mixtures. Pattern recognition within competing considerations is a part of informed simplicity. (Adapted from Frederick, 2007.)

The unaware teacher uses vague strategies for strengthening thinking

How do teachers teach students how to think? Asking learners to repeat a fact is easy; showing them the complex web each fact fits into is much harder. Teachers unaware of the need to explain complexity stick to facts rather than weaving many details into a fabric of comprehension.

Teachers sometimes tell students to think or think harder. When a teacher says such things, she has forgotten that the information is usually not clear or accessible to the child. If the child understood, she would have already used the information. Even so, mere recall is not deep thinking. Unaware teachers may not offer even simple strategies for memorization unless their own teachers or mentors used such tricks. The mnemonic device HOMES helps students remember the names of the Great Lakes, but wise teachers hope students will ultimately learn more deeply than just the memorization of facts.

Children need help puzzling out relationships among different ideas and confronting apparent contradictions. Unaware teachers don't help students follow a train of thought to its conclusion. They believe that student understanding either happens or it doesn't. Sometimes a workshop or book inspires unaware teachers to strengthen students' thinking, but these attempts are not orderly and are soon forgotten or abandoned. A single lesson on word connotations does not show literature students all the subtleties of language used by a prize-winning author. A history teacher may state that Europeans and native peoples saw things differently, but fail to ask pupils to explain the differing views of the two groups.

The unaware teacher uses a hit-or-miss approach to developing student skills

I help an 8-year-old neighbor with her math homework. Melinda often arrives with incomplete information. One day her teacher told the class that the greater than or less than signs are like alligator mouths, but Melinda did not realize the importance of the direction the signs point. For many problems she knew the right answer, yet drew the sign facing the wrong direction. Another day, she brought home an assignment that asked her to use an odometer to relate math skills to real life, but she didn't know what an odometer was or what purpose it served. We sat in the car learning about odometers before she could make sense of the worksheet. Her teacher had good intentions but forgot to fill in necessary information for students before turning them loose to independent practice.

Failing to offer guided practice is a common problem related to this hit-or-miss approach. Students need to perform operations under supervision so teachers can determine whether students' assumptions are correct and complete. After teachers see students succeed, they can allow independent work. Otherwise, students may lock errors into memory, instead of accurate answers.

The unaware teacher expects students to develop thinking skills on their own

Often we hear phrases like "Everyone knows that" or "You know better than that." To the contrary, students may be unaware—after all, they are young and inexperienced. Why assume that students will absorb knowledge and effectively apply it without guidance? Students need systematic help to achieve deep understanding.

At a fast food restaurant, I recently saw "prize-winning" drawings of menu items, each tagged with a child's name, a teacher's name, and a grade level. I wondered what the educational goal of this activity had been—recognition of menu items? Did teachers or principals see this activity as meaningful? Were the activity's implications discussed with students? Using instructional time for this activity seemed hard to justify; I wondered whether the adults involved thought about the complexity of issues surrounding even simple tasks.

At the unaware level, teachers ask their students few meaningful questions. Students tend to take ideas at face value. If they don't intuitively grasp complex issues, their teachers may say that they just don't get it, without giving any help to ensure they do. Unaware teachers don't see that building understanding is possible, no matter how complex the subject.

Questions to grow by

☐ Do you ever unpack your thinking so students can follow your reasoning?

☐ Do you invite students to give reasons for ideas and opinions they express?

☐ Can you make it a practice to mention multiple reasons and contributing factors for every issue?

The Aware Teacher

Aware teachers recognize that students need assistance in order to master complex subject matter. They seek ways to break information into pieces that kids can successfully absorb, often deciding to separately introduce the parts of a complex subject. They may hope that the relationship among the parts will then become clear; however, that intuitive leap doesn't always happen, especially without guidance from the teacher.

The aware teacher promotes segmented thinking and seeks correct answers

Did you have to memorize the periodic table of elements in chemistry? Most chemistry teachers assign it. Some kids immediately memorize every element, without question. Others reject the assignment as tedious. The rest are in between, trying to learn most of it but thinking the assignment rather pointless.

Teachers probably believe that without knowledge of the periodic table the rest of the chemistry course will be impossible, so they insist students memorize it. Quizzes, daily practice, reviews, models of elements—teachers try hard to instill the elements in students' minds. Teaching one element at a time through memorization is a segmented approach. But what choice is there other than memorization? Oxygen always has the same number of electrons; there's only one correct answer. What other possible way is there to teach it?

What if the teacher taught the periodic table as a history of human efforts to understand the invisible world? Teaching how scientist Dmitry Mendeleyev laid out the table according to atomic mass is the story of one human's leap of understanding.

A teacher could help students discover complex relationships between elements by providing copies of the periodic table, explaining the table's layout, and then playing with those relationships.

"Why is hydrogen in the first row, class?" The teacher checks for basic understanding. The answer is that hydrogen has only one ring of electrons.

"What if it had six electrons? What row would it be in? How many electrons would hydrogen need to be in line four?"

These questions stretch thinking. Students must grasp the meaning of the chart to correctly answer.

"Pretend you want a molecule that bonded four hydrogen atoms; which elements could you consider?" This question has several answers. Students must look for atoms that have an outer ring that meets the requirements for hooking onto hydrogen. Clever teachers might ask questions that yield differing results from potential combinations. A poison? A lubricant? A refrigerant? Students grasp the relationships among parts of the chart and the real world. Inspired teachers formulate approaches that challenge and intrigue in this manner. Aware teachers, however, are more likely to stick to simple memorization assignments.

The aware teacher guides the development of thinking skills with worksheets and assignments

Because aware teachers haven't yet found creative assignments that guide and stretch student thinking, they often turn to worksheets to convey each set of facts, without pointing out important relationships and complexities. When there is no time to check student understanding through personal contact, written assignments can be useful. Some teachers manage to meet individual needs by differentiating tasks using worksheets.

But worksheets rarely convey the complexities in a given field of study. Discussions of possibilities, implications, difficult choices, and unsolved mysteries stretch the mind with new ideas.

A teacher who senses that students need to think more analytically may not know how to achieve that goal. *They aren't thinking logically,* he observes. *They need to know about fallacies and how to recognize propaganda. I'll teach them about that.* He introduces seven common types of propaganda, easily taught by definition and examples. Knowing the names of common errors, however, does not ensure students will apply that knowledge to real-life situations. Though the teacher is trying to teach clear thinking, simply presenting definitions and asking students to demonstrate comprehension is not enough. Learners need dynamic interaction with real material. Students need guided practice through written work and extended discussions—activities that reinforce new thinking skills.

The aware teacher focuses student thinking on one skill at a time without making connections

Segmentation occurs when a teacher teaches facts or skills separately without showing relationships between related ideas. Until a teacher absorbs and explores the complexities of the subject matter, he can hardly impart it. There are dozens of details to consider every moment and thousands of interactions each day. Even veteran teachers are still learning more in-depth information from broadcast interviews, casual reading, research, formal training, and personal curiosity.

Most educators believe there is a sequence of learning and using knowledge, as discussed by Jean Piaget (1952), Benjamin Bloom (1984), and others. This sequence represents a developmental hierarchy in thinking that we can use to help students achieve deep understanding.

Consider Bloom's taxonomy. According to Bloom (1984), the most basic level of learning is naming, the awareness of the existence of something nameable. We call it knowledge. We can name cats, dogs, molecules, and people before we fully understand them. Listen to a toddler: "Unca Joe!" he crows, without any sense of what an uncle is.

Next is comprehension. We can explain or define the idea that the name represents. At some point we can tell others what an uncle, a tuba, or a molecule is.

Third is application. We can use the knowledge to interact with other information or connect ideas. That's why computer programs are called applications. We use such programs to record information, pay bills, and send notes. Application is what we do after we have been introduced to something and mastered a few of the fine points.

Fourth is analysis. We are aware of many fine points of a given topic. We can compare and contrast various aspects of the material.

The highest orders of thinking are synthesis and evaluation. Together they form a feedback loop. Synthesis involves gathering all we know, recombining it, and even adding to it, to generate original connections. This is creative thinking. Evaluation involves assigning value to various aspects of learned material and to our own recombinations in order to make judgments about each part. This is critical thinking. After synthesis and evaluation, we may conclude that we need to refine our thinking further, so we again synthesize and then reevaluate as many times as necessary.

All students need to use all these levels of thinking in every area. As we move forward to look at teachers who operate at the capable or inspired level, we observe practitioners who help learners go further and further up this ladder to more complex understanding.

Questions to grow by

☐ Do you invite students to explain how they reached a conclusion?

☐ Do you point out relationships between today's lessons and previously covered material?

☐ Have you used questions with many possible answers to introduce ambiguity to students?

Self-Development

• "And ...?" may be the most powerful question you can ask. Adults and young people alike tend to come up with a quick answer and feel they have answered the question. Almost all issues contain complexity if you invite yourself and others to go beyond surface considerations.

• Take time to be curious. Look up key terms or unfamiliar words just to broaden your own understanding. Ask why. Consider possibilities. Play with alternatives. Question your habits. Do something out of the ordinary. Share the fruits of your inquiries with students.

Collegial Support

• Use staff meetings, departmental meetings, and professional development sessions as platforms for growth. At each meeting, ask someone to prepare a short brief on an important issue or new discovery or to share an effective lesson. Unless teachers know the complexities of a subject, they cannot share it with students. Teachers must be lifelong learners who keep up with new developments in their fields.

• Start an informal support group. Subscribe to a magazine and discuss it with a peer. Start a book group with one or more colleagues and discuss one chapter at each meeting. Divide the supplemental materials that come with your text and hold meetings to critique content and applicability.

The Capable Teacher

Capable teachers show students the relationships between various facts and issues. They teach strategies students can use to think more analytically, and they ask students to practice using them. These strategies allow students to grasp tough or unfamiliar material without feeling overwhelmed.

The capable teacher encourages connecting new information to prior learning

When capable teachers present new material, they first find out what students already know. Sometimes this is formal, as in a pre-test. If a pre-test with four parts reveals that most students know about sections one and three, some know about section four, and almost no one can answer section two, this allows teachers to accordingly adjust lessons.

Sometimes the assessment is done in the teacher's mind, using an intuition based on experience. The internal conversation may sound like this: *What have we covered so far, and what do I know that 9th graders almost never know about this material?* Ten years of experience may tell this instructor that 9th graders don't know what primary sources are and that they will need a demonstration.

Capable teachers deliver intellectual honesty in a way that isn't discouraging. A Spanish teacher who teaches language through stories and acting still understands that she has to teach stem-changing verbs. She doesn't skip the hard skills; she believes her students can and should learn about these verbs.

"OK, class," she announces on a Monday. "You may not like this as much as our stories, but we need to learn stem-changing verbs. We're going to work on them for two weeks. I'll help you see how they work. After that, when we go back to our stories, you'll be able to use a whole new set of verbs, and use them correctly. You'll need these if you go on in Spanish. So stick with me. I promise you will understand by the end of next week."

The teacher clearly states the class goals and how they will benefit students—allowing them to create more complex stories, for instance. She has a time line and promises to guide them past their confusion into a new comfort zone. Students believe that she has the expertise to help them succeed by next Friday. If one approach doesn't work, she will find another, because she is intent on making sure every student moves to a new level of competence.

As capable teachers cover complex material, they relate it to students' existing knowledge. Sometimes this involves a brief restatement of background material to orient the listener to where the new material connects. Teachers who are good at teaching complexity use various analogies in their instruction. Certain parts of topics parallel other aspects of daily life or common knowledge. Wise teachers build bridges between lessons and real-life knowledge.

For example, Sharon Bowman, a corporate training leader, explains the "reticular activator" to executives and professors who need to teach more compellingly.

The reticular activator is the size of your pinkie, she says, but "it acts as the brain secretary." She tells her audience that it is designed to handle the routine stuff like driving that you've done before so your thinking brain can go off duty. If a dog darts in front of your car, the brain secretary "bangs on the door of the thinking brain" so it can swing into action (Sonner, 2005). When you teach in a routine, the brain secretary tells the thinking brain to take a break. So mix it up. Surprise students. Move. Whisper. Shout. Keep that thinking brain aware.

Bowman uses two familiar ideas—pinkies and secretaries— to introduce the reticular activator, clearly an unfamiliar and complex topic. And she provides tips for trainers that they will not soon forget.

The capable teacher focuses student thinking on the relationships among facts

Teachers can note related ideas in a subject area only when they themselves become highly informed about the details of subject-matter relationships.

The first year I taught English, I faced my own shaky understanding of the difference between adjectives and adverbs. I got As on all my grammar tests and could recite the definitions. But the idea of standing in front of a class and declaring positively that the words they had written in their homework sentences were one or the other—yikes! I did some very focused studying to learn the complexities of those two parts of speech to master my skills.

Two decades later, I was thinking differently. I became fascinated by words that are shape-shifters—acting as one part of speech in one sentence and as a different part of speech in another. I saw students flawlessly use these words in their sentences but become confused if I asked them to look at the roles the words played—in other words, to name the parts of speech. By then I was working on a color-coded way to point out the roles words played in sentences. I had developed clearer ways to point out these word relationships than when I first taught the subject. Color-coding became one tool among many for deepening my students' understanding.

The capable teacher shows strategies for comparing and contrasting

When we use analogies we are comparing and contrasting. Analogies show us how two unlike things are alike in at least one way. Teachers point out similarities to increase learners' understanding. They admit there are also differences, so as not to mislead learners. Rather than teaching facts at the level of naming or defining, teachers ask students to think about the implications of these facts. This strategy moves students higher on the thinking ladder, to applying or analyzing what they have heard, and thus helps students create deeper understanding.

For a familiar approach, consider using Venn diagrams. Students can fill this sort of graphic with appropriate facts and thus consider the relationship between two things.

Venn diagrams differ from simple worksheets because learners have to generate their own data, not just move information around. A Venn diagram has many right answers. Students commonly include ideas the teacher hasn't considered. Thus, the diagram allows learners some creativity and the chance to think broadly. The diagram may generate some argument if students disagree about the similarities of two topics. Such intellectual arguments are good; they allow students to defend their definitions and consider different interpretations.

Venn diagrams are effective in many subjects—science, math, social studies, sports—but there are other ways to encourage students to compare and contrast. English teachers have long assigned essays to compare or contrast plots, authors, characters, and styles. Debates and well-guided discussions can uncover useful differences and similarities. Asking students to describe and evaluate two points of view can do the same, as in, "List the beliefs of the U.S. government in 1941 regarding Japanese Americans and contrast them with the beliefs of the Japanese Americans who were sent to internment camps." Discussing such beliefs offers a rich opportunity to discover how groups differ and agree in their interpretations. Students gain a more complex understanding of topics through such activities. They come to better understand the decisions and actions of others and even their own understanding.

Questions to grow by

☐ Is connecting to prior learning a part of your thinking and teaching?

☐ Do you highlight comparisons and contrasts between facts and ideas you are teaching?

☐ Have you taught students ways to independently compare and contrast?

☐ Do you refer to connections between today's lesson and the subjects students are covering in other classrooms?

The Inspired Teacher

Inspired teachers have grasped the complexities, contradictions, unknowns, and paradoxes of the subjects they teach. Further, their lessons invite students to see the complex nature of the subject without feeling overwhelmed. Such teachers easily move among details, big pictures, and underlying concepts; they teach students to do the same.

The inspired teacher plans for, teaches for, and inspires deep thinking

When teachers impart complex understanding to students it's no accident. A sudden insight or student comment may help teachers over a rough spot in the lecture or experiment, but only wise teachers carefully note the new information, elaborate on it for the next hour, and use it in some form for years to come. Inspired teachers search for and discover ways to encourage deep thinking day after day, unit after unit.

How does a teacher plan for deep thinking? First, he recognizes that facts alone are not enough and broadens his approach. He remembers that experiences best teach students and so creates a series of experiences in the classroom or beyond its walls. He may surprise, delight, annoy, anger, or soothe, but he keeps students involved. He weaves a web of intellectual connections that are challenging and memorable. He develops new lessons, experiments, assignments, and field trips every year of his career.

Inspired teachers purposefully frame their instruction to elicit higher-level thinking. The assignments and activities offered by inspired teachers require varied and complicated responses from students. Inspired teachers study student responses with objectivity. They point out inconsistencies, misstatements, and errors of fact along with insights and useful connections to stretch students' minds.

Inspired teachers take delight in imparting the details of their field to newcomers. Students can sense this passion for a subject, and they are often inspired to love it and think about it as rigorously as inspired teachers.

A government teacher, two decades into his career, walked his government students down to the courthouse on a yearly field trip to observe a trial.

"Where are the black people?" a black student asked as she looked at the all-white jury pool.

"I don't know," Mr. Bentley answered, "but we'll find out."

The search for the answer lasted seven years and involved hundreds of students. The circuit court claimed that jury selection was random, yet every jury pool they saw contained few blacks. Students observed trial selections and trial juries, kept detailed records, and calculated the proportion of minorities in juries. They compared those figures with census data using statistical methods. They challenged local officials and signed petitions. They examined mailing procedures and the computer programs that churned out summonses. They filed a suit.

Mr. Bentley and his students finally found the problem. A zip code glitch in the computer program that generated the jury summons paperwork eliminated a sizable segment of the eligible population before randomly selecting jurors. Eventually, due to their efforts, the problem was fixed. The complexity of their research and the difficulty of discovering the source of the problem were immense. In the face of officials who discounted the idea that a problem could even exist, students who participated in the multiyear endeavor became aware of the difficulty, yet possibility, of a deeper understanding. Mr. Bentley took them on a memorable journey of discovery through analysis, evaluation, and synthesis.

Helping Students Understand Complexity

Roger Taylor (1999) suggests the regular use of dilemmas to help students understand complexity. He encourages teachers to develop questions that push students to consider the various issues within a situation. For instance, a teacher could present the following:

> "Imagine you are a wartime pilot. You are scheduled to take off when a panicked native interpreter describes a threat to his life and asks for passage out of the area. You know the rules do not permit you to take him, but that he may die if you do not. How do you decide what to do?"

Discussion of such questions allows students to confront how people make difficult decisions. There are endless quandaries, challenges, and dilemmas that teachers might present that are appropriate to any subject matter. Taylor suggests forced associations ("How is a carrot like a submarine? How is a skyscraper like the human brain?"), involvements as imagined participant, reorganization, and others. In each case, the fact that no single, certain answer exists allows students to grapple with complexity deeply and often.

The inspired teacher helps students generalize or transfer knowledge

If we observe inspired teachers, we hear a series of examples, analogies, anecdotes, current event and historic references, and made-up scenarios. Such inclusions not only keep listeners interested, they also illustrate connections. These references help students form links between new and previously held knowledge.

If a science teacher says, "Thank President John Kennedy for your sunglasses," he arouses curiosity. He then explains how the moon mission required the development of new materials and that Kennedy was the first to challenge the United States to go to the moon. Asking pupils to think about polycarbonates that darken in the sun encourages a class to consider physics and chemistry in a new way. Another teacher weaves an elaborate and dramatic story:

> "You wake up and realize you overslept. The bus will be here in four minutes. You leap out of bed, jerk on yesterday's jeans, run your fingers through your hair, grab a candy bar from your nightstand, and dash out the door. You run a block and a half. As you come within sight of the bus stop, you see the bus pulling up, so you accelerate. You leap into the bus, the driver closes the door behind you, and you collapse into a seat, panting heavily. What just happened in your body? Why do we pant after exertion?"

The teacher connects students' daily lives to science. To consider the respiration and the circulatory system, students generalize from their own experiences.

If a math teacher wants to teach volume, she might bring in cereal or snack boxes filled with goodies. By asking students to calculate how much the box could hold and measure how much product it actually does hold, the lesson connects to students' real-world interests. Issues like product settling, marketing, and misleading advertising may arise, and the teacher can use topics that suit the goals she has for today's class or pursue them all. In a follow-up assignment, she may give students sheets of heavy paper to create boxes with dimensions that meet different goals. What shape will look the largest to the consumer? Which box will sit on the shelf with the most stability? What shape will best protect the product inside or hold the most? Even the design of a cereal box is complex, warranting deep observation. The teacher who leads students to thoroughly approach subjects forms deep thinkers.

Teachers help students build on prior knowledge within the context of the course. In the classrooms of great teachers, students are never finished with a topic. Issues are revisited over and over again. Reading teachers know that prediction is a trait of readers with high comprehension, so they will teach and reteach this skill, offering practice all year to create a class with high comprehension. Almost every day the idea will appear: "How do you think this will turn out? Will his wish come true? How might she solve this problem? What do you predict will happen at the end? Make a guess about what the father will do next. Tell me what you would do and if you think this girl will do the same."

Teachers may also have posters or guides on the walls that remind students of important habits of mind they can use to think more deeply. Such guides are not mere wallpaper; they are tools. Teachers encourage students who are stuck to look at a chart to find ideas on how to proceed and invite students to add new guidelines that they discover in their problem-solving experiences.

Many teachers actually develop a long-term theme for the month or year to facilitate student thinking. If a history teacher uses the Declaration of Independence, the U.S. Constitution, or the Magna Carta to provide a reference for historic decisions throughout history, he provides students with a tool for thinking deeply. If students learn about the Constitution and its amendments during the first weeks of a U.S. history course, they can attempt to apply the principles throughout the course. Doing so provides time to compare different periods and ask why actions were taken by the government and its citizens, generating many interpretations of historical facts. How does slavery fit into the Declaration of Independence? Why did women get the right to vote 50 years later than former slaves? Does the First Amendment apply during wartime? Should it? How well do we live up to the ideas expressed in our foundational documents? Students who experience history in this way think differently than those who memorize dates, events, and facts.

The inspired teacher models many strategies for integrating knowledge and forming generalizations

Teachers can be good examples of how students can learn to wrestle with complexity. By verbalizing their own process of generating answers, teachers can demonstrate deep thinking.

Although there may be instances when a teacher has to postpone answering a student question, questions are generally too valuable to forego. Teachers may not be sure of the answer, but even a partial answer is useful to students, especially if teachers reveal how they reach their conclusions. One may say, "I'm not certain, but I know a part of the answer." After listing known facts, the teacher posits an answer and a reason for it, modeling how to approach situations where an answer will have to be discovered, not simply recalled. This approach usually models forming a hypothesis and checking its accuracy, showing students how to productively guess.

Because most children, and many adults, seem to think that teachers should know everything, discovering that teachers must think things through can be surprising. Students appreciate teachers brave enough to say, "I don't know," especially if they add, "But I promise to find out," and then keep that promise.

Expert teachers encourage all learners to understand course content at increasingly complex levels. These teachers expect everyone to be intellectually engaged and to experience the sense of accomplishment that comes with mastering challenging material. Because of the assistance offered by and modeled by these teachers, students identify the structure of a problem, guess wisely, and move toward a stronger and deeper understanding of the subject.

Actions to grow by

☐ Challenge your own thinking by reading the work of writers with whom you disagree, seeking areas of disagreement and agreement. Try to develop a more complex understanding of contributing factors and differing viewpoints, as well as the reasons behind them.

☐ Audit an advanced college course in your chosen subject to observe how the instructor explains new concepts, approaches, and relationships that have emerged since your own training was completed.

☐ To stretch your own thinking, ponder ways to connect your hobbies and personal interests to the subject you teach. How is quilting like the U.S. Constitution? How does sailing or fishing or carpentry relate to math or physical education or business? How is chess parallel to psychology?

For Information and Inspiration

Baker, K. (2007, October). Are international tests worth anything? *Phi Delta Kappan, 89*(2), 101–104.

Bloom, B. S. (1984). *Taxonomy of educational objectives.* Boston: Allyn and Bacon.

Bond, L., Smith, T., Baker, W. K., & Hattie, J. A. (2000). *The certification system of the National Board for Professional Teaching Standards: A construct and consequential validity study.* Greensboro, NC: Center for Educational Research and Evaluation, University of North Carolina.

Chuska, K. R. (2003). *Improving classroom questions* (2nd ed.). Bloomington, IN: Phi Delta Kappa Educational Foundation.

Frederick, M. (2007). *101 things I learned in architecture school*. Cambridge, MA: MIT Press.

McCleelan, T. (2000, May 2). The verdict: Teacher helping to change courtrooms. *Grand Rapids Press*, p. B3.

Piaget, J. (1952). *The origins of intelligence in children* (M. Cook, Trans.). New York: International Universities Press.

Sonner, S. (2005, February 27). How to prevent "death by lecture". *Grand Rapids Press*, p. F4.

Taylor, R. (1999, March). Cutting edge strategies and practical classroom techniques for gifted and highly capable students: A differentiated approach [Seminar]. At Crowne Plaza Hotel, Grand Rapids, MI.

Teaching students to think. (2008, February). *Educational Leadership*, *65*(5).

Afterword

We can all agree that the purpose of teaching is for students to learn. If we don't achieve that end, we might as well save our breath, our time, and our energy. Our goal is to do what is best for our students and their growth and achievement, and to nurture what they bring to the classroom. When we improve as teachers, they reap the benefits.

At the same time, I think it is fair to look at the challenge of teaching more selfishly for a moment. What is the benefit to us, the instructors, when we go through the strain of learning new facts, new interpretations, and new techniques? Actually, the benefits to us are just as great as those that our students accrue; growth keeps us fresh and enthusiastic.

In order to do what is best for students, we also need to do what is best for ourselves. We must attend to our own growth and achievements, and continually improve—if possible, dramatically so. We are always capable of forming new knowledge. The brain constantly modifies itself by building new pathways as needed or reinforcing and broadening commonly used paths.

The fact that the brain is so capable of changing is reassuring; if we haven't become inspired teachers yet, we still can. Being inspired teachers requires that we keep learning so we can make progress toward the inspired level of performance we aspire to. By putting forth effort in our everyday teaching, we can show our inspired natures more and more often. Perhaps no one can be inspired in every way all the time, but inspired teaching remains the goal that motivates and challenges us. My hope is that you keep growing for as long as you are teaching.

Most people have a great teacher in their past who still holds a revered place in their memory. A lot of us chose teaching in part because we wanted to be like that honored individual. We intuitively knew they were special individuals whether or not we could fully articulate the reasons. While these teachers may have been very different, and certainly were not perfect, they each had personal strengths, developed over time, and they consistently did their best, even when difficulties arose.

When we continue to grow in knowledge and skill we too can handle more of those unexpected moments we face in ways that, while not perfect, are effective. Increased skill and growing competence give us a greater sense of control over our work. Difficulties don't disappear, but they are more like hiccups than earthquakes. No matter what a rude or hurtful student may say, we can deal with it. No matter how many interruptions occur—announcements, fire drills, you name it—we can realign ourselves and continue to teach successfully. As we become inspired teachers, we learn to prioritize events so that student growth remains in sharp focus.

Perhaps the *most* important reason to keep growing is that if we don't, we will never believe that our students can. In my experience, individuals who continually berate others, saying they are "not trying" or "will never get this," are themselves people who rarely try and don't believe there is any use in attempting new approaches. Unless *we* are learners—people who don't give up in the face of challenge and who believe the impossible merely takes longer—how can we believe our students to be capable of sustained effort and memorable achievement? When we are learners, we model the behavior we want to see in our classrooms. If we don't live change, we confound our own best visions of tomorrow. We will believe in students only when we can truly believe in ourselves.

Inspired teachers are inspired learners. They make curiosity their constant companion. They wonder, inquire, read, listen, demand, hypothesize, challenge, and question—themselves and others. Becoming an inspired teacher is a journey that takes years or even decades. It requires both self-analysis and interaction with other skilled practitioners who offer suggestions and support.

The growth paths summarized in the charts in the Appendix, adapted from the NBPTS study rubrics (Bond et al., 2000, Appendix F.1), are offered for guidance and inspiration. They provide a supplementary way to look at the descriptive material covered in the chapters.

Use the paths in ways that fit your own style. One person might wisely decide to work first on personal strengths because those are most instinctive and central to one's own skill set. Another may decide to attack areas of personal weakness to weed out serious lapses. A third may follow personal curiosity, while a fourth makes the decision cooperatively with a group of coworkers who plan to work together. All these approaches can be effective because each of us chooses what we need and where to begin.

The most important thing is to take continual action. There may be some discomfort in challenging ourselves to do the unfamiliar, but a new comfort level lies on the other side. Remember that we are never done learning. Even revisiting a path we traveled in the past will yield new insights because we are no longer the same person who traveled it the first time.

Most of us choose to teach because of a sense of idealism and purpose. We genuinely hope to help children and contribute to the future. Not all of us, however, are able to hold onto that optimism. Unaware of many necessary skills and much needed knowledge, and sometimes working in counterproductive environments, we encounter tough realities and become demoralized. At that point, whether days, months, or years into a career, we may question our choice to become teachers and may feel little hope. We lose sight of the difference we've made. We have only three choices at that crossroads: quit (nearly 50 percent of teachers do within five years), become disconnected, or work our way up a steep—but rewarding—growth curve that will eventually allow us to become the teachers we hoped to be from the beginning. This last choice is the one I wish for all teachers, and the one this book is designed to support. May you experience the joy of inspired teaching.

For Information and Inspiration

Danielson, C. (2006). *Teacher leadership that strengthens professional practice*. Alexandria, VA: ASCD.

Pausch, R., & Zaslow, J. (2008). *The last lecture*. New York: Hyperion.

Sherin, M. G. (2000, May). Viewing teaching on videotape. *Educational Leadership, 57*(8), 36–38.

Shulman, L. S. (2004). Teaching as community property: Putting an end to pedagogical solitude. In S. Wilson (Ed.), *The wisdom of practice: Essays on teaching, learning, and learning to teach* (pp. 455–462). San Francisco: Jossey-Bass.

Sykes, G. (1999). Teacher and student learning: Strengthening their connection. In L. Darling-Hammond & G. Sykes (Eds.), *Teaching as the learning profession* (pp. 151–180). San Francisco: Jossey-Bass.

Taylor, J. B. (2006). *My stroke of insight: A brain scientist's personal journey.* New York: Viking.

Teachers as leaders: To help and not hinder. (2007, September). *Educational Leadership, 65*(1).

Wall, B. (2007). *Coaching for emotional intelligence: The secret to developing the star potential in your employees.* New York: Amacom.

Appendix

Summary of Growth Paths

The Path to Knowing the Subject

Unaware →	Aware →	Capable →	Inspired
Knows the subject and organizational methods incompletely	Knows the subject adequately but organizes poorly for learning	Knows the subject and organizes for learning	Understands the subject and organizational methods deeply
Fails to link what students know to the subject	Sometimes checks prior knowledge	Connects information to prior knowledge	Guides students to link prior knowledge to the subject
Rarely makes connections	May link the subject with other knowledge	Connects the subject with other knowledge	Integrates knowledge of the subject with other fields

Adapted from an NBPTS validity study (Bond et al., 2000, Appendix F.1). Reprinted with permission from the National Board for Professional Teaching Standards, www.nbpts.org. All rights reserved.

The Path to Using Knowledge of Teaching and Learning

Unaware →	Aware →	Capable →	Inspired
Sees events in a disconnected way	Sees events and issues one at a time	Sees patterns in student understanding and events	Notices detailed responses to instruction
Rarely makes sense of classroom events	Recalls surface details of events or timing	Uses student reaction patterns to plan lessons	Uses response patterns to predict what will help students learn
Adjusts lessons randomly	May see the need to make minor adjustments	Varies methods and materials based on student responses	Adapts, enriches, and expands instructional connections for students

The Path to Solving Instructional Problems

Unaware →	Aware →	Capable →	Inspired
Is blind to most instructional and curricular problems	Grasps only the surface of problems	Uses classroom data to find problems	Seeks outside information to grasp problems completely
Takes a chance at solving problems	Looks for quick fixes	Searches systematically for solutions	Addresses problems comprehensively
Attempts hap-hazard solutions	Uses partial solutions	Finds workable solutions for the entire class	Finds solutions for the entire class and for individuals

The Path to Improvising

Unaware →	Aware →	Capable →	Inspired
Uses straightforward plans with no flexibility	Plans little flexibility	Plans for some flexibility	Plans opportunities for unexpected learning
Is frustrated or confused by the unexpected	Follows pre-planned lessons with little variation	Makes some instructionally useful changes during lessons	Adjusts readily and effectively to student responses
Resists changes in planned instruction	Changes plans during lessons if a major need arises	Changes instruction in response to general patterns of reaction	Makes useful adjustments throughout lessons

Adapted from an NBPTS validity study (Bond et al., 2000, Appendix F.1). Reprinted with permission from the National Board for Professional Teaching Standards, www.nbpts.org. All rights reserved.

The Path to Managing a Classroom

Unaware →	Aware →	Capable →	Inspired
Uses muddled directions and procedures	Provides procedures based on compliance	Uses procedures that encourage engagement	Uses procedures that focus on student learning
Uses procedures in ways that confuse students	Leaves students unclear about procedures	Consistently communicates expectations	Creates procedures that promote mastery and learning
Reacts instead of preventing	Rarely uses preventive strategies	Sometimes uses preventive strategies to encourage engagement	Uses prevention to promote engagement
Deals ineffectively with disruptive students	Ignores early signs of disruptive behavior	Addresses and redirects most disruptions	Consistently addresses and redirects disruptive students

Adapted from an NBPTS validity study (Bond et al., 2000, Appendix F.1). Reprinted with permission from the National Board for Professional Teaching Standards, www.nbpts.org. All rights reserved.

The Path to Interpreting Events in Progress

Unaware →	Aware →	Capable →	Inspired
Feels overwhelmed by the complexity of the classroom	Sees classroom events globally	Understands simultaneous events	Maintains focus while noting simultaneous events
Cannot sort relevant from irrelevant perceptions	Struggles to discriminate among perceptions	Distinguishes between relevant and less relevant information	Consistently sorts the relevant from the less relevant
Makes little or no response to student cues	Responds inconsistently to cues	Consistently responds to cues from students	Sees patterns in verbal and nonverbal responses
Views events as separate and unrelated	Focuses on gaining compliance	Connects some student behaviors with instruction	Links responses to instructional priorities

Adapted from an NBPTS validity study (Bond et al., 2000, Appendix F.1). Reprinted with permission from the National Board for Professional Teaching Standards, www.nbpts.org. All rights reserved.

The Path to Being Sensitive to Context

Unaware →	Aware →	Capable →	Inspired
Sees situations and students simplistically	Uses categories to describe students and groups	Plans for contextual situations and student needs	Seamlessly interacts with social and cognitive contexts
Rarely modifies activities regardless of changing situations	Weakly modifies in response to students or situations	Modifies activities and instruction for changing needs	Generates specific modifications that address students' needs
Uses one-size-fits-all instruction	Occasionally adapts to individual needs	Uses responsive instructional practices	Differentiates instruction for specific students, groups, and situations

Adapted from an NBPTS validity study (Bond et al., 2000, Appendix F.1). Reprinted with permission from the National Board for Professional Teaching Standards, www.nbpts.org. All rights reserved.

The Path to Monitoring Learning

Unaware →	Aware →	Capable →	Inspired
Ignores lack of engagement	Monitors student engagement to gain compliance	Observes and listens to monitor understanding	Uses strategies for reengagement
Fails to see student misunderstandings	Misses small misunderstandings	Focuses on learning and task completion when monitoring	Assesses student understanding
Responds inconsistently	Limits feedback to "correct" or "incorrect"	Reports correctness and adds feedback	Guides students to higher levels of understanding

Adapted from an NBPTS validity study (Bond et al., 2000, Appendix F.1). Reprinted with permission from the National Board for Professional Teaching Standards, www.nbpts.org. All rights reserved.

The Path to Testing Hypotheses

Unaware →	Aware →	Capable →	Inspired
Rarely thinks about ways to enhance learning	Modifies goals based on curriculum guidelines	Uses guidelines to enhance learning in top areas of need	Analyzes information to form specific hypotheses for improving instruction
Uses incomplete, superficial solutions	Seeks one quick solution, not several possibilities	Reflects on lessons using general hypotheses	Tests hypotheses during lessons and makes adjustments
Rarely tests any solutions	Tries solutions in general, intuitive ways	Modifies instruction based on general reflection	Uses the results of hypotheses testing to alter priorities for curriculum and instruction

Adapted from an NBPTS validity study (Bond et al., 2000, Appendix F.1). Reprinted with permission from the National Board for Professional Teaching Standards, www.nbpts.org. All rights reserved.

The Path to Demonstrating Respect

Unaware →	Aware →	Capable →	Inspired
Demonstrates lack of respect	Unevenly applies respect	Encourages students to overcome obstacles	Commits to overcoming barriers
Maintains physical and psychological distance	Maintains primary control over learning	Interacts with students in supportive ways	Demonstrates openness and trust
Owns all access to learning	Trusts students with some of their own learning	Trusts students with their own learning	Shows high regard and high expectations

Adapted from an NBPTS validity study (Bond et al., 2000, Appendix F.1). Reprinted with permission from the National Board for Professional Teaching Standards, www.nbpts.org. All rights reserved.

The Path to Showing Passion for Teaching and Learning

Unaware →	Aware →	Capable →	Inspired
Rarely shows a positive attitude toward teaching or learning	Sometimes shows positive feelings toward teaching or learning	Shows enthusiasm for student learning and teaching	Shows passion and dedication for teaching and student learning
Discourages excitement about learning	Rarely encourages enjoyment of learning	Sometimes encourages enjoyment of learning	Actively promotes student enjoyment of learning
Rarely assumes responsibility for student learning	Takes limited responsibility for student learning	Generally assumes responsibility for student learning	Personally assumes responsibility for student learning

The Path to Helping Students Reach Higher Levels of Achievement

Unaware →	Aware →	Capable →	Inspired
Rarely challenges students to think	Encourages some students to think some of the time	Often encourages thinking, but in inconsistent ways	Consistently and systematically challenges students to think
Promotes the idea that lessons are tedious and time-consuming	Promotes the idea that lessons are necessary, though not exciting	Promotes some lessons as interesting to some students	Varies lessons to make them engaging, appropriate, and challenging
Believes learners will sink or swim	Offers little support to students who try to meet challenges	Offers general support for meeting challenges	Structures activities to ensure students can meet challenges

The Path to Helping Students Understand Complexity

Unaware →	Aware →	Capable →	Inspired
Uses vague strategies for strengthening thinking	Promotes segmented thinking and seeks correct answers	Encourages connecting new information to prior learning	Plans for, teaches for, and inspires deep thinking
Uses a hit-or-miss approach to developing student skills	Guides the development of thinking skills with worksheets and assignments	Focuses student thinking on the relationships among facts	Helps students generalize or transfer knowledge
Expects students to develop thinking skills on their own	Focuses student thinking on one skill at a time without making connections	Shows strategies for comparing and contrasting	Models many strategies for integrating knowledge and forming generalizations

Index

Note: The letter *f* following a page number denotes a figure.

About the Author

A National Board Certified Teacher since 2002, **Carol Frederick Steele** holds a BA in English from the University of Michigan and an MA in Communication from Western Michigan University. Her teaching career includes work in public school at various grade levels, adult education, business and industrial programs, Job Corps, and English language instruction.

She has served on the Michigan Department of Education's Commission for Professional Teaching Standards and as a mentor teacher and field instructor for Michigan State University. She has written and directed teacher training films and was awarded a Michael Jordan grant to provide urban students with basic TV production skills. She currently provides workshops and convention presentations for fellow teachers.

Her interests include reading, quilting, and volunteering for Habitat for Humanity. Born in Kansas, she lives and writes in Michigan. She may be reached at her Web site: www.carolsteele.net.

Related ASCD Resources: Effective Teachers

At the time of publication, the following ASCD resources were available (ASCD stock numbers appear in parentheses). For up-to-date information about ASCD resources, go to www.ascd.org.

Networks

Visit the ASCD Web site (www.ascd.org) and click on About ASCD and then on Networks for information about professional educators who have formed groups around topics, including "Quality Education." Look in the "Network Directory" for current facilitators' addresses and phone numbers.

Print Products

The Art and Science of Teaching: A Comprehensive Framework for Effective Instruction by Robert J. Marzano (#107001)

ASCD Infobrief 22: Ensuring Teacher Quality by Carol Tell (#100297)

Educational Leadership: Improving Professional Practice (Entire Issue #106041)

Handbook for Qualities of Effective Teachers by James H. Stronge, Pamela D. Tucker, and Jennifer L. Hindman (#104135)

Improving Student Learning One Teacher at a Time by Jane E. Pollock (#107005)

Qualities of Effective Teachers, 2nd Edition by James H. Stronge (#105156)

Videos and DVDs

Qualities of Effective Teachers (three video programs on one DVD, plus a facilitator's guide) (#604423)

A Visit to Classrooms of Effective Teachers (one 45-minute DVD with a comprehensive viewer's guide) (DVD #605026; Video #405026)

The Whole Child Initiative helps schools and communities create learning environments that allow students to be healthy, safe, engaged, supported, and challenged. To learn more about other books and resources that relate to the whole child, visit www.wholechild education.org.

For more information: send e-mail to member@ascd.org; call 1-800-933-2723 or 703-578-9600, press 1; send a fax to 703-575-5400; or write to Information Services, ASCD, 1703 N. Beauregard St., Alexandria, VA 22311-1714 USA.